Improving Health Care in Low- and Middle-Income Countries

Lani Rice Marquez

Editor

Improving Health Care in Low- and Middle-Income Countries

A Case Book

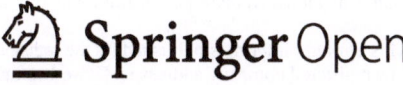

Editor
Lani Rice Marquez
University Research Co., LLC (URC)
Bethesda, MD, USA

This book is an open access publication.

ISBN 978-3-030-43111-2   ISBN 978-3-030-43112-9   (eBook)
https://doi.org/10.1007/978-3-030-43112-9

This Springer imprint is published by the registered company Springer Nature Switzerland AG
The registered company address is: Gewerbestrasse 11, 6330 Cham, Switzerland

Acknowledgments

This book is the product of many hands, hearts, and minds. First and foremost, I want to acknowledge Dr. James (Jim) R. Heiby, who conceptualized, spearheaded, and led the development of this book until his retirement from the US Agency for International Development (USAID) in October 2017. For more than 30 years, he designed, oversaw, and evaluated USAID flagship projects dedicated to improving the quality of health care in low- and middle-income countries. He also provided technical guidance and encouragement to a large number of individuals and USAID-funded projects, and this book would not have been possible without his vision for what this collection of cases could be and his passion and thought leadership for this subject. His insights and wisdom infused every case presented in this book.

Appreciation goes to USAID colleagues Rhea Bright and Ariella Camera for their instrumental role supporting Jim with the establishment of the case study narrative development guidance. Rhea and Ariella traveled to Uganda in 2014 and interviewed frontline improvers and the USAID Applying Science to Strengthen and Improve (ASSIST) Uganda team to gather descriptive details about how best to tell the story behind improvement initiatives. Jim, Rhea, Ariella, Trenton White, and Aimee Desrochers conducted the USAID reviews of all of the case study submissions. Together, they provided insightful critiques and thoughtful additions to the cases. A special thank you goes to Cassandra (Cassie) Zieminski for developing evaluation criteria for the case study submissions, providing guidance to case book authors, and reviewing case studies during her 3-month internship at USAID.

I would also like to thank USAID leaders—Karen Cavanaugh, Kathryn Panther, Kelly Saldana, and Bob Emery—for their management support to turn Jim's dream of this book into something concrete. Lisa Maniscalco at USAID continued to move this project forward after Jim's retirement when she took over as Agreement Officer's Representative for the USAID ASSIST Project. Appreciation also goes to Gayle Girod at USAID for legal counsel throughout the publication process.

I greatly appreciate the contributions of a number of USAID ASSIST Project colleagues to the development of this book. Alison Lucas played a major role: identifying and reaching out to potential publishers, managing the review process for individual cases, and working closely with me to edit and standardize the final cases selected for the book. Other members of the USAID ASSIST Project Knowledge Management team also played an important role in editing cases and shaping the overall structure of the book: Sid Deka, Mayssa el Khazen, Kate Fatta, Silvia Holschneider, and Julia Holtemeyer. Feza Kikaya, Vicky Ramirez, and Karina Valenzuela of the USAID ASSIST Project provided excellent organization and administrative support of the QI case book at various stages. I also want to thank Janis Berman for her dedicated editorial support on several cases and Kurt Mulholland, Director of Media Services for University Research Co., LLC (URC), for laying out the figures used in the cases. Sarah Earle and Yousri Hanna of URC skillfully shepherded the publishing contract negotiation process with Springer Nature. And finally, special thanks to USAID ASSIST Project Director and URC Senior Vice President M. Rashad Massoud for his support and promotion of this project.

Thank you to Janet Kim, Senior Editor, Books, Public Health and Social Work, Springer, for guiding this book through the publication process and to Shabib Shaikh of Springer Nature Book Services for supporting the final submission of the manuscript.

In our effort to provide a balanced geographic and clinical area distribution of cases in this book (and to ensure the book did not become an unreadable tome), we were forced to cull many excellent case studies from the final manuscript. A big thanks to all the authors who submitted cases for this book; your contributions strengthened the final product.

I want to recognize the chapter lead authors who worked with us over several years to bring this final product to life: Maria Elena Banegas, Joshua Bardfield, John Byabagambi, Tamar Chitashvili, Taroub Harb Faramand, James Heiby, Elena Hurtado, Nigel Livesley, Edgar Necochea, Flora Nyagawa, Nilufar Rakhmanova Pollard, Barton Smith, and Nicole Spieker.

Finally, all of us involved in this project want to acknowledge the frontline health workers in Georgia, Guatemala, Haiti, Honduras, India, Kenya, Kyrgyz Republic, Mozambique, Tanzania, Uganda, and Ukraine whose efforts to improve care are the bedrock of these cases.

The critical work described in these cases and the development of this book were made possible by the generous support of the American people through USAID. This book was developed with the support of USAID and its Bureau for Global Health, Office of Health Systems, through the USAID Applying Science to Strengthen and Improve Systems Project, managed by University Research Co., LLC under Cooperative Agreement Number AID-OAA-A-12-00101.

The contents of this book are the sole responsibility of URC and the authors and do not necessarily reflect the views of the US Agency for International Development or the US Government.

December 2019   Lani Rice Marquez, Editor

Contents

Abbreviations

AIDS	Acquired Immunodeficiency Syndrome
AMR	Antimicrobial Resistance
AMTSL	Active Management of the Third Stage of Labor
ART	Antiretroviral Therapy
ARV	Antiretroviral
ASSIST	USAID Applying Science to Strengthen and Improve Systems Project
BMO	Block Medical Officer (India)
CDC	US Centers for Disease Control and Prevention
CD4	Cluster of Differentiation 4
CME	Continuing Medical Education
CMO	Chief Medical Officer (India)
CP	Clinical Protocol (Kyrgyz Republic)
CSaZ	Congenital Syndrome Associated with Zika Virus
DIC	District Improvement Coordinator (India)
DSW	Department of Social Welfare (Tanzania)
EB	Evidence-Based
EMR	Electronic Medical Record
ENT	Ear, Nose, and Throat
FGPNA	Family Group Practice and Nurses Association (Kyrgyz Republic)
FMC	Family Medicine Centers (Kyrgyz Republic)
FP	Family Planning
GBS	Guillain-Barré Syndrome
HAART	Highly Active Antiretroviral Therapy
HAKR	Hospital Association of the Kyrgyz Republic
HCI	USAID Health Care Improvement Project
HCT	HIV Counseling and Testing
HIV	Human Immunodeficiency Virus
HMIS	Health Management Information System
HSC	Health Subcenters (India)

ICD-10	International Classification of Diseases, 10th Revision
IHSS	Honduran Institute of Social Security
IPC/C	Interpersonal Communication and Counseling
KAP	Knowledge, Attitudes, and Practices
Ksh	Kenyan Shilling
KSMIRCE	Kyrgyz State Medical Institute for Retraining and Continuing Education
LQAS	Lot Quality Assurance Sampling
M&E	Monitoring and Evaluation
MMI	Model Maternities Initiative (Mozambique)
MNCH	Maternal, Neonatal, and Child Health
MOH	Ministry of Health
MoLHSA	Ministry of Labour, Health and Social Affairs, Republic of Georgia
MSPP	Ministère de la Santé Publique et de la Population, Haiti
MVC	Most Vulnerable Children (Tanzania)
NCDC&PH	National Center for Disease Control and Public Health, Republic of Georgia
NGO	Nongovernmental Organization
NHIF	National Hospital Insurance Fund (Kenya)
Non-EB	Nonevidence-Based
PDSA	Plan-Do-Study-Act
PEPFAR	US President's Emergency Plan for AIDS Relief
PHC	Primary Health Care (Kyrgyz Republic)
PHC	Primary Health Center (India)
PHFS	Partnership for HIV-Free Survival
PLHIV	Persons Living with HIV
QI	Quality Improvement
QIP	Quality Improvement Plan
RDT	Rapid Diagnostic Test
RMNCH+A	Reproductive, Maternal, Newborn, Child, and Adolescent Health
RTI	Respiratory Tract Infection
RT-PCR	Reverse Transcription Polymerase Chain Reaction
RUA	Rational Use of Antibiotics
SBCC	Social and Behavior Change Communication
SBM-R	Standards-Based Management and Recognition
SMC	Safe Male Circumcision (Uganda)
SWO	Social Welfare Officer (Tanzania)
TB	Tuberculosis
TBA	Traditional Birth Attendant
TSH	Tanzanian Shilling
UCSF	University of California, San Francisco
UNAIDS	Joint United Nations Programme on HIV/AIDS
URC	University Research Co., LLC
USAID	United States Agency for International Development
USD	United States Dollar

VMMC	Voluntary Medical Male Circumcision
WHO	World Health Organization
ZSC	Zika Strategic Command

About the Editor

Lani Rice Marquez, MHS is the Knowledge Management Director for the USAID Applying Science to Strengthen and Improve Systems (ASSIST) Project at University Research Co., LLC (URC). A health management and evaluation specialist, Lani has worked for over 30 years in international health programs, where much of her work has focused on strengthening the performance of facility-based and community-based health workers in low- and middle-income countries through improvement methods. For the past 10 years, she has led URC's efforts to apply knowledge management concepts and techniques to strengthen quality improvement program efficiency and impact.

Contributors

Bruce D. Agins HEALTHQUAL, Institute for Global Health Sciences, University of California San Francisco (UCSF), New York, NY, USA

Maria Elena Banegas Arnold Formerly with University Research Co., LLC, Tegucigalpa, Honduras

Jean Gabriel Balan ITECH-Haiti, Port-au-Prince, Haiti

Joshua Bardfield Bard College, Formerly with HEALTHQUAL, Annandale-On-Hudson, NY, USA

Yves Marie Bernard CDC, Port-au-Prince, Haiti

Bruno Bouchet FHI 360, Washington, DC, USA

John Bekiita Byabagambi John Snow Inc., (formerly with University Research Co., LLC in Uganda), Pretoria, South Africa

Nicasky Celestin U.S. Centers for Disease Control and Prevention (CDC), Port-au-Prince, Haiti

Ekaterine Cherkezishvili Formerly with University Research Co., LLC (URC), Tbilisi, Georgia

Tamar Chitashvili University Research Co., LLC, Chevy Chase, MD, USA

Maria da Luz Vaz Jhpiego, Maputo, Mozambique

Ernestina David Jhpiego, Maputo, Mozambique

Nirva Duval Ministry of Health and Population, Port-au-Prince, Haiti

Taroub Harb Faramand WI-HER, LLC, Vienna, VA, USA

Alyona Gerasimova Pact Inc., Kyiv, Ukraine

James R. Heiby United States Agency for International Development (Retired), Annandale, VA, USA

Elena Hurtado Formerly with University Research Co., LLC, Guatemala City, Guatemala

Margareth Jasmin HEALTHQUAL-Haiti, Port-au-Prince, Haiti

Patrice Joseph CDC, Port-au-Prince, Haiti

Emily Keyes FHI 360, Durham, NC, USA

Norma Aly Leitzelar Formerly with University Research Co., LLC, Tegucigalpa, Honduras

Nigel Livesley University Research Co., LLC, Abuja, Nigeria

Alison Lucas Formerly with University Research Co., LLC, Palo Alto, CA, USA

Lani Rice Marquez University Research Co., LLC (URC), Bethesda, MD, USA

Pablo Moreira Formerly with University Research Co., LLC, Guatemala City, Guatemala

Edgar Necochea Jhpiego, Baltimore, MD, USA

Flora Pius Nyagawa Formerly with University Research Co., LLC, Dar Es Salaam, Tanzania

Nilufar Rakhmanova Pollard FHI 360, Phnom Penh, Cambodia

Lilian Ramírez Formerly with University Research Co., LLC, Guatemala City, Guatemala

Jim Ricca Jhpiego/Maternal and Child Survival Project, Baltimore, MD, USA

Igor Semenenko FHI 360, Kyiv, Ukraine

Praveen Kumar Sharma Formerly with University Research Co., LLC (URC), New Delhi, India

Barton Smith Virginia Mason Edmonds Family Medicine (Formerly with Abt Associates), Edmonds, WA, USA

Uliana Snidevych FHI 360, Kyiv, Ukraine

Nicole Spieker PharmAccess Foundation, Amsterdam, The Netherlands

Jean Solon Valles CDC, Port-au-Prince, Haiti

Roman Yorick Pact Inc., Dushanbe, Tajikistan

Chapter 1
Introduction

James R. Heiby

Abstract The Introduction by Dr. James R. Heiby frames this Case Book as intending to fill a gap in the current health-care quality improvement literature by distilling the experience and lessons learned by health-care improvers based on decades of experience seeking to improve health-care services and outcomes in low- and middle-income countries. Each of the 12 cases included in this book was written by practitioners of quality improvement and provides real-life examples of the challenges, strategies, and benefits of improving health-care processes in low-resource settings. These cases are intended to demonstrate what quality improvement approaches look like in practice and to demystify quality improvement methods for those making their own attempts at improving health care.

Keywords Health care · Low- and middle-income countries · Model for improvement · Plan-Do-Study-Act · Quality improvement · United States Agency for International Development

Early in my career at USAID, I had a meeting with a visiting health official from Ghana. When I told him, "I want to talk to you about a new project that's doing quality improvement," he laughed in my face. He thought that was really ridiculous, the idea of using modern improvement methods to improve health care in Ghana. He thought it was just an absurd idea and one that was bound to fail.

Yet, we persisted in our efforts to introduce and apply quality improvement methods to tackle gaps in health services – in Ghana and in other low-resource health systems worldwide. We were soon able to demonstrate the success of this approach through improved care and outcomes.

When I speak with health officials from low- and middle-income countries now, they are not incredulous that these methods will work in their countries because they have seen them work. But there are still a lot of doubts and questions about how these methods are applied in practice.

To date, most of our attempts to explain quality improvement have been abstract or theoretical, which has not led to an awareness of quality improvement methods

J. R. Heiby (✉)
United States Agency for International Development (Retired), Annandale, VA, USA
e-mail: jamesheiby@aol.com

© University Research Co., LLC 2020   1
L. R. Marquez (ed.), *Improving Health Care in Low- and Middle-Income Countries*, https://doi.org/10.1007/978-3-030-43112-9_1

among the broad population of health-care providers. It's not easy or practical for our target audience – frontline health-care providers and managers – to understand and learn improvement methods from these models. Health-care providers and managers will be much more likely to buy into, learn, and apply these methods if they're shown concrete examples of what we're talking about.

This book is a collection of case studies capturing decades of experiences from low- and middle-income countries in improving health-care services and outcomes. Each case study is written by health-care improvers who have been at the forefront of this work and provides real-life examples of the challenges, solutions, and benefits of improving health care. My intention is that these cases will clearly demonstrate for readers what quality improvement looks like in practice and help demystify these approaches for those making their own attempts to improve care.

What Is Improvement?

What do we mean by health-care improvement? Basically, we know a lot about how to improve health care. Over the years, we've seen remarkable improvements in health care by increasing providers' knowledge and using new tools, technologies, and medicines to prevent disease and diagnose and treat patients. But what is meant by "improvement" as a methodology is a little different. *Improvement* is a directed effort to take what we know can improve health – proven, high-impact interventions like active management of the third stage of labor or keeping newborns warm – and ensure that those are implemented reliably, in different contexts, every time, for every patient who needs them. Because this is the problem: known evidence-based interventions are either not being implemented at all, not being implemented consistently, or not being implemented on a broad scale.

While there is no single best way to improve the quality of health care, there are several basic principles that underlie the most successful improvement efforts (Langley et al. 2009; Perla et al. 2013). These are:

- Engaging health workers in teams to improve their own work.
- Knowing why improvement is needed and why it matters.
- Developing effective ideas for changes that will result in improvement.
- Testing and adapting changes before implementing at large scale.
- Having a feedback mechanism to show if improvements are occurring.
- Knowing when and how to make changes sustainable by integrating them into the system of interest.

How Has the Field Evolved in the Last 30 Years?

When reading this book, it is important to remember that improving the performance of a system or process is not a new concept. Most of what is now called the "science of improvement" stems from the work of Dr. W. Edwards Deming, a statistician who proposed that improving the quality of the manufacturing production process and eliminating delays, duplications, and errors would result in higher quality products and services at lower unit costs. Dr. Deming took his ideas to Japan in the 1950s, where they were embraced and applied to manufacturing automobiles, electronic appliances, and other consumer goods.

The same ideas began to be applied to improving the quality of health care in the United States in the 1990s. At the same time, programs supported by USAID to improve health-care quality in assisted countries began to adapt traditional strategies to incorporate process improvement approaches (Massoud et al. 2001). These approaches were applied to the delivery of priority health services, including obstetric care; immunizations; management of diarrhea, pneumonia, and malaria; and family planning (Heiby 1998).

Based on results achieved, interest in improvement grew rapidly, with many organizations developing branded models and applying them in donor-supported programs. While these models use different terminology, they often share common core elements, such as process analysis, use of standards, identification of key barriers, and closure of gaps between ideal and observed performance through active change to care processes, defining priorities for the improvement effort, empowering providers to identify problems and find solutions, and monitoring results (Tawfik et al. 2010). The proliferation of methods with different names has frequently resulted in confusion about definitions, terms, and jargon describing similar methods or concepts to achieve quality in health care and improve health outcomes (Walshe 2009).

Improvement Methods

Over the years, many approaches to improvement have been developed and used in low- and middle-income countries. Some approaches have centered on evidence-based standards and guidelines and making sure that providers use them, often linked with audit and feedback processes. Others have emphasized regulatory approaches, such as accreditation, certification and re-certification of professionals and facilities, and professional licensure and renewal. Most approaches include some form of training of health-care providers, yet few today would argue that training alone is sufficient to assure care quality. More recently, donor

> *I think it is a disservice to the sciences of improvement to reify the term "quality improvement" as if it were a device or even a stable methodology. Making patient care better is always a good idea, and there is no harm at all in using the term "improvement" to describe that quest. However, treating the pursuit of improvement (no initial caps) by searching for a boxable, boundable formula… is misleading. The ways in which people and organizations try …to continually improve the work that they do on behalf of patients are numerous and, thank goodness, will forever evolve.*
> —Donald Berwick, *JAMA* 2012; 307(19): 2093–2094

agencies in particular have promoted performance-based incentives as the solution to quality issues.

These are all valuable approaches, but when applied alone are usually not enough to resolve all quality issues. Experience has shown that multipronged improvement strategies produce better results than single-focused ones (Wensing and Grol 1994; Wensing et al. 1998). Moreover, improvement approaches that lack active mechanisms to change processes of care have had limited impact, largely because such efforts tend to address only inputs to health systems with little or no focus on processes of care delivery (Davis et al. 1992; Oxman et al. 1995; Wensing et al. 1998; Massoud et al. 2006).

The right approach for a particular setting and quality of care problem depends on many contextual factors, such as resources available, improvement expertise, leadership support, time, and scale of effort.

One widely used approach to improve health care in resource poor settings – and one that was used in many of the cases in this book – is the Model for Improvement, which uses the Plan-Do-Study-Act (PDSA) cycle.[1] The PDSA cycle guides tests of change by health-care teams to determine if a change leads to improvement. Improvement teams typically comprise frontline health-care workers, supervisors, and others involved in care, either as providers or recipients, who identify and test feasible changes to usual processes to improve care in their local setting. The model offers practical steps to improve care, including the following:

- Choose a problem to address by using data or observation to identify gaps in care.
- Develop improvement aims to focus on what you are trying to accomplish.
- Set up a team that understands and can address the problem.
- Analyze the issue to understand the problem better.
- Develop change ideas by hypothesizing about what changes will improve the problem.
- Test changes using PDSA cycles to see whether the hypothesized solution yields improvement.

About This Book

This book is a series of case studies that show how improvement can happen at the national, regional, community, and facility levels in limited-resource settings and across a variety of service areas, including maternal and child health, HIV, chronic disease care, and services for vulnerable children. The authors have decades of experience in working on quality improvement, and their cases provide detailed examples of their own experiences and those of frontline providers they have worked with.

---

[1] Developed by *Associates in Process Improvement* [Access: http://www.apiweb.org/].

The cases summarize their persistent effort to identify gaps in care, propose changes to address those gaps, and test the effectiveness of their changes to improve health processes and outcomes throughout Africa, Eastern Europe, South Asia, Latin America, and the Caribbean. This, as the reader will see, often led to dramatic improvements in health-care processes and outcomes, including improving respiratory tract infection diagnosis and management practices for children; HIV testing for TB patients; and improving uptake of high-impact maternal care practices, among many others. In some instances, their efforts did not achieve the expected outcomes, or they faced obstacles that kept them from fully reaching their goals. Reflections at the end of each chapter provide an opportunity for the reader to learn from both the successes and the challenges of each case.

Most publications on health-care improvement focus primarily on results, with less emphasis on how specific actions in health-care improvement were initiated and completed. Moreover, most books on quality improvement in health are based on work and research conducted in the United States and Europe. This collection of cases aims to increase our understanding of the mechanisms and the context by which quality improvement interventions in the health sector work in low-resource settings. Each case focuses on how specific actions in health-care improvement were initiated, the processes and steps of the improvement effort on the ground, and the results of those efforts.

Our stories of improvement are wide-ranging. While some cases focus on the experience of one facility team that tested changes and then shared its successes with other sites, often through a deliberate collaborative improvement strategy linking the work of many facilities, other cases highlight the work of multi-facility improvement teams working simultaneously on a common goal or describe national-level strategies, like the use of electronic information systems.

Each case highlights different details in the design, implementation, and methods used to improve care. A case from Tanzania about strengthening accessibility of services for vulnerable children focuses on the steps needed to organize improvement efforts, including how improvement teams were formed, external support provided to initiate district- and ward-level efforts and conduct baseline assessments, and actions required to build the improvement capacity of frontline service providers. A case from Georgia on improving the quality of care for respiratory tract infections in children highlights the importance of coaching in supporting improvement teams. A case from Uganda shows how gender issues were integrated into improvement efforts. A case from India explores the role of leadership and early successes in creating buy-in for a quality improvement intervention. In Haiti, we see how data from an electronic medical records system helped inform improvement priorities at both the national and facility levels.

This book is for anyone who is interested and wants to learn more about health-care improvement, but my hope is that it will be most useful to those engaged daily in the noble task of making health care better: health-care providers and administrators; those managing health improvement projects within Ministries of Health in low- and middle-income countries; US government and other donor agency staff;

and other key decision-makers. The book will also be useful as a teaching text in schools of medicine, public health, public policy, or other related majors.

Those looking for detailed information about quality improvement methods and theories will not find that in this book. Instead, I would refer readers to some excellent resources on this subject (see Box 1.1).

Box 1.1 Resources on Quality Improvement Methods and Theories
The Improvement Guide: A Practical Approach to Enhancing Organizational Performance (second edition). Langley GL, Moen R, Nolan KM, Nolan TW, Norman CL, Provost LP. Jossey-Bass (2009)

Curing Health Care: New Strategies for Quality Improvement. Berwick DM, Godfrey AB, Roessner J. Jossey-Bass (2003)

Quality Improvement. Technical Reference Materials. Published for the United States Agency for International Development (USAID) by the Maternal and Child Health Integrated Program (2014). Available at the USAID Development Exchange Clearinghouse: https://pdf.usaid.gov/pdf_docs/PA00M5FQ.pdf

---

For over 30 years, I have worked on adapting modern quality improvement approaches from industrialized countries for use in the health systems of low- and middle-income countries. In my work with USAID, I have had the honor of working with some of the greatest minds and practitioners in applying improvement to health-care quality. It is my hope that this sample of improvement case studies will show the reader the power of improvement methods, expand their evidence base, and most importantly, encourage a better understanding of the culture and practice for improvement in order to achieve better health outcomes for all.

References

Davis DA, Thomson MA, Oxman AD, Haynes RB (1992) Evidence for the effectiveness of CME: a review of 50 randomized controlled trials. JAMA 268(9):1111–1117

Heiby JR (1998) Quality improvement and the integrated management of childhood illness: lessons from developed countries. Jt Comm J Qual Improv 24(5):264–279

Langley GL, Moen R, Nolan KM, Nolan TW, Norman CL, Provost LP (2009) The improvement guide: a practical approach to enhancing organizational performance, 2nd edn. Jossey-Bass Publishers, San Francisco

Massoud MR, Nielsen G, Nolan K, Schall M, Sevin C (2006) A framework for spread, from local improvements to system-wide change, Innovation series. Institute for Healthcare Improvement, Cambridge, MA. Available at www.IHI.org

Oxman AD, Thomson MA, Davis DA, Haynes RB (1995) No magic bullets: a systematic review of 102 trials of interventions to improve professional practice. Can Med Assoc J 153(10):1423–1431

Perla R, Provost L, Parry G (2013) Seven propositions of the science of improvement: exploring foundations. Qual Manag Health Care 22:170–186. https://doi.org/10.1097/QMH.0b013e31829a6a15

Tawfik Y, Segall M, Necochea E, Jacobs T (2010) Finding common ground: harmonizing the application of QI in MNCH programs. Technical report. Published by the USAID Health Care Improvement Project. University Research Co., LLC, Bethesda. Available at: https://dec.usaid.gov/dec/content/Detail_Presto.aspx?ctID=ODVhZjk4NWQtM2YyMi00YjRmLTkxNjktZTcxMjM2NDBmY2Uy&rID=MTcxODkw&qrs=RmFsc2U%3d&q=KERvY3VtZW50cy5JbnN0aXR1dGlvbl9vcl9VU0FJRF9CdXJlYXVfQ29yZXVfQ29yZ2yPSgiMDA0MjkzIC0gVW5pdGVkIFN0YXRlcyBBZ2VuY3kgZm9yIEludGVybmF0aW9uYWwgRGV2ZWxvcG1lbnQi

Walshe K (2009) Pseudoinnovation: the development and spread of healthcare quality improvement methodologies. Int J Qual Health Care 21(3):153–159

Wensing M, Grol R (1994) Single and combined strategies for implementing changes in primary care: a literature review. Int J Qual Health Care 6(2):115–132

Wensing M, Weijden TVD, Grol R (1998) Implementing guidelines and innovations in general practice: which interventions are effective? Br J Gen Pract 48:991–997

Chapter 2
Improving Quality of Care for Respiratory Tract Infections in Children: The Role of Capacity Building and Coaching in Supporting One Multifacility Improvement Team in Samtredia District, Georgia

Tamar Chitashvili and Ekaterine Cherkezishvili

Abstract In most quality improvement (QI) experiences, QI teams work in a single facility or community. This case describes the experience of a multifacility QI team in the Republic of Georgia that sought to improve the diagnosis and treatment of respiratory tract infections, the most frequent reason for seeking medical care among children. The QI team for Samtredia District drew members from the ambulatory clinic and Pediatrics Department of the district hospital as well as individual doctors' practices that were all part of the same private medical service delivery network, Geo Hospitals. Geo Hospitals management also participated in QI team meetings to help address gaps in availability of essential inputs such as diagnostic tests and evidence-based medications. The case study details the design and implementation of the improvement effort and provides details about the capacity building and coaching support provided to the team that helped lead to improved health outcomes.

Keywords Coaching · Compliance with clinical standards · Cost savings · Evidence-based treatment · Georgia · Rational use of antibiotics · Respiratory tract infections

T. Chitashvili (✉)
University Research Co., LLC, Chevy Chase, MD, USA
e-mail: tchitashvili@urc-chs.com

E. Cherkezishvili
Formerly with University Research Co., LLC (URC), Tbilisi, Georgia

© University Research Co., LLC 2020
L. R. Marquez (ed.), *Improving Health Care in Low- and Middle-Income Countries*, https://doi.org/10.1007/978-3-030-43112-9_2

9

Background

Respiratory tract infections (RTIs) are the most frequent reasons for seeking medical care at the ambulatory as well as at the hospital level in the Republic of Georgia. In 2012, RTIs accounted for 36% of pediatric hospital admissions and 45% of ambulatory visits for children (NCDC&PH 2013).

According to the World Health Organization (WHO), RTIs, particularly pneumonia, remain one of the leading causes of under-five child mortality globally. Diagnosing and curing RTIs do not require advanced technologies. Yet, despite effective interventions to treat these infections, provision of appropriate care remains very low, particularly for appropriate medication prescription practices, including antibiotics (WHO and UNICEF 2013).

In Georgia, RTIs are the most common clinical condition for which children seek medical care. In 2012, approximately 46% of all outpatient pediatric (patients ages 0–15 years) clinical encounters were diagnosed with RTIs; pneumonia accounted for 7% of all pediatric hospitalizations. Due to the high burden of RTIs among children in the country, addressing the quality of diagnosis and treatment of RTIs became a priority focus area in Georgia. While many health-care quality improvement (QI) interventions have been successfully implemented in resource-limited settings, the evidence of their effect on improving RTI care and particularly rational prescription practices remains scarce. In addition, there is limited information about how these QI interventions have been planned, tested, implemented, and sustained in low- and middle-income countries, including Georgia.

To support the Government of Georgia's strategic direction on improving the quality of medical services for priority clinical conditions, including RTIs in children, in February 2012, a United States Agency for International Development (USAID)-funded technical assistance project with decades of expertise in QI began to address challenges related to quality, consistency, and continuity of pediatric respiratory infections in the country.

To improve the quality of RTI diagnostic and treatment practices, the project, in close consultation with the Ministry of Labour, Health and Social Affairs (MoLHSA), selected the Imereti Region and a sample of its 82 facilities and 212 village doctor practices to implement improvement activities. The focus of the QI activities was to improve the quality of care of the highest disease burdens in the country, including cardiovascular disease, chronic obstructive pulmonary disease, and diagnosis and management of RTIs and asthma. Sites were chosen based on the political feasibility and representation of all levels of the health service delivery system to address continuity and timeliness of care. In addition, the project supported the formation of several QI teams in the region (i.e., teams of health workers from those facilities and doctor practices) who worked to improve health provider performance related to these clinical conditions. This was done by reviewing current client data, conducting problem analyses, developing and testing ideas to change their current processes, and measuring data to determine if their changes were leading to improvement.

Designing the Improvement Effort

Background on Georgia's Health System

In recent years, Georgia's health system has transitioned from a highly centralized Soviet Semashko model toward privatization of health service delivery infrastructure and liberalization of regulations. Consequently, health services are now predominantly provided by the private sector, including medical care corporations, stand-alone outpatient clinics, hospitals, and village solo practitioners.

Inherited from the Soviet system, the number of physicians in Georgia is the highest in the European region (4.8 per 1000 population in 2012), yet the utilization of outpatient and inpatient services is the lowest (NCDC&PH 2013). While coverage and reimbursement of health services by the Government of Georgia have changed several times in recent years, the state does not generally cover outpatient medications, the cost of which is the largest share of total health expenditures. Despite the Government's coverage of selected outpatient and hospital services, implemented through various state health programs, out-of-pocket payments contributed to 70% of total health expenditures in 2012 (Chanturidze et al. 2009). The lack of affordability of medications and of access to quality medical care for high-burden clinical conditions thus posed significant challenges to patients and society in Georgia.

Site Selection and Formation of the QI Team

During the design stage of the project, medical facilities in the Imereti Region were undergoing changes in ownership and operations. Most of the facilities were owned by two of the largest private medical service delivery networks in the country (My Family Clinics and Geo Hospitals) and were financed on a per capita reimbursement system. Given this structure, the project deliberately selected medical facilities in these two networks to implement improvement activities. It was expected that when their central management saw the benefits of quality improvement in project-supported sites owned by these corporations, they would scale up successful QI practices to other facilities in their networks.

The QI team in Samtredia District included representatives from all levels of care under the management of Geo Hospitals, which was managing the State Program on Village Doctors and was the implementer of the main publicly funded health programs in the district. The QI team comprised two pediatricians from a Geo Hospitals ambulatory clinic, one pediatrician from a 35-bed district hospital in the Geo Hospitals network, and seven doctors from village clinics that were functionally and programmatically linked to Geo Hospitals. Due to a shortage of nurses and their limited role in providing clinical care in Georgia, nurses were not included in the improvement team. The composition of the QI team was deliberate in order to: (1)

strengthen referral and counter-referral linkages between the different levels of care at the district level; and (2) fit into the objectives of Geo Hospitals to improve communication and care coordination between village doctors and their newly established ambulatory clinic and hospital within the district. Involvement in QI activities as part of the multifacility improvement team was a welcome opportunity for village doctors since they had limited information on recent changes in implementation of the State Program on Village Doctors and the organization of health service delivery within the district. In addition, strengthening the quality of the medical care for the most frequent reasons for children's ambulatory visits, particularly in the villages, responded to the needs of Geo Hospitals to reduce medical care costs by managing the risk of overutilization of their primary care and specialty outpatient services.

Choosing Improvement Priorities

At the start of the QI intervention in June 2012, unpublished data from the National Center for Disease Control and Public Health (NCDC&PH) and the WHO suggested that in contrast to many other developing countries where lack of access to the health-care services is a core problem in the delivery of high-quality RTI care, in Georgia the main issue was the overutilization of diagnostic tests, specialist services, and medications, particularly antibiotics. The latter led to unjustified out-of-pocket expenses and adverse health and economic outcomes for families and society.

Before the improvement work began in Samtredia, a baseline assessment was carried out by the project implementing organization from April to August 2012 to identify critical quality gaps in the diagnosis and management of RTIs and other priority clinical areas. The assessment was part of a larger unpublished study conducted by the project in 9 hospitals, 10 ambulatory clinics, and 26 village primary care practices to assess the cost-effectiveness of QI interventions. The study included intervention and control facilities and gathered information on existing gaps in care processes and supporting system functions from review of patients' medical charts, an observation checklist to assess key inputs/inventory, and interviews with care providers, managers, and patients/parents. Results from the medical record review revealed irrational and non-evidence-based use of medications during ambulatory management of RTIs and hospital management of pneumonia in children. At the ambulatory care level, a child with an acute RTI received, on average, 3.4 (95% confidence interval, 3.17–3.65) medications, with 2.6 (95% confidence interval, 2.37–2.75) of them irrelevant to his or her clinical condition and without any medical justification (i.e., non-evidence-based). Similarly, at the hospital level, a child received, on average, 7.5 (95% confidence interval, 7.14–7.87) medications, with 5.46 (95% confidence interval, 5.13–5.80) of them irrelevant to his or her clinical condition and not compliant with up-to-date scientific evidence. As shown in Fig. 2.1, non-evidence-based medications (including cough medications,

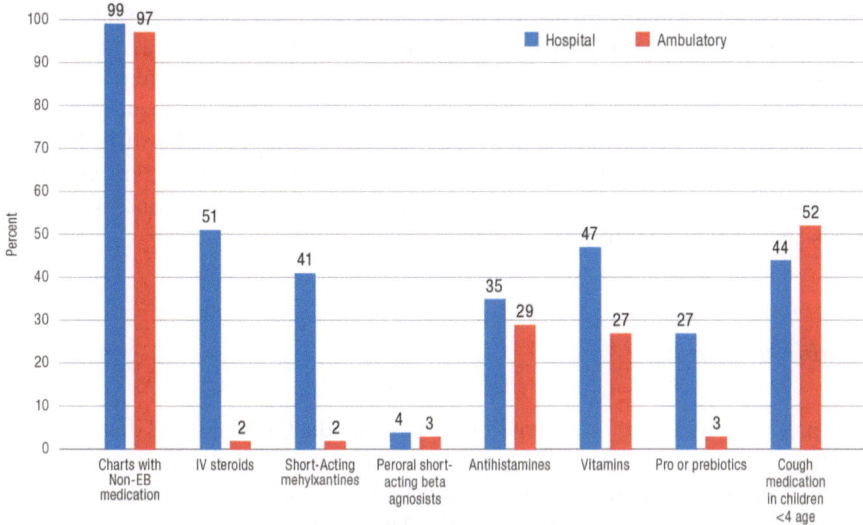

Fig. 2.1 Use of non-evidence-based (Non-EB) medications in children diagnosed with pneumonia or RTIs at discharge and at last ambulatory visits (October 2010 to March 2012). Percent of medical charts with specific groups of non-evidence-based medications. (Source: Ambulatory ($n = 212$) and hospital ($n = 274$) medical charts)

probiotics, vitamins, antihistamines, and intravenous steroids) were prescribed to almost all children presenting with RTIs. Some non-evidence-based medications (e.g., vitamins) are associated with mild patient safety risk while others (e.g., intravenous steroids) are associated with high risk of adverse events and call for immediate action.

The baseline assessment helped the Samtredia QI team, as well as the other project-supported QI teams delivering care for pediatric patients, to develop and refine their improvement aims.

Carrying Out the Improvement Intervention

The quality improvement intervention started with the project team and facility managers visiting each intervention facility and identifying members for the QI teams in the Imereti Region, including the Samtredia QI team presented in this case. After identifying all QI teams in the region, in March 2012 the project organized a 2-day learning session for all the QI teams in Imereti Region, with the participation of local, regional, and national key stakeholders. The purpose of the learning session was to introduce QI concepts and methods as well as ways to plan, implement, monitor, and refine changes in their health-care processes. The emphasis on health systems rather than individuals was new and unexpected for the members of the QI teams as they were used to top-down supervision that seeks to find bad performers and individuals to blame. In addition to QI methodologies, learning session participants received up-to-date information on evidence-based best practices for the management of RTIs in ambulatory and hospital settings. Participants were assisted in developing improvement aims, objectives, changes, and measurement criteria by working through a clinical case study. The sections below outline how the QI teams worked to choose their improvement priorities, how they set their aims and measures for improvement, and the changes they tested to improve the quality of diagnosis and management of RTIs.

Problem Analysis

The project provided clinical support for the Samtredia QI team's RTI diagnosis and management improvement work through an external technical expert in RTI – the head of the Georgian Respiratory Association, who was also a professor of the Tbilisi State Medical University Pediatric Department and Clinical Director of the largest children's referral hospital in Tbilisi.

The project supported the team with biweekly coaching visits from the technical expert, which included technical assistance on problem solving and clinical capacity building. The creation of one multifacility improvement team in Samtredia allowed the project team to achieve cost savings by avoiding separate coaching visits to each facility and instead providing coaching in one location to the multifacility improvement team. This allowed the project to increase the frequency of the coaching, which in turn proved to be a precondition for successful and sustainable improvement.

During the QI team meetings (lasting on average 2–4 hours), village doctors and pediatricians from the ambulatory clinic and the Samtredia District hospital selected medical charts to identify gaps in diagnosis and management of RTIs at individual doctors' practices, as well as coordination of care at different levels. In addition to randomly selecting medical charts with standard RTI diagnoses, members of the QI team also brought for discussion, rare cases of RTIs among children from their clinical practice. They discussed possible interventions/changes in their local health-care processes to close the gaps and improve care. The coaching visits were usually conducted on the weekends (due to unavailability of other free time). The value of the visits was so high for individual provider teams that none of the providers objected to sacrificing their personal time to work on improvement activities without any remuneration for participation from the project or health facilities (e.g., overtime, per diem, or travel costs). Geo Hospitals management was also invited and regularly participated in QI team meetings. Their involvement was instrumental to address gaps in availability of essential key inputs (e.g., diagnostic tests, equipment, and other medical commodities) at medical facilities.

The first coaching visit in June 2012 included a brief overview of QI methodology as well as a clinical lecture on best practices in pediatric pneumonia management. As part of the coaching visit, the project's technical expert presented a typical medical chart of a child in Georgia diagnosed with pneumonia, for whom 11 medications were prescribed. After careful analysis of each prescribed medication, the team agreed that only one medication was necessary. After presenting this typical case, the expert presented the results of the baseline assessment of RTI management that clearly showed the scope of the problem of overprescribing medications. This was followed by a discussion on the impact of such excessive use of medications on antibiotic resistance, patient safety, and costs associated with medical treatment. Team members realized that excessive use of antibiotics and other medications to treat pediatric RTIs was part of their routine practice. They wanted to change this practice but felt unsure and ill equipped to do so.

To help team members use systems thinking, the project helped QI teams use improvement tools such as a problem tree, fishbone (cause-and-effect) diagram, and driver diagrams, to help delineate the root causes of the problem related to irrational use of medications and systematize them according to the six WHO health system building blocks (WHO 2012). Despite being inexperienced and having very limited exposure to QI concepts and methodologies, the providers enthusiastically started identifying the root causes of the irrational prescription practices. Specifically, they identified these four root causes:

- Poor knowledge of evidence-based guidelines and inadequate skills to manage acute pediatric respiratory tract infections
- Inadequate ability to locate and evaluate current scientific evidence and apply it to their clinical practice
- Limited availability of evidence-based medications in the hospitals, in a recommended dosage and form (e.g., amoxicillin)
- Parental misconceptions and beliefs (e.g., their demand for multiple medications, antibiotic prescriptions, parenteral medications, and specialist consultations and additional tests)

Development of Aims and Measures of Improvement

At the first coaching visit, the Imereti teams also discussed and reached initial agreement regarding the overall aim of the improvement intervention as well as improvement objectives, changes to test out, and proposed indicators to assess their progress. The QI teams identified their improvement aim as "decrease morbidity and mortality among children two months to five years of age due to acute upper (rhinitis, sinusitis, pharyngitis) and lower (bronchitis, pneumonia) respiratory infections through improved case management." Since case management of RTIs was identified as a universal challenge among all QI teams supported by the project, all QI teams (including the Samtredia QI team) identified the same overarching goal of improvement interventions, while changes tested to reach the improvement objectives were not always the same. To accurately measure the progress toward this aim, specific improvement objectives and indicators to assess care at all stages (assessment and diagnosis, treatment, parent counseling, and follow-up) were also discussed (Chitashvili and Cherkezishvili 2014).

For example, to evaluate the progress in the quality of clinical assessment and diagnosis, the teams tracked the following two indicators:

- Percent of medical charts of children that had documentation of vital signs, weight, and height
- Percent of medical charts of children with RTI with justified diagnosis (defined as at least one relevant symptom of the disease with duration and objective clinical finding documented in the chart)

The rationale for choosing these indicators was an identified gap found during the baseline assessment of documenting clinical symptoms and their duration in medical charts. For example, to diagnose bronchitis, the provider should at least find out whether that patient has a cough as the main symptom, record its duration, and record relevant lung sounds on both sides. However, even this elementary standard was met in only 5% of medical charts with diagnosis of bronchitis. The same problem was observed across all RTI diagnoses. Poor assessment and documentation of the diagnosis of symptoms and their duration make it impossible to assess the quality of diagnosis/differential diagnosis of RTIs and consequently, clinical decisions around disease management.

Along with improvement aims and indicators, during the first few coaching visits, the QI team also agreed on the sources for data collection, frequency, and sampling for routine monitoring, keeping in mind the need to balance resource (human and financial resources, time) availability and statistical rigor. Specifically, progress in improved RTI practices was routinely assessed through random sampling of medical charts with relevant diagnosis from the facility registries. The project's regional coordinator visited each facility monthly to help health-care providers to select the charts and perform routine monthly monitoring. This monthly monitoring support continued throughout project implementation. In addition, the regional coordinator conducted spot checks of routine monitoring results for at least 25% of selected medical charts at each facility (requiring on average 3–4 hours of work per each facility). Routine monitoring results were entered into Excel by the regional coordinator, and the data from different QI teams were aggregated by the project team.

Testing and Implementing Changes

The changes tested by the team and progress on the indicators were analyzed by using Excel-based annotated time series charts, discussed during the learning sessions, which were held quarterly (eight sessions in all). Progress on indicators during these sessions was shown through poster displays of time series charts showing two or three of the best performing indicators as well as those with the least improvement. The team analyzed the factors and changes that contributed to the improvement and the remaining challenges to address to improve the gaps in quality of care.

The changes introduced were mostly associated with improving the knowledge, skills, and practices of care providers and knowledge and attitudes of patients related to overutilization of medications to treat pediatric RTIs. Patients' attitudes were addressed by counseling parents and families about rational medication use. Based on knowledge and practice gaps, providers identified specific clinical topics for which they needed clinical trainings and information on up-to-date, evidence-based best practices. Table 2.1 details examples of the changes the Samtredia QI team tested to improve RTI diagnosis and management. The full set of changes tested and the evidence-based clinical interventions implemented is available (Chitashvili and Cherkezishvili 2014).

Support for Improvement

To build individual, institutional, and systems capacity (Focal Area #2 of USAID Georgia's Global Health Initiative plan), the project supported continuous strengthening of human resources for health by providing integrated, competency-based clinical and QI trainings for medical care providers and coaching visits to facility-based QI teams participating in the improvement work in Imereti (Chitashvili 2015).

The most frequent format for improving problem solving during the coaching visits, which were usually conducted every 2 weeks, was peer review of medical charts. To conduct these reviews, under the supervision of the external advisor, the QI team members were assigned different roles, which were rotated. For example, while one team member's role was to summarize and critically evaluate the medical chart of his/her peer, other team members discussed the case, identified gaps and best practices in the charts according to agreed indicators, and documented the medical chart review results in the routine monitoring Excel database. Project coaches identified the cases from medical charts that had the most gaps or the best compliance with clinical practice guidelines and used these as a basis for discussion with the QI team. Discussions, usually facilitated by the QI coach, centered on comparing the current care with evidence-based best practices, identifying gaps and their root causes, and discussing changes needed to improve the care. Peer review of medical charts with RTI diagnosis and case discussions were a routine part of each coaching visit.

Initially, at the hospital level, the project planned to improve hospital management of pneumonia (which occurs in about 20% of all RTI cases). However, due to rapid improvement in ambulatory management of respiratory tract infections and hospital management of pneumonia, in September 2012, the project team and QI teams decided to expand the scope of the QI intervention to the whole spectrum of respiratory tract infections at both ambulatory care and hospital levels.

To improve the clinical knowledge and practices of care providers, during the coaching visits, the QI teams received clinical and improvement capacity building through interactive lectures and presentations on evidence-based management of selected clinical conditions by the project's external advisor. These clinical training

Table 2.1 Examples of gaps and changes introduced by the Samtredia QI team to improve the quality of diagnosis and management of RTIs

Problem addressed	What was the change tested and how was it implemented?	Evidence of success
Poor knowledge and skills of care providers to manage acute pediatric respiratory tract infections according to evidence-based guidelines	During coaching visits, engaged care providers in developing new skills and attitudes by: • Assessing gaps in quality of RTI diagnosis and management by regular peer review of medical charts • Dissemination of condition-specific "change packages" focused on high-impact, cost-effective interventions • Alternating roles on the QI team (case presentation, case review and discussion, filling out the routine monitoring sheet) • Using medical chart review and directly observed consultations to assess progress • Organizing regular on-the-job clinical and QI trainings • Promoting high-performing providers within the geo hospitals network by assigning them higher responsibilities, such as clinical supervision of other care providers (no financial incentives were used by the project) and participation in quarterly meetings with other QI team members to learn from each other's experiences	Provider interview results before and after 18 months of project interventions revealed that in addition to improved clinical practice, basic knowledge and skills of providers were also significantly improved. For example, the percentage of doctors who correctly answered all four knowledge assessment multiple-choice questions about pneumonia and RTI management increased from 3.6% (April 2012) to 96.8% (November 2013), while in control sites, it decreased from 7.4% to 0% (81% attributable improvement, $p < 0.001$)
Limited availability of evidence-based (EB) medications in the hospitals, included in a recommended dosage and form	Engaged hospital manager and geo hospitals corporation management to improve access to EB medications by: • Discussing the issue with corporate and facility management to purchase the first-choice antibiotics (e.g., amoxicillin) instead of wide-spectrum antibiotics • Proactively communicating with management about stock-outs and the need to purchase evidence-based medications in guideline-recommended dosages	During the focus group interviews, the QI team reported that since identifying the problem, management has regularly purchased EB medications
Misconceptions among parents of the need to prescribe antibiotics and antipyretic medications to treat pediatric RTIs and provider belief in parent expectations of multiple drugs and antibiotic prescription	Improved parent counseling on the importance of rational use of antibiotics and other medications and of the challenges associated with inappropriate use of medications, including self-treatment of their children with RTIs, by: • Discussing during the QI team meetings the best strategies to communicate with parents Counseling patients/parents of the children with RTIs about rational medication use at every patient visit • Counseling parents on when to give antipyretic medication and danger signs that require follow-up with the care provider • Discussing the issue of irrational use of medications at medical conferences and meetings and sharing the success of their efforts to reduce non-EB medications Sharing these messages via local media and TV by well-respected clinicians, including the head of the respiratory care association	In patient phone interviews, parents indicated improved knowledge and practice of respiratory tract infection self-management after 18 months of project interventions (from April 2012 to November 2013). The number of respondents naming medications prescribed by the doctor that are relevant to the parent-reported diagnosis increased by 28.4% (attributable difference + 20.1%, $p < 0.006$), and the average number of non-EB medications prescribed reported by patients/parents decreased from 3.8 to 1.5

Source: Chitashvili and Cherkezishvili (2014)

sessions were integral parts of the coaching visits and usually were conducted in the clinic rather than in a classroom setting. The gaps in provider knowledge and practices were regularly assessed by knowledge assessment questionnaires and directly observed during clinical visits of children with RTIs. Patients for directly observed consultations were selected based on the RTI diagnosis (to ensure full range of RTI diagnosis) and patient/parent consent. Observation was conducted by QI team members, the external advisor, and other clinical consultants of the project. During such observations, after obtaining informed consent from the children's parents, patients were invited to group consultations. During the directly observed consultations, randomly selected QI team members demonstrated their skills and knowledge by consulting with children with different RTI diagnoses. Other team members took notes and, together with the external advisor and the project team, discussed the quality of care provided after the consultations.

Another example of the on-the-job training methods used by the project was the use of local specialists to build capacity of family physicians to address the felt needs of providers. For example, during one of the team meetings, village doctors expressed their discomfort about performing otoscopy and in general based their diagnoses solely on clinical symptoms or referred patients to specialists. This created significant barriers for children in villages to access care in a timely fashion and avoid pain. All village doctors had otoscopes (distributed in 2006–2007 as part of the Primary Health Care Professionals Retraining Program funded by the European Union), but without any experience and practice, they lacked confidence and did not use this important diagnostic tool in their everyday practice. After identification of the problem, the QI team organized on-the-job trainings and a workshop on "Otoscopy in pediatric respiratory tract infections." The workshop was conducted by the otorhinolaryngologist from Samtredia Geo Hospitals (where the QI team conducted regular meetings), together with the project team. It consisted of lectures and practical training sessions on indications, execution, and interpretation of an otoscopic exam. For these purposes, the project and QI team members invited patients from all project-supported sites and conducted free testing and consultation sessions with patients during the seminar. Typically, medical trainings in Georgia were more theory-based and less applied (i.e., theoretical lectures for large audiences, usually off-site, and without the possibility to practice newly acquired skills). The new format enabled family doctors from villages and district ambulatory clinics to immediately apply skills and knowledge received during the training under the direct supervision of highly qualified experts. Because information on the number and proportion of otitis diagnosed at the primary care level was not readily available within each and across different medical facilities, the QI team was not able to document the improvement in diagnosis of otitis at the primary care level.

To address the poor knowledge of medical care providers, the project's main approach was not only to provide updates on evidence-based clinical practice but also to equip the team with the skills to search and assess clinical recommendations in terms of strength of evidence and its applicability to their clinical practice using the PICOT (Patient, Intervention, Comparison, Outcome, Types of Study) model. From passive "recipients" of updated evidence-based best practices from the project, members of the Samtredia QI team turned into active "consumers" of EB literature – skills they could use to identify best care practices/clinical content of improvement interventions in any clinical focus area. Specifically, the project:

- Invited QI team members to participate in Translating Research into Practice (TRIP) on-the-job trainings, conducted by the project, in collaboration with the New York University nursing school
- Conducted regular case study discussions and review of evidence-based medical literature during QI team meetings
- Encouraged care providers to search for and review medical literature and have them present the literature during the regional learning sessions and medical conferences organized by the project at the local, regional, and national levels
- Encouraged QI teams to organize workshops for other care providers and share the evidence updates on management of particular RTIs, comorbidities, and rare and interesting cases

In an environment of constantly updated evidence-based clinical recommendations based on new research findings, the project believed that such an approach built providers' capacity to sustain improved compliance with best care practices in any clinical area of their interest even after the end of the project-supported improvement interventions. Similarly, the providers participating on the QI team could use the improvement capacity they acquired during the RTI work and apply it to any priority clinical area.

The clinical content for the above-mentioned clinical trainings was developed through close collaboration with local professional associations, such as the Georgia Family Medicine Association, Georgian Respiratory Association, Georgian Hypertension Society, Georgian Cardiology Association, Georgian Association of Pediatricians, and Georgian Association of Allergology and Clinical Immunology.

To increase utilization of continuous learning opportunities by the greatest number of physicians in Georgia, the project also supported communication and information exchanges between medical care facility managers, providers, and organizations/individuals and invited local physicians to participate in regional learning sessions and other project events (Chitashvili 2015).

Results

After 20 months of QI interventions, the Samtredia QI team dramatically improved RTI diagnosis and management practices. For example, the indicator "percent of medical charts of children with RTI with justified diagnosis" increased from 47% to 100% (Fig. 2.2).

Improvements in proper diagnosis were also accompanied by better management and treatment of RTIs, including rational antibiotic therapy. Based on the national

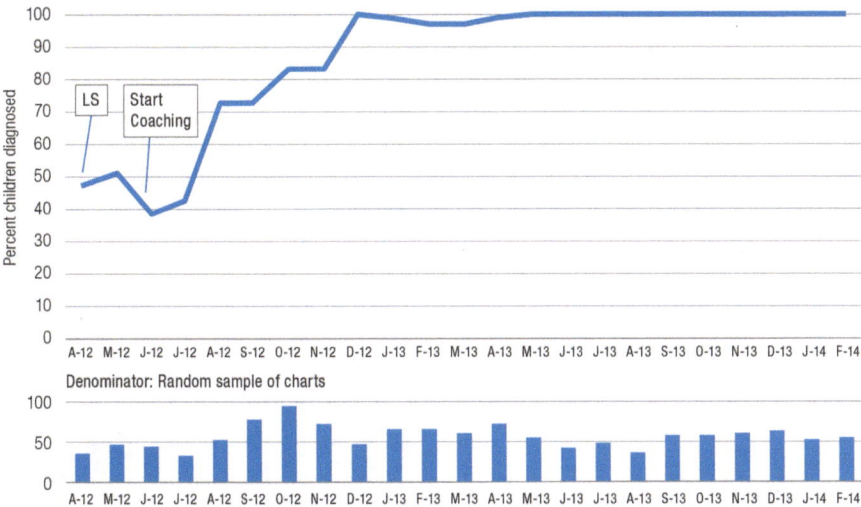

Fig. 2.2 Percent of children diagnosed with acute RTI for whom diagnosis is supported by medical chart documentation in Samtredia Geo Hospitals, its ambulatory center, and seven village family doctor practices (April 2012 to February 2014)

guidelines and their original source from the British Thoracic Society, the indicator monitored by the team requires that: (1) an antibiotic is indicated, and (2) the first-choice antibiotic is selected for the patient's age and symptoms (first-choice medication and right form, dose, and frequency). As shown in Fig. 2.3, the use of first-line antibiotics increased from 7% to 100% at project-supported sites from April 2012 to February 2014. (Note that hospital data are shown only from September 2012, when the project decided to broaden the clinical scope from pneumonia to all RTIs treated at the hospital level.)

Similarly, according to the baseline assessment, the use of other non-evidence-based (non-EB) medications (such as vitamins, short-acting methylxanthines, the so-called metabolics, expectorants, and cough depressants) was the routine practice in the region. During the project interventions, the number of non-EB medications per patient decreased from 1.12 to 0.03 at ambulatories and from 7.0 to 0.0 at the hospital in Samtredia District.

In sum, average compliance with all process indicators monitored increased by 57% from April 2012 to February 2014 (Fig. 2.4).

The cost-effectiveness analysis conducted by the project for the entire Georgia QI intervention showed that these QI interventions were effective not only in terms of improvement in evidence-based clinical practice but also from the viewpoint of rationalization of hospital pediatric pneumonia and ambulatory RTI management costs. Results showed that after 30 months of implementation of quality improvement interventions (with the assumption that the achieved level will be sustained for at least a year), the incremental cost saving per patient in the case of hospital management of pediatric pneumonia was 21.1 USD, and in the case of

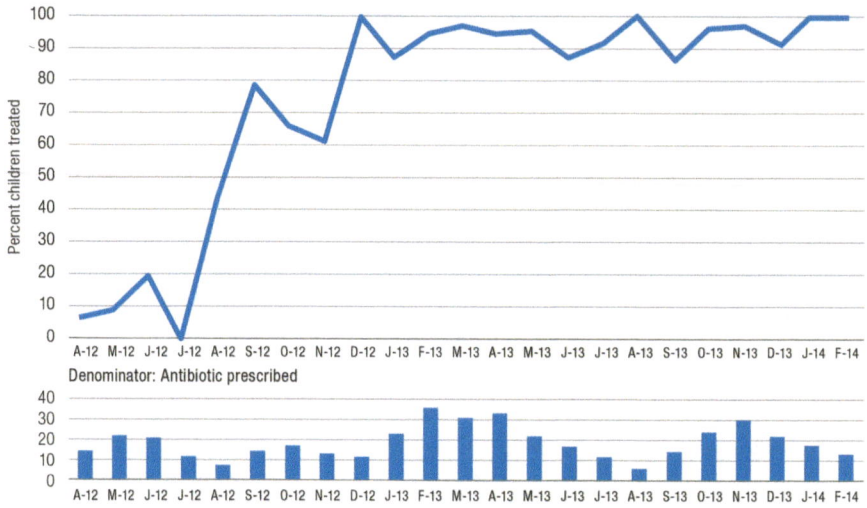

Fig. 2.3 Percent of children treated with first-line antibiotic for acute RTI in Samtredia Geo Hospitals, its ambulatory center, and seven village family doctor practices (April 2012 to February 2014)

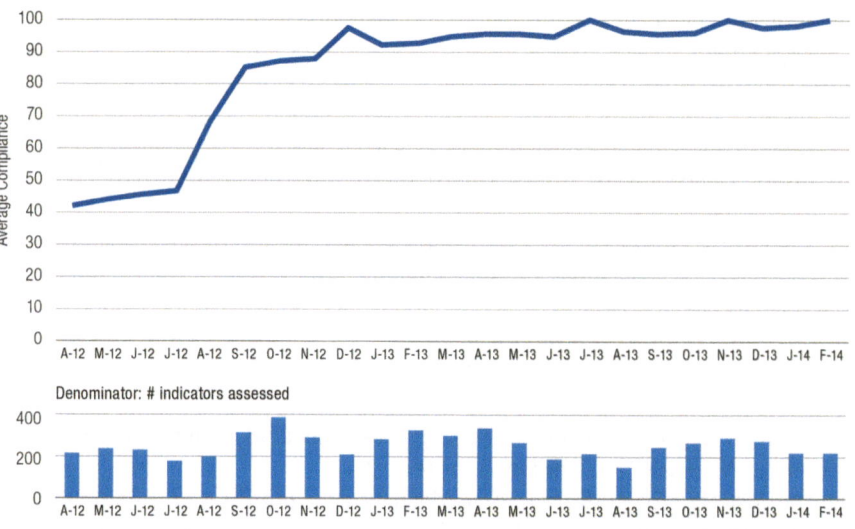

Fig. 2.4 Average compliance with all indicators in random sample of charts in Samtredia Geo Hospitals, its ambulatory center, and seven village family doctor practices (April 2012 to February 2014)

ambulatory management of pediatric RTI, it was 4.5 USD. Assessment of incremental cost savings using decision-tree analysis for each selected indicator showed that the intervention was more cost saving than the business-as-usual alternative. This means that as a result of the quality improvement interventions, the quality of care assessed with the selected indicators improved, simultaneously while eliminating the costs of non-EB practice. Specifically, while the project-related cost of the intervention for hospital management of pneumonia was 15,870 USD and for ambulatory management of RTIs was 23,807[1] USD, after the intervention (due to the decrease in prescribing of non-EB medications and diagnostic tests), 19,708 USD and 135,318 USD, respectively, were saved. The cost savings exceeded intervention-related expenses by 15,215 USD (9.8 USD per patient) for hospital and 102,032 USD (6.6 USD per patient) for ambulatory management of RTI. In other words, the intervention saved 9.8 USD and 6.6 USD per patient, for hospital and ambulatory management of RTI, respectively, and increased the likelihood of receiving better quality of care for pediatric RTIs in the intervention facilities (Chitashvili 2015).

Spreading the Knowledge

Along with the documented improvements, medical providers themselves also expressed a willingness to spread the modern evidence-based best practices outside of the project. With project support, they conducted two medical conferences for doctors not supported by the QI intervention. At the conferences, featured on regional TV channels, they presented their clinical cases along with critical analyses and justification of changed/improved practices. The fact that they gradually changed the themes for the conferences from the "Management of the Most Prevalent Pediatric Respiratory Diseases" (conducted in February 2012) to "Rare and Interesting cases of Pediatric Respiratory Clinical Conditions" (conducted in January 2013) illustrates also the evolution of their knowledge and confidence managing these cases.

Reflection

Thinking back, all decisions made at the beginning of the project regarding design and composition of the improvement team were successful; the design of the team allowed efficient use of project resources and took into account the intrinsic motivations not only of health-care providers but also of patients and

---

[1] 1 USD = 1.7 GEL.

the private corporations that owned the facilities. The choice of the project expert/coach also greatly influenced the success of the improvement effort. The expert himself attributed the success to the methodology of quality improvement: *"The format the project introduced was different from the traditional trainings we were used to in the country. Intensiveness of the interventions close to clinical practice, routine monitoring of the results achieved, and enthusiasm of our colleagues in the region enabled us to exceed expectations and reach spectacular results. At the beginning of the project, we could not imagine that our doctors would manage difficult clinical cases in resource-constrained settings and have their decisions be compatible with the current best evidence. It was a pleasure to witness the transformation of the QI team from reactive listeners to proactive planners. Quite soon they started to plan the agenda for next meetings, identify the most visible gaps in their knowledge and skills, ask for trainings, bring their cases, and suggest new activities for the group. I am really happy to be part of this project and hope that this experience as well as personal contacts will continue after the end of the project."*

In contrast with other projects implemented in Georgia, this project built not only clinical but also improvement capacity of care providers and managers. Now they are equipped with the knowledge and skills to identify and manage gaps in other processes of care, as well as identify the evidence-based content of care by searching for and critically reviewing the existing scientific evidence. As one of the Samtredia QI team members, a family physician, mentioned, these are the skills she and her colleagues value the most as an outcome of the project and use in day-to-day clinical practice, regardless of the clinical area: *"We were taught about the importance of guidelines during our family medicine training. For example, we received copies of 40 guidelines and training on some of them. But it is really difficult to return from [such] lectures and transform your practice in one day, without support and feedback. One needs guidance and assurance that complications came from the natural history of diseases and not from your mistakes, or because the guideline recommendation was wrong. Without this kind assistance, rarely anybody have the courage to go against widespread practice, doctors' and parents' beliefs [...] From today's perspective, I see that I had flaws even in understanding guidelines, for example the levels of evidence, the strength of the recommendation. When you have the deep knowledge and intensive support, it is not difficult to persuade anybody: patient, parent, colleague, employer [...] And what is more important is you have the internal assurance of doing the right thing and protecting patients from unnecessary medications and risks associated with their use."*

Finally, a huge success of the project was incorporating rigorous research into the intervention design to complement the regular QI team monitoring data. The cost-effectiveness study, yet to be published, generated evidence on effectiveness and cost impact of the QI intervention which is instrumental to make evidence-based decisions at different levels of the health service delivery system in Georgia and many similar settings. Similarly, routine monitoring of the progress and regular coaching helped clinical providers to see the progress of their efforts, better understand remaining gaps, and refine changes to continuously improve the content and process of care.

The major regret for us is that due to ongoing major health sector reform and changes in governance within the health system in Georgia, scale-up of the improvement interventions was not systematically undertaken by the state and monitoring indicators were not integrated into the routine reporting systems to promote measurement and accountability.

In the future, we feel that to scale up successful QI best practices, we could also consider limiting assistance to the demonstration QI teams for 18 months and use the project resources to spread the QI interventions to other facilities using our QI champions as coaches to their peers.

Snapshot of a Changed Practice

A 6-month-old male patient was brought for an ambulatory visit in Samtredia Geo Hospitals due to nasal discharge and fever. The doctor explained to the mother that the boy had a viral respiratory tract infection, a common condition that needed no treatment other than an antipyretic (if the fever was more than 38.5 °C), comfort, and fluids. Then the doctor explained to the patient's mother the abnormal signs for this condition and what she could do if dangerous signs occurred. The doctor explained that the drugs commonly used in previous years were not necessary. The mother later said, *"At first, I was afraid to just watch my ill child suffering and not give him anything. But, after seeing the same result as with 5–6 medications for older kids, I felt assured and happy. Now I know what is dangerous and when the treatment is just comfort and warmth of the mother. I feel confident that with the close monitoring of our pediatrician, my kids will be healthy, and we will not miss anything dangerous."*

Acknowledgments   The authors express special gratitude to Project Quality Advisor consultant Ivane Chkhaidze, regional coordinator Ketevan Jugheli, and the Samtredia QI team members – Tamar Loladze, Bela Bregvadze, Khatuna Kobakhidze, Ekaterine Dvalishvili, Marina Dondua, Irma Amaglobeli, Mzia Sakvarelidze, Olga Vashakidze, Nana Loria, and Tvalmaisa Amaglobeli – for their hard work, professionalism, and devotion to the improvement of health care in Georgia. The authors also express gratitude to the central management of Geo Hospitals – George Kvinikadze, Ia Sephiashvili, and Sergo Magradze – and to managers of the Samtredia branch of Geo Hospitals, Irakli Lagidze and Luara Kakhiani, for their exceptional support and contribution to team success. Finally, we appreciate the Ministry of Health, Labour and Social Affairs of Georgia, the National Center for Disease Control and Public Health, and USAID for supporting and financing the project and University Research Co., LLC (URC) for implementing the project.

The work described in this case was funded by the USAID Office of Health Systems through the USAID Applying Science to Strengthen and Improve Systems Project, implemented by URC under Cooperative Agreement Number AID-OAA-A-12-00101.

References

Chanturidze T, Ugulava T, Duran A, Ensor T, Richardson E (2009) Georgia: health system review. Health Syst Transit 11(8):1–116. Available at: http://www.euro.who.int/__data/assets/pdf_file/0003/85530/E93714.pdf

Chitashvili T (2015) Scaling up, sustaining and institutionalizing better health care in Georgia: results and strategic recommendations from USAID support for improving quality of priority clinical conditions during 2012–2015. Technical report. Published by the USAID ASSIST Project. University Research Co., LLC (URC), Bethesda. Available at: https://pdf.usaid.gov/pdf_docs/PA00W72V.pdf

Chitashvili T, Cherkezishvili E (2014) Tested changes and applied evidence-based clinical interventions to improve care of respiratory infections among children in Georgia's Imereti region. Published by the USAID Health Care Improvement Project. University Research Co., LLC (URC), Bethesda. Available at: https://pdf.usaid.gov/pdf_docs/PA00W72T.pdf

National Center for Disease Control and Public Health (NCDC&PH) (2013) Ministry of Labour, Health and Social Affairs of Georgia. Statistical Yearbook, 2012. Tbilisi. Available at: http://ncdc.ge/AttachedFiles/2012_ebdab6ba-1aef-45af-bb77-d087e98ebeed.pdf

World Health Organization (2012) Monitoring the building blocks of health systems: a handbook of indicators and their measurement strategies. Available at: http://www.who.int/healthinfo/systems/monitoring/en/

World Health Organization and UNICEF (2013) Ending preventable child deaths from pneumonia and diarrhoea by 2025: the integrated global action plan for pneumonia and diarrhoea (GAPPD). Available at: http://apps.who.int/iris/bitstream/10665/79200/1/9789241505239_eng.pdf

Chapter 3
Addressing Behavior Change in Maternal, Neonatal, and Child Health with Quality Improvement and Collaborative Learning Methods in Guatemala

Elena Hurtado, Lilian Ramírez, and Pablo Moreira

Abstract This case describes how two projects in Guatemala, both funded by the US Agency for International Development (USAID), applied quality improvement (QI) principles and methods to social and behavior change communication (SBCC) interventions. QI has been mostly associated with improving clinical care, where teams review medical records to determine whether caregivers complied with care quality criteria and then suggest and test process changes to address gaps. Project leaders and stakeholders were convinced that QI elements, such as the plan-do-study-act (PDSA) cycle and collaborative learning methods, could also work to improve SBCC interventions. This case recounts the experiences of a community-based improvement collaborative involving 166 health posts and 429 community centers in Guatemala. The initiative focused on improving processes of care and nutritional results during the first 1000 days of life (from pregnancy to the child's second birthday) to improve the effectiveness of interpersonal communication and counseling and other SBCC strategies to increase the health knowledge of women and their families and achieve change in 19 health and nutrition-related behaviors.

Keywords Behavior change communication · Guatemala · Interpersonal communication and counseling · Lot quality assurance sampling · Maternal, newborn, and child health · Nutrition · Quality improvement · Traditional birth attendants

Background

From 2007 to 2014, the two USAID-funded projects worked with the Ministry of Health (MOH) of Guatemala to strengthen maternal, neonatal, and child health (MNCH) and nutritional care. Both projects relied heavily on the use of quality improvement collaboratives to improve health-care services and SBCC. A quality

E. Hurtado (✉) · L. Ramírez · P. Moreira
Formerly with University Research Co., LLC, Guatemala City, Guatemala

© University Research Co., LLC 2020
L. R. Marquez (ed.), *Improving Health Care in Low- and Middle-Income Countries*, https://doi.org/10.1007/978-3-030-43112-9_3

27

improvement collaborative consists of a large number of improvement teams from multiple health-care facilities working together and meeting often to promote mutual learning and data exchange in a specific area of care to trigger even more rapid health-care improvement (USAID Health Care Improvement Project 2008). Teams in the MNCH collaboratives in Guatemala conducted PDSA cycles to test process changes to improve compliance with health care and SBCC standards.

While the collaboratives produced recognizable results in facility-based clinical care during the projects' initial stages, project leaders, stakeholders, and participants realized that most deliveries and maternal deaths occurred in the communities – outside the clinical care setting. They, therefore, decided that the way forward was to focus on improving MNCH-related knowledge and skills within communities by improving: pregnant women's recognition of danger signs; individual, family, and community preparation of emergency plans; traditional midwives' participation in referrals; and culturally appropriate, patient-centered delivery services. Project leaders, subsequently, looked to develop community collaboratives that focused on using QI to improve SBCC interventions.

To do this, the projects had to take into account the organization of the health-care system, the number and type of health personnel working at the primary level (see Box 3.1), and the nature of the SBCC strategies that were being implemented at the time. Among the many channels in which SBCC interventions are carried out, interpersonal communication and counseling play a particularly critical role. Project leaders and participants realized that the data yielded by current SBCC documentation left them unable to measure the quality of counseling and, more importantly, its effects on pregnant women's knowledge and practices. For example, while clinical teams had added checklists in their registers as reminders or ways to measure quality of care indicators, such as development of a birth/emergency plan, provision of postpartum family planning counseling, and delivery of communication materials to clients, these forms did not provide the evidence needed to ascertain quality or measure results. In addition, although this type of counseling was also conducted in home visits, no records were kept of counseling provided during home visits, and results were never measured or analyzed by auxiliary nurses and community health workers.

Box 3.1 Snapshot: The Health Care System in Guatemala

From 1996 to 2014, primary health-care services in Guatemala were provided in health posts directly managed by the MOH, a few health facilities were supported by municipalities, and community centers were managed by NGOs. The NGOs operated in the Extension of Coverage Program, which was part of the government's primary health-care program, under contracts with the MOH. In the health posts and the community centers, a single auxiliary nurse provided health care, and occasionally, a professional nurse or a last-year

Box 3.1 (continued)

medical student provided health care in health posts. In the community, mostly in areas covered by the Extension of Coverage Program, auxiliary nurses, rural health technicians, and health educators were in charge of health promotion and SBCC activities. In some places, volunteers or health promoters and mother counselors supported by different NGOs or projects also participated.

Designing the Improvement Effort

After a first community-based collaborative proved critical in effecting changes to maternal health knowledge and practices in a demonstration area, the project introduced, in 2012, a second community-based collaborative in 166 health posts and 429 community centers. The initiative focused on improving processes of care and nutritional results during the first 1000 days of life (from pregnancy to the child's second birthday). They were able to introduce the collaborative at a large scale because leaders promoted the community effort as one that would build upon earlier successes with clinical and community collaboratives.

All improvement starts with an aim. The primary objective of the second large-scale community-based collaborative was to improve the effectiveness of interpersonal communication and counseling and other SBCC strategies in order to increase the health knowledge of women and their families and achieve change in 19 health and nutrition-related behaviors. These behaviors were the core of the SBCC strategy and the focus of a strategic counseling tool known as the "Wheel of Practices for Better Living"[1] that was introduced by the project to promote maternal health and prevent chronic malnutrition (Fig. 3.1).

To generate interest in expanding the QI collaborative's focus on SBCC for MNCH, the project initially used a local advocacy approach. Project leaders worked with social workers, rural health technicians, and health educators from the MOH Health Promotion and Education Department, the mandate of which was to implement SBCC interventions. Project leaders showed MOH staff how information and data on health promotion activities and behavioral outcomes was critical to improving their ability to communicate with and interact with clients in the community. Further, they sought to demonstrate how the QI methods being used to improve clinical health care could be used to improve community SBCC. To garner buy-in from the central-level MOH, the project invited the authorities to the health districts' quarterly learning sessions, where health-care improvement data on selected

---

[1] The Wheel of Practices for Better Living (*Rueda de Prácticas Para Vivir Mejor* in Spanish) is available at https://dec.usaid.gov/dec/content/Detail_Presto.aspx?ctID=ODVhZjk4NWQtM2Yy Mi00YjRmLTkxNjktZTcxMjM2NDBmY2Uy&rID=NTU1Nzk4&inr=VHJ1ZQ%3d%3d&dc=Y WRk&rrtc=VHJ1ZQ%3d%3d&bckToL=

Fig. 3.1 The wheel of practices for better living

process indicators for maternal and neonatal care were presented and discussed by primary health-care worker teams. Conducted as celebratory events with activities to recognize and highlight accomplishments, the learning sessions proved effective in instilling enthusiasm for QI work. In addition, the sessions provided an opportunity for the MOH Health Promotion and Education Department officials to learn about QI methods that could be used to support SBCC.

After MOH officials observed and participated in sessions and talked with participants and project staff, they began to envision how applying QI methodology could support health promotion. Support for using improvement methods to strengthen SBCC messaging and campaigns grew among officials of the department as they became convinced of the effectiveness of this approach. Their advocacy for this work was critical to the ability of the project to work with health area technical teams on indicators, sampling, data collection instruments, analysis, coaching, and improvement interventions.

Formation of Collaborative Teams

The establishment of the 2012 community collaborative's quality improvement teams was a participatory process. At first, the project attempted to form teams in each primary health-care facility. However, frequently there was only one auxiliary nurse in a facility, especially in health posts, which made collaborative learning difficult or impossible. Therefore, Municipal Health District authorities and project staff decided instead to create "supervision areas" that joined auxiliary nurses from contiguous health posts within each health district and all personnel in each nongovernmental organization (NGO) jurisdiction. These supervision areas typically had a population of 10,000 inhabitants who were expected to be covered by the health facilities in the area.

The project also envisioned the formation of two QI teams in each supervision area: one devoted to the improvement of clinical health care, led by the auxiliary nurses, and the other devoted to SBCC initiatives, led by the rural health technicians or the health educators. However, district authorities and health providers found this was not feasible for several reasons. First, in these settings, the auxiliary nurse was responsible not only for clinical care but for health promotion as well, and thus participated in SBCC initiatives. In addition, there were too few staff members in these rural areas, and many had very limited education. Learning to apply QI methods also requires a certain amount of training in data collection, recording, analysis, and planning in order to be implemented successfully; on top of this, there was a high number of coaching visits and learning sessions needed. As a result, project leaders strongly recommended assembling only one QI team in each supervision area, but having different actors lead an effort, depending on whether it was a clinical or community initiative.

In the end, the health districts defined 104 supervision areas,[2] 38 of which were MOH jurisdictions, composed of 4–6 health posts each, and 66 of which were NGO jurisdictions, composed of 4–5 community centers. Supervision areas, rather than the municipal health center, became the locus of activity. Each one had a QI team with up to five members of different types of health personnel – auxiliary nurses, health educators, rural health technicians, and community facilitators – depending on the types of personnel available in the different health-care delivery models and at the various facilities. These teams examined both clinical quality of care in records and maternal knowledge and practices indicative of the quality of behavior change interventions.

The project also organized 30 higher level health district QI teams comprised of a physician coordinator, a professional nurse, a rural health technician, and the

---

[2] Supervision areas were composed of 4–6 contiguous MOH health posts (each health posttheoretically covered a population of 2000) or one NGO jurisdiction with 4–5 community centers (a jurisdiction theoretically covered a population of 10,000). At the beginning, there were 38 health posts and 66 NGO jurisdiction supervision areas. At the most active point of the collaborative, there were 112 supervision areas – 40 MOH health postsupervision areas and 72 NGO jurisdiction supervision areas.

NGO teams in charge of monitoring the collaborative effort (Hurtado et al. 2011). In 2012, the project signed agreements with 19 NGOs and trained NGO staff, generally professional nurses, in facilitation techniques and tools for community-based collaboratives under the Extension of Coverage health-care delivery model. In turn, NGO staff often conducted training of their community QI teams.

Within a single QI team in each supervision area, the auxiliary nurses conducted the collection and analysis of the health-care data from clinical records, while the rural health technicians, health educators, and/or community facilitators collected and consolidated data from community-based interviews. All staff were considered members of the QI team and participated in both clinical and community QI efforts, especially in analyzing results and planning changes that would lead to improvement.

Understanding SBCC Processes

Assessing the quality of SBCC processes such as interpersonal communication and counseling cannot be performed entirely through record review, as is typically done for assessing clinical health care. It is uncommon to find records of counseling, and even less so with enough detail to determine quality. As mentioned, checklists on counseling and for registering graphic materials provided to clients had already been added to clinical records (prenatal, postnatal, neonatal, and child) and were being reviewed in the clinical QI component, but data were insufficient to ascertain quality and effectiveness to improve SBCC activities.

The project then considered using other techniques such as direct observation and/or individual exit interviews to determine quality of counseling. Although the teams agreed that direct observation would be the gold standard for QI monitoring, they had to be realistic about the requirements to gathering these data, as it would require considerable training and standardization, time, effort, and resources. Instead, they decided that the community-based behavior change component would focus on changes in knowledge and practices of pregnant women and/or mothers in the community. These changes were theorized to occur as outcomes of improved interpersonal communication and counseling primarily through home visits by community health workers (see "Outputs/Outcomes" in Fig. 3.2).

It is fair to say that with the approach taken (measuring outcome knowledge and practices), the project relied on the validity of indicators to reflect the quality and effectiveness of SBCC. Also, it relied on the validity of the indicators in improving the health and nutrition of the people who are in the coverage area of health facilities. However, these assumptions are often made in QI work; specific appropriate studies would have needed to be conducted to firmly establish the link between QI collaborative efforts and health outcomes in the population.

Based on the available evidence and the health and nutrition situation in Guatemala, the MOH and the SBCC QI collaboratives developed indicators for selected key essential behaviors or practices for families with pregnant women and/ or children under 2 years of age. Most of these were topics already included in the

Inputs	Processes (Activities)	Outputs/Outcomes (Products or effects)
Persons, staff	Implementation of	Provision of health care/
Infrastructure	evidence-based	nutrition services
Material supplies	intervention or set of	User satisfaction
Medicines	interventions	**Changes in knowledge, attitudes, intentions and/or practices**
Information and Communication technology	IPC/C in clinic and home visits; health talks	

	Clinical Health Care QI Collaborative Indicators	SBCC QI Collaborative Indicators

Fig. 3.2 SBCC inputs, processes, and outcomes

Table 3.1 Standards and indicators in the community-based collaboratives

Standard	Indicator	Description
All families should have a hand-washing station at home	Percentage of families with children under 2 years of age that have a specific place to wash hands, with soap and water	The hand-washing station can be inside the house, but it can also be on the corridor or patio of the house; presence of water and soap required
Every pregnant woman should recognize at least three danger signs during pregnancy, delivery, and postpartum	Percentage of pregnant women who can name at least three danger signs during pregnancy, delivery, and the postpartum	Danger signs common to pregnancy, delivery, and postpartum are hemorrhage, blurred vision, constant headache, abdominal pain, difficult breathing, and fever
Every pregnant woman should have an emergency plan filled out	Percentage of pregnant women who have an emergency plan filled out	Evidence of having card filled out: place and money rows filled out, and emergency plan is signed by family member or friend in charge of putting it into action in case of a danger sign

MOH counseling protocols and SBCC strategies, but they were turned into standards and indicators with specific descriptions. Examples of standards and the indicators developed are presented in Table 3.1.

Measuring indicators entailed that each quarter a sample of 19 pregnant women or mothers of children 0–2 years of age from each supervision area were selected to interview[3] using Lot Quality Assurance Sampling (LQAS). The project trained the teams in the sampling method, provided the tools, and supervised teams in the selection of households and respondents and the LQAS interview process. After measuring knowledge and practice indicators, the QI team consolidated and

---

[3] The Lot Quality Assurance Sampling (LQAS) methodology was used to draw samples of 19 pregnant women or mothers of children under 2 years to provide information on maternal knowledge and practices in each supervision area.

Table 3.2 BEHAVE format for planning improvement changes in the community-based collaboratives

To help _____ (target group)	To: _____ (behavior)	We will focus on: _____ (use weaknesses or factors identified)	By doing: _____ (activities)	Detailed description of activities	Quarter		
					1st mo	2nd mo	3rd mo
Pregnant women	Recognize at least three danger signs during pregnancy, delivery, and postpartum (indicator)	Increasing perception of risk and knowledge of six common danger signs for pregnancy, delivery, and postpartum	In each home visit, health talk, and prenatal care visit, mention "six dangers" to pregnant women	1. Create a recall material (ended up being rhyme and mimic)	X		
				2. Train health providers to use it		X	
				3. Use it in every home visit, talk, and prenatal consultation		X	X

Source of the BEHAVE format: FHI 360 (who purchased the assets of the Academy for Educational Development in July 2011); released with permission under a Creative Commons Attribution 4.0 International License (CC BY 4.0) https://creativecommons.org/licenses/by/4.0/

analyzed results and identified those indicators that scored lower. Then, they discussed the reasons for low performance and planned changes in SBCC activities to improve results that could be implemented during home visits, health talks, and even mass media campaigns.

To plan these changes, the community-based collaboratives initially used tools from the behavior change field[4] and adapted them for use in QI. An important tool was the BEHAVE model developed by the Academy for Educational Development (Table 3.2). The BEHAVE model focused health workers on specific actions to convey danger signs to pregnant women.

Later on, the community collaborative used the standard QI "planning matrix" being used in the clinical health-care collaborative to plan changes and improve results. It contained six columns: (1) gap found, (2) proposed change, (3) activities to be conducted, (4) where, (5) when, and (6) person responsible for leading the effort.

Example of Carrying Out the SBCC Improvement Effort in Chichicastenango, Quiché

The QI team in one supervision area of Quiché applied QI methods to improve the indicators related to pregnant women having an emergency plan and recognizing danger signs. The team noted that they were not meeting their targets regarding

---

[4] The BEHAVE Framework was originally developed by the Academy of Educational Development, which later became part of FHI 360.

pregnant women recognizing danger signs and having an emergency plan to respond to them. Therefore, they decided to follow a major QI principle: Always involve in the improvement effort those who directly perform the process, in whole or in part. This meant including traditional birth attendants (TBAs) in the intervention and inviting them to be part of the QI team. In Guatemala, TBAs are generally illiterate older women, experienced and well respected in the community, who care for women from pregnancy to the postpartum period. In rural indigenous communities, they can attend as many as 80% of deliveries.

The intervention required challenging a perception that TBAs would be reluctant or unwilling to talk about emergency birth plans with their patients lest the family think they were incapable of attending women in their homes. Whether or not this perception was valid, the teams knew they had to find a way to get the TBAs to assume ownership of the intervention.

MOH guidelines required only that TBAs be taught about danger signs and that they refer to the hospital pregnant women who displayed those symptoms. However, trainings had not covered having TBAs review the specific components of an emergency plan, such as identifying the referral hospital, preparing for transportation, designating a person to help at home, and how to put the plan into action. Women were filling out the plans in the prenatal clinic, but TBAs were not encouraged to discuss the plans with the women.

The QI team, in partnership with representatives of the TBAs (e.g., better known TBAs, those with more patients, and/or those with closer ties to health services who represent the other TBAs), developed a new approach to emergency plans. The new procedures required that each TBA visit the referral hospital to develop an understanding of the components of the plan including:

- Knowing the cost of transportation and vehicles available in the community
- Designating someone to help at home, if they accompanied the woman to the hospital
- Communicating with the community health commission to activate the community emergency plan

In addition, TBAs were given emergency planning cards to provide their patients in case their patients had not received such a card in the health post or community center.

The QI team tested the interventions during two quarters by training TBAs, organizing guided visits to the appropriate hospital, and meeting with the health commission to discuss the community emergency plan.

After this intervention began to yield successful results (see Box 3.2), the health district continued to actively work with the TBAs to address other obstacles. One challenge was the low number of women receiving prenatal and neonatal services. In particular, very few pregnant women were initiating prenatal care in the first trimester. This lack of care during the first 12 weeks delays the initiation of micronutrient supplementation, nutritional counseling, and other interventions and puts women at risk of worse health and pregnancy outcomes. Again, TBAs were involved since they usually have contact with pregnant women before the official health services do.

Box 3.2
During 2013 our NGO target of pregnant women detected before 12 weeks of pregnancy was 25, but it was not met. In 2014, our target was set at 30, something which worried us very much. In our analysis meetings of both clinical and community results, we observed that the referral of pregnant women with complications had increased after actively involving the TBAs. Therefore, we proposed a strategy of involving the TBAs in wider referral of women and children to health services and created 'the TBA's folder.'

–NGO nurse in Quiché

In addition to referring pregnant women with danger signs to health services, TBAs became involved in referring all pregnant women at the onset of pregnancy, all postpartum women, newborns, and all healthy and sick children under 2 years of age to health services. In addition, they were also asked to refer nonpregnant women of reproductive age to health services for family planning or for treatment of an illness. For this purpose, each TBA in the jurisdiction received a folder with her identification details, including name, address, and a list of the communities she attended. The folder contained five different colored envelopes, each containing cards with pictures: (1) red for postpartum mothers and newborns, (2) yellow for pregnant women, (3) green for nonpregnant reproductive-aged women, (4) blue for healthy children under 2 years; and (5) gray for a sick child or woman, or a pregnant woman showing a danger sign.

TBAs gave their clients an appropriately colored card to give to the facility health provider. The health provider registered the referral, signed and stamped the card, and gave it back to the TBA who had sent it. At the end of the month, the TBAs got together at the health facility and counted the number of cards of each color that had been signed and stamped by the facility personnel. The TBAs explained to the nurse the cases referred, received feedback, and were acknowledged and congratulated for their work (see Box 3.3). Those with the largest number of referrals at the end of the quarter also received a certificate of accomplishment from the health facility.

Box 3.3
These folders are a useful and productive tool for us. Before I could not demonstrate my work, but with the folders I can show the work that I do... I am very happy with the folders.

–A TBA in the supervision area

The change was implemented from April to June 2014. By June 2014, in the same supervision area, 55 pregnant women had been identified in the first 12 weeks of pregnancy (above the target of 30). Similarly, the health facilities observed a rise in the number of postpartum mothers and newborns returning for care, family planning clients, and children attending growth-monitoring checkups due to TBA referrals.

The card and colored envelope referral system also permitted a certain amount of discretion. A TBA said that she gave the yellow cards to pregnant women who did not want to attend prenatal care because they did not want to make their condition known. These women liked the fact that they just had to present their card and were attended by the nurse. The same was true, she explained, for women wanting family planning services; they could just give the green card to the health provider and get the service. After observing these initial successes, two other health districts in the health area decided to implement the change.

Documentation and Job Aids

In QI projects in Guatemala, especially in community-based collaboratives, documentation of results and change interventions has presented a formidable challenge. The formal educational level of the staff is generally low: auxiliary nurses have 2 years of secondary education, while community facilitators generally have completed only primary education. To show quantitative results, the project experimented with visual tools where health providers colored columns with results according to an established color scheme. These were pasted on the wall for analysis and presented at learning sessions.

Documenting the qualitative results on changes implemented presented an even greater challenge. The project tried various means, including giving oral presentations, recording and transcribing these presentations, presenting panels, providing photographs of improvement changes, and photocopies of each facility's notebook (containing notes that were taken on meetings held, visits received, comments, decisions taken, and recommendations from coaching visits). Project staff produced copies for team members and staff whenever possible, whether through photo or carbon copies and/or notes describing interventions and lessons learned.

Measurement and Results

To measure indicators and identify those that were not reaching the quality targets, the collaborative used LQAS, a relatively low-cost and simple sampling method that could be used locally in the health posts' and NGOs' supervision areas. Sampling was carried out more easily by the NGOs than by health posts, since the NGOs were required to update their population census annually as part of their contracts with the MOH.

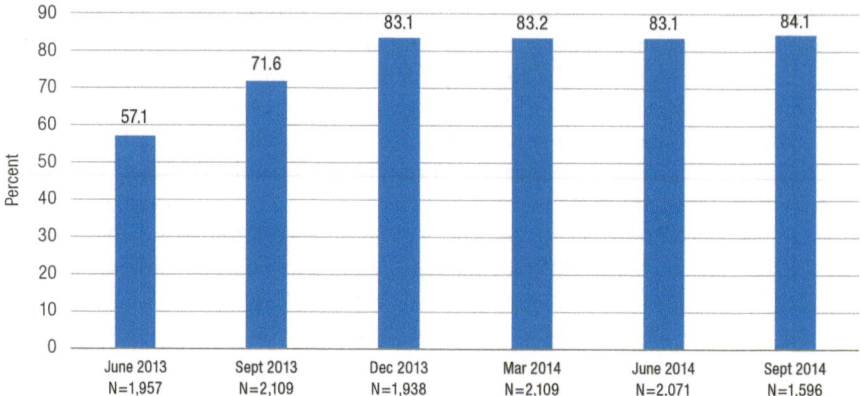

Fig. 3.3 Percentage of mothers who correctly mentioned optimal birth spacing period (3–5 years), Community SBCC collaborative, Guatemala (June 2013 to September 2014)

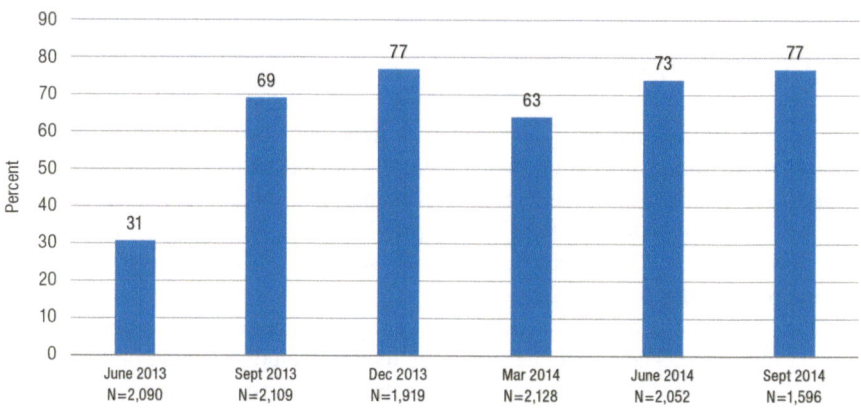

Fig. 3.4 Percentage of mothers who received a postpartum home visit within 48 hours after delivery, community SBCC project, Guatemala (June 2013 to September 2014)

Most indicators showed increases after successive QI cycles of measuring, planning, trying out changes, and adopting those that resulted in improvement. For example, the percentage of mothers who could correctly state the ideal birth interval (3–5 years) rose from 57% in June 2013 to above 80% (LQAS QI target) in September 2014[5] (Fig. 3.3). The percentage of clinical records[6] showing that postpartum women received a home visit within 48 hours of birth rose from 31% to 77% during the same time period (Fig. 3.4). Improvement plans and activities that

---

[5] The last measurement had fewer supervision areas reporting due to the cancellation by the MOH of contracts with the NGOs. The Extension of Coverage Program through NGOs was ended by the MOH in November 2014.

[6] Using LQAS, 19 clinical records were selected in each supervision area; records came from the different facilities that made up the supervision area.

community QI teams carried out to achieve these outcomes included developing key messages and talks on the ideal inter-pregnancy interval for use at every clinic visit and during household visits, as well as conducting postpartum exams at home and bringing clinical records to register findings.

Support for Improvement

Coaching Visits

Coaching visits to supervision areas were conducted each quarter for both the clinical and the community-based collaboratives. Because transportation restrictions such as lack of vehicles or gasoline and lack of per diem affected district level staff's ability to make regular coaching visits, the NGOs' professional nurses often accompanied the project staff to make visits. They followed coaching guidelines jointly developed by the MOH and project staff.

Before a visit, project coaches reviewed data on the supervision area, the type of facility, the composition of the QI team, as well as previous measurements and visits. Data were available in the supervision areas' project information system which also included open source Google maps with all supervision areas. Coaches coordinated with the health district and NGO, since they were required to be accompanied by MOH staff.

The QI team, which included staff from four to five community centers or four to six health posts, met at one facility to verify and exchange results and share change plans and experiences. Among the activities in which teams participated, guided by coaches, were to:

- Explore – through open-ended questions – the team's knowledge and use of QI methods.
- Review baseline or current measurement of indicators and the forms used, identify low-performing indicators, and prioritize one or two for improvement.
- Reinforce PDSA cycles.
- Use the improvement-planning matrix to register and monitor improvement activities.
- Identify gaps by comparing the improvement-planning matrix with implementation documentation or by having the team describe the methodology used.
- Take notes of knowledge of the methodology and application and the aspects that needed to be improved, leaving a record of the visit in the facility's notebook.
- Use the planning matrix to note where and when changes had been implemented.

As the QI intervention progressed, the coaches recognized that teams often required more intensive coaching in how to apply LQAS to draw the community samples. Coaches supported team members by accompanying them on visits to selected households to observe how they identified the household and selected the respondent(s), as well as the interview process and recording of responses.

Due to limited resources, the USAID-funded project provided copies of the questionnaires and planning matrices to all supervision areas. Coaches found that they often had to supply the QI teams with tools, such as instructions on how to select a sample or fill out questionnaires, and information, education, and communication materials for SBCC activities.

During coaching visits, teams verified data quality under the guidance of coaches. The coaches guided team members in checking records to ensure that the numbers correctly added up. Following visits, coaches summarized results in the project's quarterly report disseminated to USAID and the MOH central and health area level technical teams.

Institutionalization

Since 2014, there have been profound changes in Guatemala. The health-care system has faced budgetary and staff challenges that have produced a climate in which it is hard for institutional changes to take root and for spread and scale-up to take place. Changes within the top ranks of the MOH and at the central and health area levels have made it difficult to sustain positive change.

The government's termination of the NGO health delivery model dramatically curtailed the collaborative's growth plan which had relied heavily on continuing to involve community organizations' representatives in measurement, analysis of results, and subsequent planning of improvement.

Even in the face of these challenges, QI methods and tools have become part of MOH guidelines and are being used by other cooperating agencies and projects. QI methodology has taken root with some health providers who participated in QI efforts and remained in their posts. They continue to use them to measure and improve processes and results, even when, in practice, the central-level MOH does not actively promote and support their use any longer.

Reflection

Collaborative participants emerged with lessons learned about how to apply QI interventions to the SBCC cycle and how the process differs from applying the methods to clinical care. For clinical interventions, the project typically defined standards and indicators of prenatal, postnatal, and neonatal childcare; measured them in a sample of each type of clinical record; and undertook planned actions to improve the levels of compliance with these standards and indicators.

Because SBCC documentation was not sufficient to measure progress, teams had to define indicators based on maternal knowledge and practices. These indicators were best measured through sampling the population through lot quality assurance sampling.

Due to the large number of primary health-care facilities and dispersed areas of coverage and community-level personnel, the collaborative had to be prescriptive in the organization of supervision areas, timing of measurement, the amount of time for the action period, and scheduling learning sessions. Participants found that PDSA improvement cycles that could be done rapidly in clinical interventions were only able to be performed "relatively rapidly" in community settings. Community-based teams needed at least one quarter between measurements to effectively implement changes planned.

Through trial and error, project participants came away with significant lessons learned about the formation of community QI teams. They found that organizers of QI efforts would be well served to first consider the structure of a country's health-care system and the number and type of health providers available. In addition, in this primary health-care setting, clinical and community-based collaboratives had to work together to optimize involvement of the limited number of personnel and achieve results.

Project participants also found that it was sometimes critical to challenge existing perceptions when implementing a QI intervention. The QI intervention with TBAs described in this case study required that the team trust that TBAs would be willing and able to assume ownership of the strategy.

Acknowledgments The authors express gratitude to the Ministry of Public Health and Social Assistance, Guatemala; staff at the central level, in the health areas of Chimaltenango, Huehuetenango, Ixil, Quetzaltenango, Quiché, San Marcos, Sololá, and Totonicapán, and in the health districts from 2008 to 2012; staff from the 30 selected health districts from 2012 to 2017; personnel of the Extension of Coverage Program; and staff of the 19 NGOs from 2012 to 2014.

The authors also express gratitude to Baudilio López, Program Officer, USAID/Guatemala.

Many people contributed to the design of this improvement effort as staff of the USAID-financed projects implemented by URC in Guatemala: Elena Hurtado, Senior Technical SBCC and Research Advisor since 2005 and Nutri-Salud project director 2012–2014; Lilian Ramírez, USAID Health Care Improvement Project (HCI) Community Monitoring and Evaluation (M&E) Advisor, Nutri-Salud; Pablo Moreira, M&E Advisor, Nutri-Salud; Axel Moscoso, M&E, Nutri-Salud; Carlos Díaz, M&E, Nutri-Salud; Gustavo Barrios, HCI and Nutri-Salud; Coralia Cajas, Health Area Technical Advisor, HCI and Nutri-Salud; Carlos León, Health Area Technical Advisor, HCI and Nutri-Salud; Mélida Chaguaceda, Health Area Technical Advisor, HCI and Nutri-Salud; Cristina Maldonado, Health Area Technical Advisor, Nutri-Salud; Juan Carlos Mansilla, Health Area Technical Advisor, HCI and Nutri-Salud. Janis Berman of University Research Co., LLC served as technical reviewer for the case.

The work described was funded by the USAID Office of Health Systems through the USAID Applying Science to Strengthen and Improve Systems Project, implemented by URC under Cooperative Agreement Number AID-OAA-A-12-00101, and the USAID Health Care Improvement Project, implemented by URC under the terms of Contract Numbers GHN-I-01-07-00003-00, GHN-I-02-07-00003-00, and GHN-I-03-07-00003-00.

References

Hurtado E, Insua M, Franco LM (2011) Performance of quality improvement teams in Guatemala. Research report summary. Published by the USAID Health Care Improvement Project. University Research Co., LLC (URC), Bethesda. Available at: https://pdf.usaid.gov/pdf_docs/PNADZ394.pdf

USAID Health Care Improvement Project (2008) The improvement collaborative: an approach to rapidly improve health care and scale up quality services. Published by the USAID Health Care Improvement Project. University Research Co., LLC (URC), Bethesda. Available at: https://pdf.usaid.gov/pdf_docs/PNADM495.pdf

Chapter 4
Haiti's National HIV Quality Management Program and the Implementation of an Electronic Medical Record to Drive Improvement in Patient Care

Joshua Bardfield, Bruce D. Agins, Margareth Jasmin, Nicasky Celestin, Nirva Duval, Jean Gabriel Balan, Patrice Joseph, Jean Solon Valles, and Yves Marie Bernard

Abstract This case describes the development and application of a national electronic medical record system, iSanté, to drive improvement as part of Haiti's national HIV quality management program. The Haiti Ministry of Health, with support from donor agencies and local implementing partners, developed iSanté in 2008 to support public health, specifically to facilitate and prioritize use of data for quality improvement and real-time monitoring of HIV care and treatment nationwide. This case describes the development and implementation of the HIV quality management program at the facility level and the development of the iSanté electronic medical record system to record and tabulate data to facilitate evidence-based decision-making about patient care in order to improve patient outcomes.

J. Bardfield (✉)
Bard College, Formerly with HEALTHQUAL, Annandale-On-Hudson, NY, USA
e-mail: jbardfield@bard.edu

B. D. Agins
HEALTHQUAL, Institute for Global Health Sciences, University of California San Francisco (UCSF), New York, NY, USA

M. Jasmin
HEALTHQUAL-Haiti, Port-au-Prince, Haiti

N. Celestin
U.S. Centers for Disease Control and Prevention (CDC), Port-au-Prince, Haiti

N. Duval
Ministry of Health and Population, Port-au-Prince, Haiti

J. G. Balan
ITECH-Haiti, Port-au-Prince, Haiti

P. Joseph · J. S. Valles · Y. M. Bernard
CDC, Port-au-Prince, Haiti

© University Research Co., LLC 2020
L. R. Marquez (ed.), *Improving Health Care in Low- and Middle-Income Countries*, https://doi.org/10.1007/978-3-030-43112-9_4

Keywords Electronic medical record · Haiti · HIV · Prevention of mother-to-child transmission · Quality management · Retention

Introduction

HIV/AIDS first emerged in Haiti in the late 1970s, an era of minimal defenses against the onset of the emerging epidemic. By 2016, there were 150,000 people living with HIV in Haiti (prevalence of 1.7% 15–49 years), with only a little over half receiving antiretroviral therapy (UNAIDS 2016). Key affected populations include sex workers (8.4% prevalence), men who have sex with men (18.2% prevalence), and incarcerated people (4.3% prevalence) (UNAIDS 2016).

As a response to the HIV/AIDS epidemic, in 2007 the country's Ministry of Health (Ministère de la Santé Publique et de la Population, MSPP), with funding from the US President's Emergency Plan for AIDS Relief (PEPFAR) through the US Centers for Disease Control and Prevention (CDC) and in coordination with other donor agencies and local implementing partners, initiated a national HIV quality management program, HEALTHQUAL-Haiti, to systematically measure and improve the quality of adult and pediatric HIV care and treatment services.

Designing the Improvement Effort

Haiti's Quality Management Program

In 2007, the MSPP launched the national HIV quality management program with PEPFAR support at 19 clinics focusing on adult and pediatric HIV care, initially using paper-based records; it was later expanded to a total of 135 HIV clinics nationally. In 2012, the national HIV quality management program expanded its focus beyond HIV to include other public health priorities, including maternal and child health, nutrition, and mental health. At that time, the program increased the number of quality measures collected from the initial 10–19 indicators, which were revised and expanded to cover outcomes and processes of care for HIV-TB comorbidity, maternal health, immunization, nutrition, and mental health.

The quality management program implemented by the Haiti MSPP is based on a public health approach to government-led HIV improvement programs developed in 1992 by the New York State Department of Health AIDS Institute (Agins et al. 1995) and now implemented in 10 countries in Africa, Asia, South America, the Caribbean, and the South Pacific (UCSF-HEALTHQUALa).

The quality management program encompasses the structures, functions, and processes required to support sustainable implementation of quality care at the national level including:

- Leadership involvement
- Development of a national quality management plan, workplan, and sustainability plan
- Human resource management
- Patient and community involvement
- Performance measurement: collecting, reviewing, analyzing, and using data for improvement
- Organizational infrastructure (including management committees, systems for QI documentation, and national QI projects)
- Knowledge management and peer exchange
- Capacity building, including coaching, mentoring, and training
- Patient safety
- Focus on patient outcomes

Quality improvement coaching is a key component of a national Quality Management Program and imperative for the deployment of any large-scale improvement initiative. Coaching is the primary strategy through which the national Quality Management Program develops, enhances, and refines systems at site level to improve health-care processes and patient outcomes. In Haiti, an initial cadre of 19 coaches was trained by experienced quality improvement advisors/coaches using a formal training continuum that included Training of Trainers, Training on Coaching Basics, and Training of Quality Leaders didactic and experiential modules (UCSF-HEALTHQUALb). The trainings were facilitated through funding from PEPFAR with the support of the MSPP, the national HIV program, and implementing partners and included capacity building support in key areas of improvement (rooted in the model for improvement) (Langley et al. 2009):

- *Performance measurement*, including data collection, analysis, and reporting
- *Quality improvement*, including:
    - Reviewing and analyzing performance data
    - Developing project teams
    - Investigating the process (root cause analysis)
    - Planning and testing changes/improvement strategies, using the plan-do-study-act (PDSA) improvement cycle or more formal implementation strategies
    - Evaluating and adapting changes and developing sustainability plans

- The elements of the *quality management program*

This first group of coaches then trained and coached the first group of 19 facilities that were selected to be part of Haiti's national HIV quality management program. These facilities were selected to include a diverse mix of facility types and sizes (hospital, clinic, community health center) and geographic areas (urban/rural and departmental region). As the program expanded, coaches were assigned to facilities based on the facility's needs in the three core areas noted above—performance measurement, quality improvement, and the quality management program. Gradually, new coaches from the MSPP and implementing partners were trained as new facilities were integrated into the HIV quality management program.

Coaches come from diverse professional backgrounds—medical and paramedical, information system, program management, etc.—and are all trained using the previously mentioned training continuum and a more recently developed formal coaching curriculum for QI (http://www.healthqual.org/coaching-toolkit). Coaches are generally recruited from within the health sector and often from within the MSPP, implementing partners' or donor agencies' staff.

Coaches can be assigned to one or more facilities depending on seniority. The implementing partners' coaches are assigned to facilities supported by that partner. The CDC regional coaches and the MSPP Departmental coaches support all facilities in the region/district where they are assigned. Even if a coach is assigned to a specific facility, they usually plan joint visits with other coaches—especially when conducting the organizational assessment, which is a formal validated scoring tool that measures facility-level progress in core areas of the quality management program. The coaches are encouraged to work together to ensure harmonization of improvement activities across the national program.

Coaches visit each facility at least once every quarter. These visits can occur more often depending on need, level of engagement, performance, and staff turnover. Visits are generally scheduled but can happen ad hoc, if needed. In the beginning, the HIV quality management program focused primarily on improving HIV care, and coaches generally focused their technical assistance efforts in that area. As the quality management program transitioned to a broader public health approach, designed to leverage improvement principles from HIV to other infectious and chronic diseases across the health system, QI training and support have expanded to all the facility personnel. All facility-based programs can be involved in QI depending on facility performance and priorities.

In addition, the MSPP established a national-level Core Team, comprised of MSPP staff and implementing partners and led by the MSPP General Director, to act as the executive arm of the national quality management program. The Core Team provides support, guidance, and technical assistance to the national HIV quality program. National QI projects, in which the MSPP identifies national priorities for clinics to target their QI activities, are selected by the Core Team according to epidemiologic data, PEPFAR recommendations, and gaps identified in the facility performance reports, which are generated by each facility based on patient-level data.

Implementing the Quality Management Program at the Facility Level

As a first step in the implementation of the HIV quality management program at the facility level, an organizational assessment[1] is conducted to identify programmatic gaps and weaknesses. Based on findings from the assessment and informed by recommendations shared by QI coaches, the facility leadership and staff develop a formal quality plan and workplan to address those gaps. Next, based on clinic resources, a formal Quality Committee may be formed to manage QI activities. The Quality Committee is usually tasked with reviewing data and selecting facility-level QI projects to be conducted, with consideration of national priorities. The Quality Committee also selects the members of the QI teams. At the facility level, QI teams are comprised of existing facility staff.

Once a facility is integrated into the national HIV quality management program, the staff are trained on QI methodology. Initial training happens at formal training sessions, which typically include multiple facilities, with 2–4 personnel from each participating facility. Subsequent training to spread QI knowledge to all staff takes place on-site at the facility and is led by the coaches. The QI coaches provide experiential training at the facility level in each of the key areas of improvement listed above, which prepares a facility to move a quality improvement project through each step from initiation to completion and enables them to repeat the process with new opportunities identified for improvement.

Facility-based QI projects are selected based on facility performance data, national priorities, and feasibility based on human resources at a given facility. Once iSanté was introduced, performance data could be readily extracted from the platform and reviewed by the facility team. The facility-based QI project team would then conduct process analysis, often using a fishbone diagram, to diagnose the underlying causes of gaps in their processes and systems of care delivery and suggest effective and sustainable strategies for change that are tested through PDS cycles. Successful strategies are then adopted after approval of the Quality Committee and the facility leadership.

Developing an Electronic Medical Record System in Haiti

Systematic collection of routine patient-level clinical data in health-care facilities in low- and middle-income countries is an essential component of HIV quality management. In addition, analysis of data, at all levels of the health system, is key to

---

[1] https://healthqual.ucsf.edu/sites/healthqual.ucsf.edu/files/HEALTHQUAL%20OA_February%202018.pdf

improve patient care and outcomes and to facilitate evidence-based decision-making. Increasingly, developing countries throughout the world are adopting electronic data collection systems as an effective strategy to improve care with the limited resources available (Forster et al. 2008). iSante offers real-time access to patient data to guide decision-making at the individual patient, facility, and national levels. In many contexts, data are collected but not used due to lack of knowledge, data quality issues, or both. Successful improvement of HIV care and treatment programs requires actionable data, and knowledge and skills for analysis and reporting.

In 2008, additional PEPFAR funding became available to design and deploy an electronic medical record (EMR) for Haiti's HIV care and treatment program, building on and improving upon the existing paper-based record. The MSPP collaborated with the CDC Global AIDS Program, through its implementing partners, to develop an EMR as a coordinated strategy to ensure access to real-time data that could be used for improvement. The national quality Core Team and the team tasked with developing the EMR collaborated to ensure that the system was equipped to address the needs of the nascent HIV quality management program.

A development team (comprised of an electrical engineer, database specialist, programmer analyst, and network specialist) then developed the system using the paper patient record designed by the MSPP and CDC-funded implementing partners. They programmed the system using a software bundle comprised of free and open-source software (LAMP: Linux OS, Apache web server, MySQL database, and PHP scripting language). Development and programming of the system took approximately 1 year, split into three phases (Fig. 4.1).

A task force comprised of key staff from the MSPP, the national program, and implementing partners developed and defined indicators, chose the pilot facilities for rollout of the EMR, and developed an organizational system to maintain

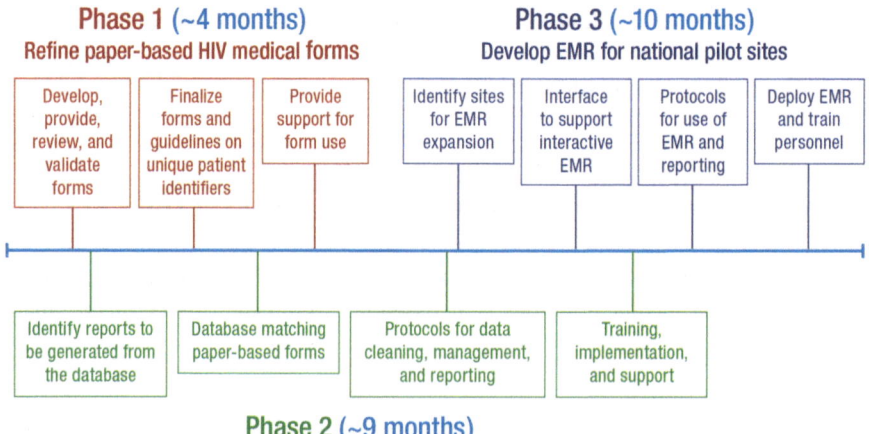

Fig. 4.1 Timeline for development and implementation of the EMR system in Haiti

oversight. The task force initially selected and programmed 19 indicators into the EMR, covering HIV treatment, tuberculosis, maternal and newborn health, nutrition, and immunization, to assess the quality of care (based on national guidelines) received by HIV patients (Appendix 1).

The new electronic medical record, iSanté, facilitated data collection and analysis through its built-in capacity to integrate and extract QI data, accelerating national and local quality improvement work. iSanté was designed to address challenges associated with paper patient records and to streamline separate data collection and reporting processes; it eases constraints associated with formatting data for reporting by automating reports of QI measures. iSanté has improved data integrity through automation and data security, including redundant data back-up, and it facilitates the searching, analysis, and sharing of information. This, in turn, supports health-care workers and clinics to manage and utilize patient data and facilitates timely and accurate reporting. Since iSanté was first implemented, its mandate has been expanded beyond HIV to also include primary health-care and women's health consultations in the same facilities.

Using Electronic Medical Record Data for Improvement

In each of the health-care facilities where iSanté is in use, the trained data manager, or Disease Reporting Officer, is responsible for data entry, data reconciliation, and reporting. At most of these facilities, iSanté is used at point of care in real time, and data entry is completed directly by a health-care worker. Technical issues will occasionally require facilities that operate iSanté at point-of-care to temporarily revert to paper charts. Once a given problem is fixed, a task force is formed to clear the backlog while reverting to data collection at the point-of-care.

Data managers, or Disease Reporting Officers, generate routine reports on select indicators, which can be easily produced daily, weekly, monthly, quarterly, or annually via preprogrammed reports embedded in iSanté. Daily, the data manager reviews iSanté for data entry errors and reports back to the appropriate health-care worker for reconciliation. Missed visits are displayed in a visit report provided to the MSPP-coordinated community team for patient follow-up. Monthly reports are generated by the site coordinator or other QI staff to evaluate performance progress in core areas of care based on facility and/or national priorities. Monthly clinic-level data reports are printed and shared with all service staff and facility leadership and can be generated by any health-care worker or member of the QI team.

Reports communicate performance scores for all performance measures. Performance scores are reviewed and discussed during regular QI team or staff meetings and during QI committee meetings, where gaps in care and improvement strategies are identified. Regular and immediate access to data through iSanté is used by QI teams and other facility staff to continually monitor effectiveness of improvement interventions and to adapt as needed.

Performance data are reviewed, analyzed, and validated at the national level by the MSPP during each semester of the fiscal year. This process is designed to identify gaps in particular performance measures across health-care facilities and to inform national priorities for improvement. Semiannual national meetings of the MSPP-coordinated Core Team focus on routine evaluation and analysis of performance trends across all 19 national performance indicators by health-care facility and department within the most recent 6-month data collection period. This group of stakeholders—including MSPP delegates, staff of the national HIV program, and implementing partners—sets benchmarks for the next review period, identifies weaknesses and gaps in the public health-care delivery system, and provides feedback about quality management implementation at the clinic level. This feedback is presented to regional leadership in the geographic Departmental Directorates, who are responsible for communicating with regional coaches, who work with the facilities directly to implement improvement work based on these priorities and areas of need.

Because iSanté includes longitudinal data on all care received by patients in participating health facilities, sampling of data for improvement is not needed; performance measures are calculated based on the patient universe. The system is designed to produce multiple retrospective or prospective reports that generate case lists for appointment, lab test, and care reminders which can be used at all levels: clinic, department, and national. Mechanisms are in place to ensure patient confidentiality is protected. Patients are identified by a code, patient ID, and date of visit in the EMR; they are not identified by name. Access to patient records is only available by care team staff at the particular facility where a patient receives care, with access authorization required for each iSanté user (e.g., username and password).

Measuring Improvement and Results

Use of the EMR at National and Clinic Levels to Improve Quality

iSanté has been instrumental in optimizing use of available performance data for improvement, particularly through real-time access to patient data and automation of processes, including reporting, associated with systematic care delivery.

Between January 2008 and March 2014, Haiti's quality management program collected 13 rounds of data using the EMR, measuring care across nine indicators. In each case, performance improved between baseline (collected January to June 2008) and follow-up (October 2013 to March 2014) (Table 4.1). Complete definitions of these and other indicators are found in Appendix 1.

Electronic prompts programmed into the EMR represent a principal factor in facilitating systematic attention to core areas of care (Table 4.2). These include

Table 4.1 Mean clinic scores by round of data collection and indicator

Indicator	January to June 2008		October 2013 to March 2014	
	Mean score (%) and the number of clinics | number of eligible patients			
Clinical visits	76%	11|3111	80%	95|58,264
Antiretroviral therapy (ART)	45%	11|2520	71%	95|9723
ART adherence assessment	29%	11|2134	79%	94|44,181
Tuberculosis (TB) clinical screening	29%	16|2990	93%	93|5453
Nutrition evaluation	77%	16|8912	86%	94|56,422
Family planning	6%	16|5238	51%	94|30,730
ART for pregnant women	32%	16|289	91%	84|867

Table 4.2 Use of the EMR to identify areas for improvement and improvement tracking

Project types	EMR prompts	Changes related to EMR prompts
All	• Performance report for quality management program	Use of EMR performance reports to identify low-performance indicators for QI projects
		Use of EMR performance reports to monitor success of interventions during PDSA cycles and at the end of QI projects
Retention in care	• Active/inactive patients	List of active and inactive patients for tracking and follow-up
	• Quality of care report • Appointment reminders • Visits scheduled next 7 days	List of patients expected at clinic visits for the week to follow up with missed appointments
	• Quality of care report • CD4 information • CD4 rates	Patients status: List of active and inactive patients on ARVs; list of patients at risk of discontinuation of their medications, inactive in clinic, or discontinued care at clinic Used for updating CD4 tests and tracking ART eligible patients
ART enrollment	• Quality of care • Appropriate treatment indicators • ART enrollment among medically eligible	List of patients eligible for ART List of eligible patients enrolled on ART

automated reporting of indicators to identify low performance in specific measures and use of iSanté-generated performance reports to monitor progress in improvement interventions across PDSA cycles and at the end of specific projects. Other examples include real-time access to active patient lists for tracking and retention, identification of inactive patients and patients at risk of medication discontinuation, and identification of patients eligible for and/or enrolled on ART, among others.

Improvement Snapshot: iSanté and Prevention of Mother-to-Child Transmission of HIV

When an HIV-positive woman becomes pregnant, she needs clinical services during her antenatal care to prevent transmission of HIV to her baby. When an HIV-positive woman does not receive these services, such as antiretroviral treatment and adherence support, the likelihood of her HIV-exposed infant being infected is very high, but when antiretroviral therapy is provided to the mother during pregnancy, the mother-to-child transmission rate for HIV can drop to under 5%, which is the global target set by WHO.

National priorities in the areas of prevention of mother-to-child transmission of HIV (PMTCT) and family planning for HIV-positive women have demonstrated notable improvement in Haiti through immediate access to performance data. For example, clinical performance measurement data for PMTCT tracked nationally through iSanté between January and June 2008 for 16 clinics demonstrated notable gaps in adherence to national PMTCT standards. On average, only 32% of eligible patients were receiving ART prophylaxis, appreciably under the national benchmark of 100% for HIV-positive pregnant women.

As a result of this observed gap in care, which became possible through routine iSanté reporting, the MSPP initiated a coordinated campaign through their national HIV quality management program. In 2011, the eligibility definition for ART in pregnant women was changed from gestational age >28 weeks to >14 weeks (or 98 days from the date of last menstrual period). As of March 2012, the MSPP adopted Option B+ requiring all HIV-positive pregnant women to be systematically placed on ART.

At the clinic level, improvement teams reviewed and analyzed data from iSanté to set facility-specific priorities for improving PMTCT based on gaps identified using EMR data and causes identified using root cause analysis. They then selected interventions for pilot testing, assessed the impact of their changes, modified systems, or tested new changes and immediately integrated tested improvements into daily work by engaging staff and patients. Some interventions implemented at the clinic level included revision and dissemination of PMTCT guidelines to all staff involved in the care process, introduction of female case managers in all clinics to follow up on care of HIV-positive pregnant women, routine tracking of HIV-positive pregnant women by field agents in the community to re-engage patients in care, and early dispensing of ART to HIV-positive pregnant women.

Clinic-level obstacles to routine, consistent, and timely data entry were addressed to reinforce those systems. This included MSPP-supported QI coaching to clinic teams with annual on-site retraining on the EMR and correct data entry procedures, improving EMR access at point of care, institutional focus on immediate data entry directly into the EMR on day of care or directly after each patient visit, and systematic data entry of obstetrics–gynecology and pharmacy forms in iSanté.

The priorities identified at the national level and the changes in care initiated at the facility level to address these priorities have led to a marked improvement in the

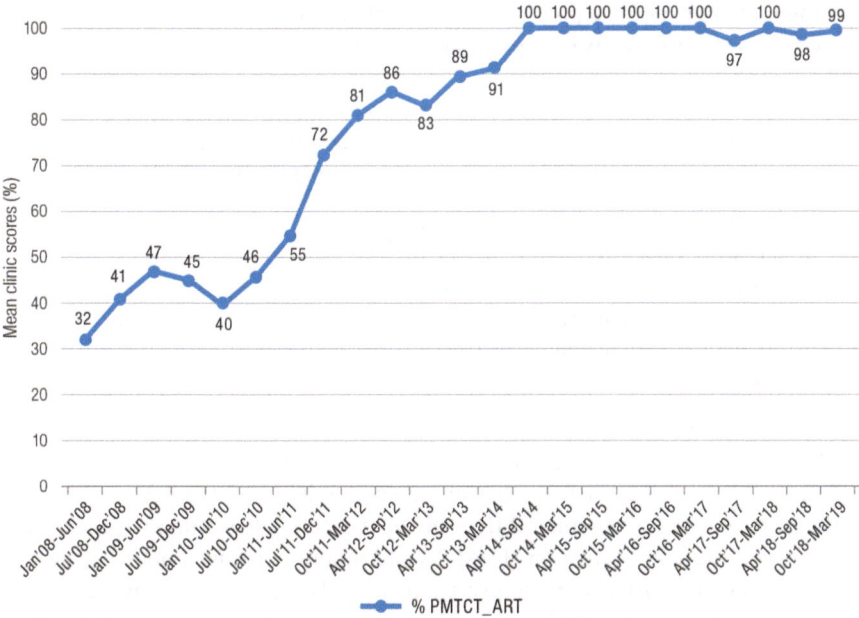

Fig. 4.2 ART enrollment for pregnant women (%) by review period, January 2008 to March 2019

number of HIV-positive women receiving appropriate care during pregnancy. Overall performance of the indicator measuring the percentage of HIV-positive pregnant women enrolled on ART has improved from an aggregate mean of 32% in January–June 2008 to an average of above 99% across review periods through March 2019 (Fig. 4.2). Since ART adherence during pregnancy is associated with reduced transmission of HIV to newborns, this improvement was likely associated with fewer HIV infections among infants born to HIV-positive mothers.

Health Facility Improvement Snapshot: Addressing Lost-to-Follow-Up at Bernard Mevs Hospital

Bernard Mevs Hospital is located in western Haiti, in the town of Delmas, serving a catchment area that includes Haiti's capital, Port-au-Prince, and the neighboring counties of Delmas, Simmons, Cité Soleil, and other low socioeconomic populations in the region. Hospital services include surgery, pediatrics, family medicine, urology, orthopedics, critical care units, and HIV. There are 1956 active persons living with HIV (PLHIV) in care at the facility.

In January 2018, a facility performance review of data from iSanté revealed that only 74% of PLHIV were retained on highly active ART (HAART) at 12 months. As a result, a QI project team comprised of a social worker, a data-reporting officer, a community field agent, a pharmacist, a data clerk, and the HIV program coordinator was convened to analyze gaps in performance and propose changes based on their findings.

The QI team, as part of robust process improvement activities, used data from tracking of lost-to-follow-up to identify root causes of poor retention. Seven primary factors were identified and quantified during that analysis, including:

- Patients who were too sick to come to facility
- Patients who transferred to another facility
- Lack of resources for transportation to the facility
- Patients seeking alternative care
- Dissatisfaction with hospital services
- Interurban travel
- Work-related barriers

A series of changes, based on the causes identified, were then tested on the February 2017 cohort. First, the list of patients enrolled on HAART in February 2017 was extracted from the EMR with their 12-month retention status. Next, patients who were not active on HAART at 12 months were telephoned or tracked in the community using community navigators. Then, on a case-by-case basis, HAART delivery was adapted to the meet individual patients' needs. For example, for patients who experienced difficulty making routine visits to the hospital, multi-month dispensing of ART or community delivery of HIV drugs (at patient's home or meeting point) was implemented.

Of 12 PLHIV enrolled on HAART 12 months who were lost to care prior to the intervention, 11 were found and 1 was declared deceased. Of the 11 PLHIV found, 2 received community delivery of ARVs and 9 received multimonth dispensing. This strategy facilitated the increase of 12-month retention from 74% at baseline in January 2018 to 92% at follow-up in February 2018. The intervention was subsequently scaled up to the broader patient population of PLHIV at Bernard Mevs, where improvement has been sustained at or near 100% through March 2019 (Fig. 4.3).

Reflection

Real-time access to patient-level, facility-level, and aggregate national-level data through iSanté has proved invaluable in supporting implementation of Haiti's MSPP-led national quality management program. With immediate access to data at the local level, and with support from national improvement coaches, improvement teams have the capability to quickly review and analyze data for improvement, assess performance of small-scale tests of change, and make adjustments to efficiently maximize effectiveness of QI activities. Nationally, production of aggregate data reports has facilitated identification of gaps in

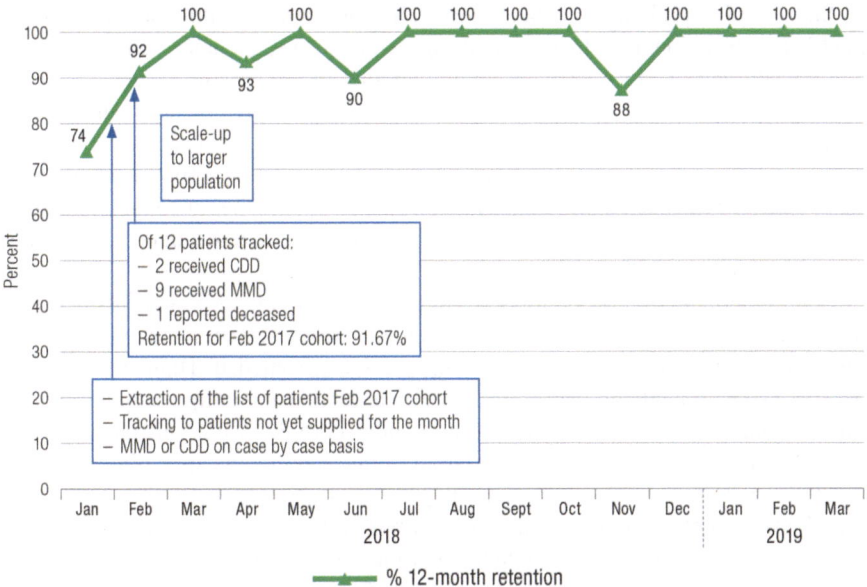

Fig. 4.3 Hospital Bernard Mevs 12-month retention on HAART

care—geographically and/or by area of care—which can be easily displayed for decision-making. This information is routinely used to inform national priorities and reinforce critical areas of care nationwide.

Through Haiti's coordinated national quality management program, which is characterized by strong leadership support from the MSPP, the electronic medical record has facilitated timely access to data for national improvement prioritization in multiple core areas of HIV care. Over the last decade, these have included prevention of mother-to-child transmission of HIV, co-trimoxazole prophylaxis, antiretroviral therapy, and family planning for HIV-positive women, among others.

Among the implementation challenges are familiar issues confronting low- and middle-income countries—issues that were exacerbated considerably in Haiti during these years due to multiple natural disasters, particularly the January 2010 earthquake that devastated much of the island's physical infrastructure and led to the death and displacement of hundreds of thousands of people. Deficiency in local infrastructure, particularly inconsistent access to electricity and information technology networks necessary to operate the EMR, has been one challenge to implementation. Nevertheless, the MSPP mitigated these issues at the onset by establishing local servers at 53 of the 108 iSanté clinics and hospitals and generators at all iSanté-equipped facilities, thus alleviating challenges associated with slow internet connections and facilitating automatic replication of patient data to a central data repository to ensure that patient information is not lost during power outages or natural disasters.

Successful exploitation of iSanté also relies on trained health-care staff within the MSPP for national deployment and support, as well as human resource capacity at the health-care facility level for daily operation of the system. Development of, and access to, an electronic medical record system is simply not sufficient; knowledge and capability for consistent and accurate data entry, analysis, and reporting are critical. The importance of local coaching support must be emphasized; coaches work directly with each facility to ensure that national priorities are understood, that QI knowledge and skills are reinforced among QI teams, and that data are routinely used to improve patient care.

The implementation of iSanté is an exceptional example of how real-time EMR data can be harnessed and used for improvement, which is even more extraordinary given the setting and multiple natural disasters confronted in Haiti over the last decade. Development and deployment of iSanté represent a unique step in improving the quality of patient care in Haiti and underscore the accomplishments of the national HIV quality management program in introducing and spreading improvement concepts around data use and analysis for quality improvement nationally. This includes noteworthy coordination and buy-in from the Government of Haiti, HIV program leadership, stakeholders, and the multiple partners and donor agencies whose support was vital for success in building technical capacity and management processes for implementation within the context of a national quality program.

Acknowledgments The authors appreciate the support provided by the Haiti Ministry of Health; the National HIV Program; the MSPP HIV QI team; Regional Coaching Teams; CDC-Haiti; the Health Resources and Services Administration; I-TECH; Kathleen Clannon; and Joan Monserratte.

Appendix 1. iSanté Indicators

Current HIV indicators in iSANTE	Definition
Patient retention in ART care	Percentage of HIV-positive patients on ARV treatment in progress excluding transferred
Isoniazid prophylaxis	Percentage of HIV-positive enrolled patients who received isoniazid prophylaxis during the analysis period, excluding patients with active TB, deceased and transferred children under 1 year of age and exposed children
ART enrollment	Percentage of HIV-positive patients enrolled on ART during the analysis period excluding deceased and transferred and exposed children
Proportion of HIV-positive patients receiving ARV therapy for more than 6 months with undetectable viral load	Percentage of HIV-positive patients who have been on ART for more than 6 months with the most recent undetectable viral load

Current HIV indicators in iSANTE	Definition
Proportion of children exposed to HIV with a negative polymerase chain reaction test during the analysis period	Percentage of children exposed to HIV aged 4 weeks to 18 months whose most recent polymerase chain reaction test is negative during the analysis period
PMTCT	Percentage of HIV-infected pregnant women who received triple ARV therapy during the analysis period, excluding deceased and transferred
Patient retention at 12 months	Percentage of adults and children who are still on ARV treatment 12 months after the start of ARVs, excluding transfers and exposed children
Adherence assessment	Percentage of HIV-positive patients on ARVs who have benefited from the pills account or completed the questionnaire in the last 6 months, excluding deceased and transferred and exposed children
Level of adherence	Percentage of HIV-positive patients enrolled on ARVs older than 3 months with ART adherence level ≥95%, excluding deceased and transferred and children exposed
TB screening	Percentage of HIV-positive patients assessed for TB during the analysis period, excluding deceased and transferred, children under 6 months and children exposed
Proportion of HIV-positive patients receiving ARV therapy who received an assessment of their viral load at 6 months after initiation of treatment	Percentage of HIV-positive patients who have been on ARVs for more than 6 months, with the most recent viral load result in the last 12 months compared to the end date of the test period, excluding deaths and transfers and children exposed
Pediatric early HIV detection	Percentage of children aged 4 weeks to 1 year who received the early polymerase chain reaction test at any time before the end of the test period

References

Agins BD, Young MT, Ellis WC, Burke GR, Rotunno FF (1995) A Statewide program to evaluate the quality of care provided to persons with HIV infection. Jt Comm J Qual Improv 21(9):439–456

Forster M, Bailey C, Brinkhof MWG, Graber C, Boulle A, Spohr M et al (2008) Electronic medical record systems, data quality and loss to follow-up: survey of antiretroviral therapy programmes in resource-limited settings. Bull World Health Organ 86:939–947. https://doi.org/10.2471/BLT.07.049908

Langley GJ, Moen R, Nolan KM, Nolan TW, Norman CL, Provost LP (2009) The improvement guide: a practical approach for enhancing organizational performance, 2nd edn. Jossey-Bass, San Francisco

UCSF-HEALTHQUALa. HEALTHQUAL. Found at: https://healthqual.ucsf.edu/. Accessed 20 Aug 2018

UCSF-HEALTHQUALb. Coaching Certification Program. National Quality Management Program Guidance. Found at: https://healthqual.ucsf.edu/sites/healthqual.ucsf.edu/files/Coaching%20 Certification%20booklet10online.pdf. Accessed 20 Aug 2018

UNAIDS (2016) Found at: http://www.unaids.org/en/regionscountries/countries/haiti. Accessed 20 Aug 2018

Chapter 5
Bridging the Gap Between Emergency Response and Health Systems Strengthening: The Role of Improvement Teams in Integrating Zika Counseling in Family Planning Services in Honduras

Maria Elena Banegas Arnold and Norma Aly Leitzelar

Abstract This case describes how QI methods were applied in an emergency response context to improve health-care delivery during an infectious disease outbreak – the Zika epidemic that affected Honduras and other countries in Latin America and the Caribbean beginning in 2016. It describes the national-level efforts of both the Ministry of Health and Social Security Institute to strengthen health services in the context of a novel and rapidly spreading epidemic and shows the process of improving care at the facility level, through the experience of the Catacamas Polyclinic in the Olancho Region of Honduras. The case illustrates how the efforts of facility-level QI teams were supported by and coordinated with national-level efforts to develop and promulgate updated standards of care and train health workers in their application. Ministry of Health support for the QI activities included coaching support by central and regional-level QI coaches, support for monitoring of performance indicators, and facilitation of peer-to-peer learning among QI teams to scale up learning about how to improve Zika-related care.

Keywords Collaborative improvement · Counseling · Family planning · Honduras · Peer-to-peer learning · Performance monitoring · Quality of care · Zika

Background

In early 2015, an outbreak of the Zika virus emerged in Brazil; within a year, the virus had spread to 21 other countries in the Americas. As the magnitude of the epidemic unfolded, new and troubling evidence emerged about an uptick in birth defects in Zika-affected regions and their potential link to this virus, causing the World Health Organization to declare Zika a public health emergency of

M. E. B. Arnold (✉) · N. A. Leitzelar
Formerly with University Research Co., LLC, Tegucigalpa, Honduras

© University Research Co., LLC 2020
L. R. Marquez (ed.), *Improving Health Care in Low- and Middle-Income Countries*, https://doi.org/10.1007/978-3-030-43112-9_5

international concern, defined as "an extraordinary event which is determined to constitute a public health risk to other States through the international spread of disease and to potentially require a coordinated international response" (World Health Organization).

The Zika virus was discovered in 1947 in the Zika forest of Uganda. It caused an epidemic in Micronesia in 2007 that spread to several countries in Oceania before reaching the Americas in 2014. The Zika virus spreads among people mainly through the bite of an infected mosquito – the same type of mosquito (*Aedes aegypti*) that transmits Chikungunya and dengue. In addition, the virus can be transmitted between people through sexual intercourse and from a pregnant woman to her baby during pregnancy or at birth. A Zika virus infection during pregnancy can cause microcephaly and other serious brain defects in the developing baby. In addition, there are a host of other possible health and development issues that are being observed in infants and children who were exposed to Zika in utero that continue to be under study.

By 2017, local transmission of the Zika virus had been detected in 148 countries in the Americas, Asia, Africa, and Oceania. Thirty-one countries or territories had reported cases of microcephaly and other central nervous system malformations, possibly associated with Zika virus infection or that suggest a congenital infection, and 23 of them have reported an increase in the incidence of Guillain-Barré Syndrome (GBS) and/or confirmation of Zika virus infection in GBS cases through laboratory tests. Thirteen countries or territories have reported incidence of sexual transmission of Zika.

In Honduras, 32,142 suspected Zika cases had been reported by 2016. Out of these cases, 665 were among pregnant women, 46% of whom were confirmed by reverse transcriptase polymerase chain reaction (RT-PCR) test to have had a Zika virus infection during pregnancy. By late 2016, 134 cases of microcephaly were reported; of these, evidence of the mother having had a Zika virus infection during pregnancy was confirmed by a laboratory test (RT-PCR or serology) in only four cases. The highest incidence of Zika virus infections was recorded in five departments (and cities): Francisco Morazán (Tegucigalpa), Cortes (San Pedro Sula, Choloma, Villanueva), Yoro (El Progreso), Olancho (Juticalpa), and El Paraíso (Danlí).

The Zika Response

As the epidemic unfolded, national governments across Latin America and the Caribbean and the international community quickly mobilized resources to respond to the threat. In Honduras, the national authorities implemented a multisectoral response, organized by the President of the Republic, which included the participation of the Ministries of Health, Education, and Social Inclusion as well as international health organizations like the Pan American Health Organization, USAID, and others. USAID provided technical and financial support through implementing organizations for a range of Zika response efforts, including vector control (ZAP Project), communication campaigns (UNICEF and Breakthrough Action), service delivery (USAID ASSIST Project), and community mobilization (PASMO, Global communities, Project CAZ). A coordination team was formed within the Honduran Ministry of Health (MOH), with the participation of technical staff from relevant MOH units (Health Surveillance, Service Networks Directorate, Primary and Secondary Care Departments, General Directorate of Standardization, among others). This group was named the Zika Strategic Command, and it became the focal point of coordination for all Zika activities in Honduras.

USAID requested in 2016 that one of its projects with decades of experience applying improvement methods to health care begin implementing activities in Latin America and the Caribbean to strengthen the ability of the health systems to respond to the Zika epidemic. Specifically, the project sought to integrate Zika care within family planning, prenatal, and newborn services to improve the capacity of the health system to deliver consistent, evidence-based, respectful, people-centered, high-quality Zika-related care to women of reproductive age, pregnant women, and mothers of newborns affected by Zika and their families. A key goal was to improve client and provider knowledge about Zika and its consequences, particularly for newborns, and about how to prevent Zika virus infection. To meet this need, in Honduras, the project coordinated with the two largest health service providers – the Ministry of Health and the Honduran Institute of Social Security (IHSS, for its acronym in Spanish) – to start an initiative to improve the quality of health services in both organizations.

Designing the Improvement Effort at the National Level

Overview of the Honduran Health System

The MOH is the largest provider of health services in Honduras, covering around 60% of the population. The IHSS serves the working population of the country that has health insurance, covering around 12% of the population (Carmenate-Milián et al. 2017). Within the MOH, there are two levels of care. Primary care is provided by teams in the community or health facilities that provide outpatient care with basic services in obstetrics, pediatrics, internal medicine, and, in some facilities, labor and delivery. Secondary care comprises inpatient services and specialized care provided through different types of hospitals.

The Zika Strategic Command (ZSC) drew on the technical expertise and experience of a multidisciplinary team that was responsible for coordinating health promotion and Zika prevention activities at the community, ambulatory, and hospital levels. The USAID ASSIST Project gave technical assistance to the ZSC to initiate its plan. One of ASSIST's first activities with the ZSC was to decide on appropriate indicators to conduct a baseline assessment of Zika care in the health facilities within the high-incidence departments. Given the recent emergence of Zika in the Americas, another important activity early in the response was to draft national guidelines for comprehensive management of patients with a suspected or confirmed Zika virus infection during preconception, pregnancy, delivery, and postpartum stages and for care of newborns affected by congenital syndrome associated with Zika virus (CSaZ).

At IHSS, the Medical Directorate created a technical team to implement activities within their institution, which included the participation of Epidemiological Surveillance and the Quality Management Unit and the coordination of the North-Western Region of the country, where more cases were concentrated. This technical team worked closely with the ZSC.

Site Selection

For implementation of Zika care improvement activities in Honduras, the USAID-funded project coordinated with the national-level Zika Strategic Command to select 42 health facilities for the initial improvement work; 12 of these facilities were hospitals (10 MOH and two IHSS), and the rest were primary care facilities (20 MOH and 10 IHSS). These facilities were selected because they had the highest incidence of suspected Zika cases. The 42 facilities were located in Atlántida, Choluteca, Cortes, El Paraíso, Olancho, Santa Barbara, and Yoro departments and the metropolitan regions of Tegucigalpa and San Pedro Sula. Within each region, a team of technical advisors from the MOH, IHSS, and the USAID-funded technical assistance project coordinated Zika service strengthening activities with the Health Region Coordinating Team and the managers of the selected primary care health facilities and hospitals. ·

Baseline Assessment

One of the strategic objectives proposed by USAID-funded technical assistance project was the integration of Zika counseling in the services provided to women of reproductive age, mothers, and families to educate clients on Zika risks and complications and to teach and encourage clients to take personal protective measures and other actions to prevent Zika. As a first step, the MOH, IHSS, and USAID-funded project conducted a baseline assessment in the 42 priority facilities to understand what health service clients knew about the Zika virus and how to prevent it. The baseline tools were prepared by the USAID-funded project's regional technical team, for use in Honduras and other countries across the Latin American and Caribbean region. They were reviewed and adapted for use in Honduras by the Zika Strategic Command, the IHSS Zika team, and country-based technical staff of the

USAID-funded project. The tools mainly focused on identifying whether Zika counseling and messages were being provided within key health services (family planning, prenatal, and postpartum care) and whether pregnant women could describe the risk of a Zika infection during pregnancy and ways to prevent Zika (including use of a condom to prevent sexual transmission of the virus), among other topics.

The baseline results showed that 20% of women of reproductive age and 22% of pregnant women could not identify Zika risks and complications (18/88). Only 43% of the women of reproductive age interviewed (40/107) could mention four or more personal protection measures to prevent Zika virus infection, but only 4% of these identified condoms as a protection measure against sexual transmission of the virus. When inquiring if the woman had received counseling on the risks of mother-to-child transmission of Zika while pregnant, 60% of patients who had visited an IHSS facility said they had received this information, but only 36% of those who had visited an MOH facility had.

At baseline, no clients were screened for Zika; however, a retrospective review of 145 patient records from the assessed facilities showed that 27% of sampled pregnant women had shown signs of an arbovirus-associated fever, 20% reported a skin rash, and 12% reported conjunctivitis – all potential signs and symptoms of Zika. At baseline, 75% of the 42 health facilities evaluated had condoms available. Less than half of health-care providers said that they had received training on Zika, and there were no standards or normative guidelines for Zika case management.

Development of and Training in Standards of Zika Care

Given the baseline results, a technical group of MOH, IHSS, and other organizations, led by the MOH General Directorate of Standardization with the support of the USAID-funded project, prepared normative guidelines for Zika-related care, which were approved at the end of 2016, for women of reproductive age with suspected or confirmed Zika infection during preconception, prenatal, postnatal, and postpartum stages and for infants or children with suspected congenital syndrome associated with Zika.

Regional MOH and IHSS coaches were identified and trained beginning in November 2016. These coaches then replicated the training on Zika guidelines for health-care providers in a two-and-a-half-day facility-level workshop, which they have delivered since January 2017. The coaches also received training on health-care improvement methods and tools.

The work to improve health care began by mid-2017. To strengthen Zika service delivery, the MOH and IHSS, with the support of the USAID project, developed collaborative improvement projects to implement Zika counseling in family planning (FP) services and in prenatal care and to screen newborns for microcephaly.

Formation of QI Teams

After the workshop for coaches, the health region management support units were instructed to organize three types of collaborative improvement teams within participating facilities: Zika prevention in family planning, Zika screening and prevention in prenatal care, and Zika screening in newborn care. Hospitals typically had all three teams. Primary care facilities organized only family planning and prenatal care teams; in facilities with a small number of staff, organization of the prenatal care team was prioritized. The regional teams sent instructions to facility managers to organize improvement teams of 6–8 persons following specific profiles. Upon implementing improvement work, many teams incorporated new personnel who were not initially considered while other team members dropped out because they were not involved in direct patient care.

Once the teams were organized, two training sessions (each lasting 2 days) were held at each facility, with a period of 2 weeks between them. In the first session, trainers addressed the general health-care improvement approach, developing improvement aims, forming the QI team, developing a flowchart of the current care process, and developing indicators to measure progress. The second session, held after teams had begun analyzing the gaps in their existing care processes, focused on measuring indicators, identifying changes to test, developing a flowchart of the ideal care process, creating time series charts, and preparing an action plan for testing changes and measuring results.

MOH Support for Improvement Teams

Coaching

After the training, QI coaches, selected by the MOH Quality Department and health region staff, followed up with each facility-level QI team to support the care improvement process they were designing and implementing. Many coaches also belonged to respective health region's management support unit. Visits were scheduled in coordination with the MOH Quality Department or IHSS and with those responsible for the Zika response in the health region. The role of the national-level staff was to provide political support; keep the Service Network Directorate informed of the progress of activities; and attend meetings with the regional team and coaching meetings with improvement teams. In the case of IHSS, members of the Zika technical team from the USAID-funded project accompanied IHSS coaches on visits to QI teams.

Coaching meetings usually lasted 1 day, and if the facility had two or three improvement teams, the meetings would be longer to allow sufficient time to assist all three teams. During these meetings, the coach guided QI teams in conducting analysis of the improvement work, asking probes like: What is the indicator result? Did the change work? Was it enough? Do we need another change? In the event that the team had not collected data for the indicator, MOH, IHSS, and the USAID project coaches participated in data collection and analysis.

Monitoring of 12 performance indicators for the Zika response was implemented nationwide by the USAID-funded project in coordination with the MOH's Information Management Unit (*Unidad de Gestión de la Información*). With technical assistance provided by the USAID-funded project, the Information Management Unit, in coordination with primary and secondary care facilities, prepared a monitoring plan and, subsequently, held workshops for regional managers in charge of health facility monitoring. They also developed an improvement database for health facility staff to use to input data collected at the facility level; facility-level data reports were then sent to the regional level, and the regional level sent them to the national-level MOH Information Management Unit.

The project, in coordination with the MOH and IHSS, conducted periodic visits to verify the validity of the data reported to the MOH's Information Management Unit and the consistency of data in the registers, the monitoring instruments, and the improvement database. Results were analyzed in conjunction with the coaching team visit.

Shared Learning

Improvement teams from different health facilities working on the same (or similar) aims have much to learn from each other. The improvement coach's role is fundamental in spreading learning. In Honduras, coaches shared successful ideas from one team with others and helped to transfer innovative change ideas from teams that had positive results to teams that did not experience such quick results. The coach's expertise and experience also played an important role in honing ideas and changes and guiding implementation.

The USAID-funded project also provided funding for QI team members from one facility to visit the QI team of another health facility to learn about and see the changes they were making in practice to help them understand the feasibility of replicating the successful changes within their own facility. The visiting teams often asked for support in replicating successful change ideas. Many requests were made to expand the improvement process to other health facilities in regions where the project worked.

In addition, the USAID-funded project and the MOH organized national learning sessions to bring teams together to exchange experiences. At these sessions, the USAID-funded project team employed knowledge management techniques to ensure that participants had an opportunity to share what they had learned and were engaged to learn from others. Through the experiences and results shared during these learning sessions, project staff were able to compile best practices implemented by teams working to improve Zika care within family planning services.

The first national learning session for the Zika family planning (Zika-FP) collaborative was held 6 months after starting the improvement process. Teams presented their changes and successful experiences in a series of interactive conversations that encouraged teams to learn from each other (see Box 5.1). The national learning session lasted for 2 days. Twenty-eight improvement teams in the Zika-FP improvement collaborative participated in the learning session, in addition to staff from the MOH, USAID, the USAID-funded project, and other implementing partners. During the session, the teams identified the changes that were currently being discussed for institutionalization. Table 5.1 shows a sample of the key changes that the Zika-FP teams recommended to others.

Box 5.1 Techniques to Foster Peer-to-Peer Learning
In preparation for the national learning session, coaches selected a few teams that had excellent results from the changes they had implemented to address their improvement aims. Coaches provided these teams with a tool to document their experiences and asked them to identify a member who would be working as the "speed consultant" during the session. Many of the teams made posters to convey their results. Session participants sat at eight tables with a speed consultant at each. The consultant would speak for 20 minutes about the experience of his or her improvement team, sharing successful changes. After 20 minutes, participants would move to a new table. Participants had the opportunity to buy – or not buy – change ideas, symbolically paying the speed consultant to purchase compelling ideas, which helped to give a value to successful change ideas. Participants at the tables could present and "sell" their changes, thus promoting learning across teams.

Improving Zika Counseling and Care Within Family Planning Services at Catacamas Polyclinic in Olancho

Catacamas Polyclinic, located in the city of Catacamas (population 40,912) in the Department of Olancho, offers specialty services for obstetrics and gynecology, prenatal ultrasonography, and pediatrics and has a special clinic to provide care to adolescents due to the high incidence of teenage pregnancy in the area served by this clinic.

The facility manager organized an improvement team composed of three nursing assistants (one of whom also served as the team coordinator), a professional nurse, and a general physician.

Table 5.1 Key changes that Zika-FP improvement teams recommend to others

Challenge	Successful changes
High turnover of personnel and management in health facilities	• Create procedures and materials for onboarding new staff that include introducing them to Zika care and prevention
High case load, busy workload, and lack of time	• Make changes to the process of care to free up provider time through more efficient provision of services (e.g., creation of designated clinics with assigned medical or nursing staff for family planning and Zika counseling, incorporation of Zika-FP counseling into pre-clinic care, use of colored cards to send clients to Zika-FP counseling through a variety of providers to distribute workload) • Involve providers with lighter caseloads or who are already trained in counseling (e.g., HIV, breastfeeding, and adolescent counselors) to provide Zika-FP counseling to distribute workload • Standardize content and methodology of Zika counseling within family planning counseling • Standardize job aids to make provision of Zika-FP counseling easier and more efficient for providers (A flipchart to guide Zika-FP counseling was developed by one improvement team and proved successful; the flipchart was then improved and standardized for use by all teams)
Monitoring and evaluating provision and quality of counseling	• Standardization of the registration of counseling in new (e.g., stamps applied to existing medical records, forms stapled to medical file) and existing (e.g., medical record, MOH data collection forms) medical documentation forms used in the health facility. An improvement made was to design an integrated counseling form that addressed topics for both pregnant and non-pregnant women
Client resistance to receiving and using condoms	• Adopt a diverse information and education communication strategy to teach clients about sexual transmission of Zika and potential complications for the baby: Individual and couple counseling Group classes and meetings (formal and informal (i.e., in the waiting room); targeted at specific groups like men, adolescents, or pregnant women) Educational materials (videos, flipcharts, posters, flyers, and handouts) • Provide condoms in discrete packages (e.g., recycled or brown paper bags, opaque plastic bags, paper envelopes, etc.) • Involve partners and other men in prevention of sexual transmission of Zika through their participation in prenatal care, group counseling, individual counseling, and follow-up of couples

Setting Improvement Aims

The improvement team decided to focus on integrating Zika in FP services for two groups: women of reproductive age and adolescents (both female and male). They set a different improvement aim for each group, based on the team's analysis of each group's needs in the context of Zika.

Given that the emergence of Zika in the Americas was so new, few health facilities had any processes in place to include Zika within existing care processes. When the Zika-FP team at Catacamas Polyclinic first started working on this topic, they found that no women or adolescents attended at the facility were receiving information and counseling on Zika and its complications.

For women of reproductive age, they set this improvement aim: "To increase Zika counseling to clients, partners, and/or men of reproductive age who attend the clinic for FP services and/or psychological services, documenting the services provided in the patient's medical record on a sheet designed for that purpose, from 0 to 100% between June 26 and December 31, 2017."

Then, they selected an indicator to measure achievement of their aim:

- Percentage of female and male family planning clients and/or partners who received FP/Zika counseling.

For adolescent care, they set this aim: "Increase knowledge about Zika virus prevention and transmission methods among the adolescent male and female population and/or partners that attend the adolescent care clinic by providing Zika counseling and/or Zika education sessions prior to clinical care (e.g., talks in the waiting room), during their medical appointment, and as they are exiting the health facility (educational room, comprehensive teenage counseling, consultation room, psychological care), documenting the care provided in the designated Zika counseling sheet, from 0 to 50% between June 26 and December 31, 2017."

They selected these indicators to measure achievement of their aim:

- Percentage of teenagers (male and female) and/or partners who attend the adolescent care clinic and receive counseling, information, and guidance on Zika virus infection.
- Percentage of teenagers (male and female) and/or partners who demonstrate knowledge of Zika transmission and prevention methods.

Analysis of the Current Care Process to Identify Gaps

The team developed a flowchart of the existing care process for women of reproductive age and identified several problems. First, FP counseling was provided at the health facility through a nursing assistant trained as a counselor but who had other duties. FP counseling was only provided for some methods because the health facility has a high patient load, leaving the provider with little time for each woman and causing delays in receiving care. The FP service at the clinic had a FP counseling tool provided by MOH, but it was not used very often. This service was provided with limitations because the same counselor provided other reproductive health care. Zika counseling was not provided within family planning services or within psychology services. Even FP activities were not recorded on any form, except for a small note written in the medical record that read: "FP counseling provided."

The team observed similar challenges with adolescent care. The adolescent care clinic had been established 2 months prior and had a private space specifically designated for comprehensive counseling and consultancy. Approximately 26–30 teenagers received care daily at the clinic, causing prolonged wait times for care. Zika counseling was not provided there either.

The adolescent counseling room already existed with sufficient privacy, but the improvement team arranged for additional furniture such as a couch and additional chairs. They decorated the room with flowers so that patients would find the space to be more attractive. They began to supply condoms to patients in small packets.

The counseling room also had a waiting area that could seat five persons, so the team decided to give group talks on Zika while patients were waiting to talk individually with the counselor. This allowed them to reduce the individual counseling time since they simply needed to review the adolescent's understanding of the Zika counseling messages, which took less time than starting the counseling from scratch.

Some of the teams found that pregnant women would reject the condoms or throw them out after receiving them because they were afraid to ask their husbands to use them. To address this barrier, the teams began engaging men, holding meetings with them to discuss their role in preventing Zika transmission by using condoms.

Measuring Improvement

Team members met to review a sample of randomly selected files obtained from the facility's statistics service. The improvement team found that the facility's current performance was 0% in their defined indicators when they made the first measurements at the time of the training workshops. The QI team created a form where they documented the clients' medical record number and listed messages on Zika signs and symptoms, transmission (mosquito bite, sexual, and mother-to-baby), prevention methods, personal protection measures, and complications, noting whether counseling was provided and whether it covered these key topics. This form served both as a means of data collection for the team and as a job aid for providers. The QI team also documented distribution of FP methods every month.

Data monitoring, which began in June 2017, was carried out on a weekly basis until January 2018, and monthly thereafter. Each week, a different person from the QI team was assigned to measure indicators. After they had collected data, the team would meet to consolidate and graph the results on a board provided by the USAID project for this purpose. The director of the health facility would include the indicator monitoring results as a topic of discussion during the monthly all-staff meeting.

Testing and Implementing Changes

Table 5.2 presents the first changes tested by the Catacamas team to reduce gaps in the quality of Zika care within family planning services.

Table 5.2 Changes tested to reduce gaps in the quality of Zika care within family planning services

Changes tested	Start date	End date	Was there improvement? (Yes/no)	Learning	Is this change recommended to other teams?
Developed form to prompt and document quality, comprehensive counseling on Zika signs and symptoms, transmission, prevention methods, and complications	June 25, 2017	July 3, 2017	Yes; indicator increased from 0% to 30%	While testing the change, we identified it was necessary to introduce another change to improve (namely, creating a designated space)	Yes
Created a designated space for FP and Zika counseling and assigned a rotating schedule of nurses (trained in counseling methods) to provide counseling within that space	July 7, 2017	July 14, 2017	Yes, increased to 100%	The goal would not have been accomplished without this change	Yes

For the first time, the facility staff began to recognize that counseling is a part of clinical care and began to understand the need to record it in order to follow up with the client. Also, around this same time, counseling services began to be recorded in the MOH official information system for the first time as part of changes initiated at the national level by the Zika Strategic Command.

Within a few weeks, the team realized that recording care was not useful if the service was disorganized. Under the original process of care, the doctor was responsible for providing Zika counseling, but patients mentioned that doctors used very technical language that they found difficult to understand. There was only one provider, an auxiliary nurse, who had been trained as a counselor, but this person was also providing other reproductive care services and could not cover everyone. In addition, counseling was not private, and family planning counseling was only provided for certain methods. The team decided to create a private space for counseling in the FP clinic. Initially, they assigned one counselor to provide counseling full time, but later, the facility trained more health-care providers as counselors (with MOH and USAID-funded project support). Currently, all nurses and the psychologist provide counseling, and there is a robust schedule of coverage to meet client demand while accommodating staff vacations, etc. The flow of care within the clinic was totally modified.

Changes introduced to improve the clients' knowledge of Zika are described in Table 5.3.

To conduct exit interviews with clients, they requested help from the psychologist (who was not part of the improvement team at the time). The team wanted someone outside the team to collect this data, so that there would be no potential bias and the result would be more reliable. The psychologist would not tell anyone

Table 5.3 Changes tested to improve the clients' knowledge of Zika

Changes tested	Start date	End date	Was there improvement? (Yes/no)	Learning	Is this change recommended to other teams?
Preparation of a flipchart to guide Zika counseling	July 3, 2017	July 7, 2017	Yes (by 100%)	Organization and teamwork in a coordinated way ensured success	Yes
Provided structured Zika educational sessions to FP clients and clients of the adolescent clinic in waiting rooms and meeting spaces	July 7, 2017	July 14, 2017	Yes	Completing activities is not enough; the most important thing is to make activities sustainable	Yes

when she was conducting exit interviews. (After some time, the psychologist became part of the team and then became the coordinator of all the teams organized and functioning in the facility.) Clients were interviewed as they left the health facility, using a survey instrument developed by the MOH and the USAID-funded project. Once the clients' knowledge had been assessed, the completed forms were shared with the improvement team for analysis and decision-making.

When analyzing the initial data from the exit interviews, the team realized that clients' knowledge was still very poor. Then, the team decided to create a flipchart with standard Zika information to teach Zika signs and symptoms, transmission methods (including sexual transmission), prevention through personal protective measures, and complications. When this change was introduced, their indicator went up to 100%. However, in subsequent exit interviews, they continued to find clients lacking important Zika knowledge, so they decided to use other information, education, and communication techniques, such as group talks, posters, and involving teenagers to educate their peers, to promote learning.

Other Activities That Contributed to Improvement

- Training counselors in long-acting reversible and permanent contraceptive methods.
- The health manager hired two facility psychologists with MOH funds to provide counseling. The QI team integrated these staff members into the clinical care process.
- Trained community leaders, educators, peer leaders, and an adolescent support committee. Because the staff in the facility had prior experience working with adolescents, the project sought to merely reinforce these activities, including training adolescents to lead group discussions with other adolescents about Zika and preventive topics. They coordinated with schools to reach those adolescents

who were already attending the clinic to train them to work with groups of adolescents to teach them about the Zika virus and how to prevent its transmission.
- Periodically during meetings with adolescents, they engaged health personnel to conduct demonstrations of correct condom use.
- They provided condoms to clients in small packages.
- Shared Zika information with the television media.
- Created murals.

Results

The improvement team introduced the identified changes and used team meetings to analyze the results of their indicators, shown in Figs. 5.1 and 5.2.

National-Level Monitoring of Zika Indicators

Apart from the indicators monitored at the health facility level by the team as part of the improvement process, indicators were also monitored for follow-up at the national level by the USAID-funded project. The MOH's Information Management Unit started monitoring 12 Zika indicators with technical support from the project in June 2017. A monitoring plan was developed, followed by a monitoring plan training workshop to train health region technical teams and those responsible for monitoring and evaluating health facilities. Then, the Excel database provided by

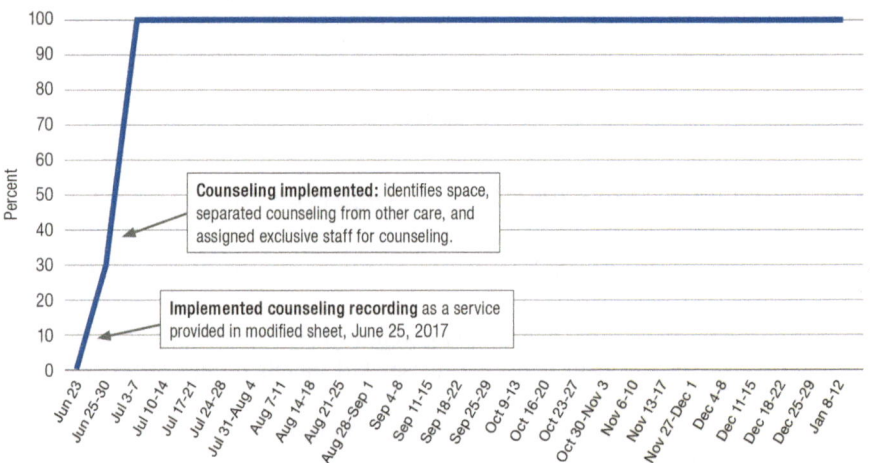

Fig. 5.1 Percentage of male and female clients and their partners attending family planning and psychological services who received Zika counseling, Catacamas Polyclinic, Honduras (Jun 2017–Jan 2018)

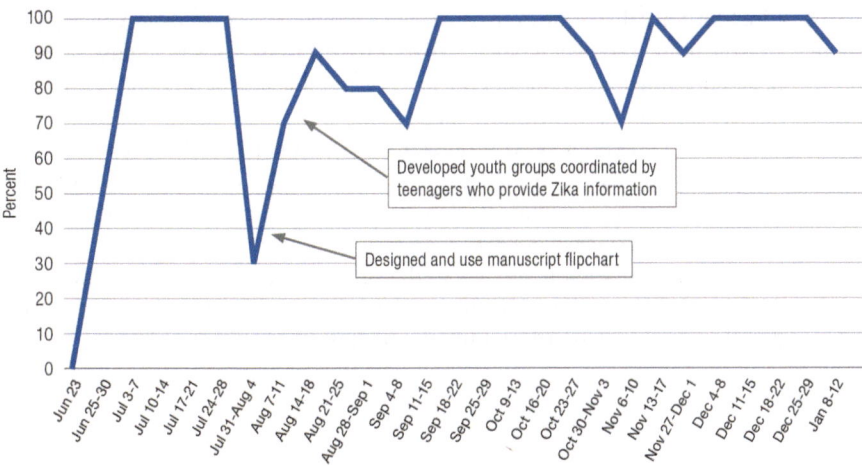

Fig. 5.2 Percentage of male and female clients of the adolescent clinic and/or partners with knowledge about Zika, Catacamas Polyclinic, Honduras (Jun 2017–Jan 2018)

the USAID project was given to health facility staff, regions, and the MOH Information Management Unit. The indicator measurement report traveled from the team, who sent it to the database at the regional level; the regional level consolidated all the facility data and then sent it to the MOH Information Management Unit. Health regions also sent a copy to the MOH Quality Unit and the USAID project. This indicator monitoring motivated the facility teams to improve other indicators when results were not satisfactory.

Spreading the Knowledge

In February 2018, the MOH, with the support of the USAID-funded project, conducted a second national learning session for teams from different health facilities to meet and share learning from their work improving Zika care in family planning services. During the learning session, the Catacamas Polyclinic improvement team presented their successful experience, and other teams spoke with them to ask how they did it and what activities they implemented.

The changes made by QI teams to improve Zika counseling in family planning services were analyzed at the national-level MOH office, with support from the USAID-funded project. To further support the efforts of the facility-level teams, the national-level technical team identified a need to improve the chapter of the National Family Planning Strategy on organization of family planning services. The National Family Planning Strategy is the official document guiding family planning activities in Honduras and was developed with USAID funding in previous years.

The flipchart for Zika counseling prepared by the Catacamas team was adapted by the USAID-funded project to standardize it for all improvement teams. The topics of Zika counseling, counseling in the pre-conception stages, pregnancy, postpartum, etc., were added to the flipchart's design.

The Catacamas Polyclinic decentralized services manager also identified successful changes made by the FP-Zika team that could be shared with lower level health facilities in the Catacamas catchment area that are part of the polyclinic's decentralized health services network.

The Olancho Health Region, in view of the success of its health facilities with the Zika care improvement process in FP services, took the initiative to expand the process to other service networks within the region.

Reflection

The Olancho Region had a nurse leader, very empowered in her role as a regional Zika quality focal point. Within her role on the regional coordination team, she advocated for the need to expand the integration of Zika counseling in FP services to other health service networks.

As a result of the experience of the Catacamas Polyclinic, improvement teams have also been organized at the San Francisco de Juticalpa Hospital, which is the referral hospital in Olancho Health Region, some 30 minutes away from Catacamas. The hospital is now also providing Zika counseling and distributing condoms to both women of reproductive age and pregnant women to prevent sexual transmission of Zika.

An interesting piece of data from one of the quality improvement teams at the San Francisco de Juticalpa Hospital is the experience they had in the beginning of 2018. The MOH Management Planning Unit, which is in charge of planning and scheduling management activities at the national level, called the hospital's improvement team to ask if there was an error in the data or why there was a difference in condom delivery, since they were surprised that the hospital had tripled the number of condoms distributed. The doctor in charge of handling the information responded, explaining that the situation was due to the fact that they were delivering condoms in the Zika prevention framework, to both women of reproductive age and pregnant women.

Other health regions also have expansion plans to implement the counseling process in FP and postnatal care services. Tulane University conducted a study in the Metropolitan Health Region of Tegucigalpa, which assessed the quality of Zika and FP services. The results indicated that health facilities that have quality improvement teams have better results than facilities that do not have them. Given these results, the Metropolitan Health Region requested the USAID project to support the expansion of improvement to other new facilities.

The work of the teams, using data and transforming their processes, does make a difference.

Acknowledgments The Zika improvement work in Honduras was supported by the USAID Office of Health Systems through the USAID Applying Science to Strengthen and Improve Systems Project, implemented by University Research Co., LLC under Cooperative Agreement Number AID-OAA-A-12-00101.

References

Carmenate-Milián L, Herrera-Ramos A, Ramos-Cáceres D, Lagos-Ordoñez K, Lagos-Ordoñez T, Somoza-Valladares C (2017) Situation of the health system in Honduras and the new proposed health model. Arch Med 9:4. https://doi.org/10.3823/1333
World Health Organization. International Health Regulations procedures concerning public health emergencies of international concern. https://www.who.int/ihr/procedures/pheic/en/

Chapter 6
Scaling Up a Quality Improvement Initiative: Lessons from Chamba District, India

Nigel Livesley and Praveen Kumar Sharma

Abstract To improve maternal and newborn survival, the Government of India launched the Reproductive, Maternal, Neonatal, Child, and Adolescent Health initiative in 2013. The initiative provided additional support to districts in states that fell within the bottom quartile on a number of health indicators, including the State of Himachal Pradesh. This case describes (1) how a USAID-supported project introduced the QI approach in Chamba District of Himachal Pradesh, (2) how the project provided initial support to form QI teams and get improvement work on maternal and newborn care started, (3) why the district government staff decided they wanted to scale up the use of QI, (4) how the district government spread QI to new blocks and facilities, and (5) what happened after the project withdrew support. The case also offers insights about key features of improvement work.

Keywords Antenatal care · Delivery care · Essential newborn care · India Maternal health · Post-natal care · Quality improvement · Reproductive health · Scale-up

Background and Setting

India is home to over 1.2 billion people. It accounts for one fifth of all deliveries in the world and one quarter of all newborn deaths. The size and complexity of India create important challenges in delivering good health care.

N. Livesley (✉)
University Research Co., LLC, Abuja, Nigeria
e-mail: nlivesley@urc-chs.com

P. K. Sharma
Formerly with University Research Co., LLC (URC), New Delhi, India

© University Research Co., LLC 2020   77
L. R. Marquez (ed.), *Improving Health Care in Low- and Middle-Income Countries*, https://doi.org/10.1007/978-3-030-43112-9_6

India is divided into 29 states and 7 union territories. States are further subdivided into districts, which range in population from fewer than 10,000 people to over 11 million. All levels of the health system are involved in providing health care: the central government sets the overall policy and provides the majority of finances, while state and district governments are responsible for service delivery.

To improve maternal and newborn survival, the Government of India launched the Reproductive, Maternal, Neonatal, Child, and Adolescent Health (RMNCH+A) initiative in 2013. The RMNCH+A initiative provided additional support to the districts in each state that fell within the bottom quartile on a number of health indicators.

Different states used different approaches to improve maternal and newborn survival. One approach used by the State of Himachal Pradesh was to request a United States Agency for International Development (USAID)-funded technical assistance project with decades of expertise in quality improvement (QI) to help specific facilities in priority districts of the state to use QI methods to deliver better care and to help the district governments develop strategies to spread and institutionalize the use of QI methods. This support started in December 2013 and ended in December 2015.

Chamba District was one of the four districts in Himachal Pradesh selected for support. With a population of 500,000, Chamba has 1 district hospital, 3 sub-district hospitals, 8 community health centers (CHC), 42 primary health centers (PHC), and 170 health sub-centers (HSC).[1]

Table 6.1 lists the key actors involved in this improvement case at each level of the health system.

Getting Started

In September 2013, the QI project started working in India. Soon after arriving, the project director met the Joint Secretary for Reproductive and Child Health for the Government of India's Ministry of Health and Family Welfare to discuss QI and introduce the approach of the project. The Joint Secretary was interested in this approach of training frontline health workers in management skills and tools to identify and fix problems at the service delivery level. He wrote a letter to the Government of Himachal Pradesh introducing the project. The Joint Secretary also introduced the project staff to senior Himachal Pradesh officials during a visit to launch the RMNCH+A initiative in November 2013. This allowed the State Improvement Coordinator from the USAID-funded project to establish contacts with the state and district stakeholders. The Chamba District Improvement Coordinator (DIC) with the project remembers said, *"Our first step was to brief the*

---

[1] Primary health centers are 6–30 bed units staffed by 1 or 2 general doctors. Health sub-centers are two to six bed units staffed by nurses. Community health centers are 30 bed units staffed by at least 4 doctors, including a gynecologist and anesthesiologist.

Table 6.1   Key actors in the Chamba District case

Position	Role
National government	
Joint Secretary for Reproductive and Child Health	Introduced the project to the state government
State government	
Mission Director, National Health Mission	Introduced the project to the district government
District government	
District Collector *Lead civil servant for all sectors in district government*	Agreed to participate in QI program Reviewed QI program progress
Chief Medical Officer *Lead civil servant in the district health sector*	Assigned QI project to initial sites Requested scale-up to a new block Assigned staff to act as QI coaches during scale-up
Medical Officer Health *Lead technical staff in district health sector*	Mobilized staff to attend QI trainings Provided oversight to QI teams
Block government	
Block Medical Officer, Pukhri Block	Provide oversight to QI teams in his block Communicate with district leadership
Medical Officer at PHC in Pukhri Block	QI team member
Staff nurse at district hospital	QI team leader
Staff nurse at PHC in Pukhri Block	QI team leader
Ward sister in civil hospital	QI team member
Health supervisors	Served as QI coaches during scale-up
Multipurpose health worker at health sub-center	QI team member
Project staff	
District improvement coordinator (DIC)	Provided QI training and mentoring at facilities Supported peer-to-peer learning Trained and mentored new coaches
State improvement coordinator	Supported the DIC Supported district to develop scale-up plan
National project director	Initiated contact with the Government of India Supported state improvement coordinator and DIC

district administration and health officials about the project and convince them of the positive impact they could achieve on maternal and neonatal mortality using the QI approach." During an initial introductory meeting in November 2013, the State Improvement Coordinator and DIC briefed the Chief Medical Officer (CMO) and the Medical Officer Health on the fundamentals of QI and talked about how the project could support facilities in Chamba to deliver better care. The CMO and the

Medical Officer Health agreed that they could benefit from the project's support. They asked the DIC to meet with the district data assistant to identify facilities that could benefit from this approach.

The following week, after reviewing facility-level data with the district data assistant, the DIC met again with the CMO and Medical Officer Health to discuss which facilities they should target for the QI work. Based on what they heard, district officials and the QI project team jointly decided to start the work at the district hospital and in one CHC, two PHCs, and one HSC within Pukhri Block. The MOH felt that Pukhri was a sensible choice to pilot the interventions due to its proximity to district headquarters, making it easier to monitor, and because most facilities in Pukhri were sufficiently staffed. In addition, nearly 60% of all institutional deliveries in the district occurred in the five facilities listed above, thus providing a good opportunity for the project to demonstrate the effectiveness of the QI approach across all four periods of maternal and newborn health – antenatal, intrapartum, postnatal, and neonatal.

After the initial planning, the District Collector and CMO introduced the DIC and other staff from the project to the leaders and staff at the initial facilities, so that they could present the QI project and discuss what would be required of health facility staff participating in the intervention. Project staff explained that they planned to come to the facilities to form QI teams, and then facility staff and project staff would work together to improve quality of maternal and newborn health. A staff nurse at the regional hospital recalled, *"After meeting the QI project staff, some of us were a bit skeptical because we were already providing services 24 × 7, but others were excited by the possibility of doing something new!"*

In particular, the Block Medical Officer (BMO) for Pukhri was not initially enthusiastic about the selection of his block. He complained to the CMO, *"Why always Pukhri? How is it that we are the first block to get selected for any pilot in the district? Our teams are already overloaded with deliveries and newborn services."*

There was also considerable skepticism about external people providing support. The staff were initially distrustful of the DIC and viewed him as an outsider since he was not from the local health system. Many worried that he would highlight gaps in care to district and state leadership, creating "new problems" for them. Others questioned his ability to effect change and improve care in the facilities, given that he is not a doctor or nurse and therefor lacks the medical training that the facility staff have. *"Who is he to tell us what to do?!"* staff protested. However, the DIC persevered. Slowly, he earned their trust by continuously interacting with them in a respectful manner and taking all decisions in consultation and through mutual agreement, which reduced resistance. The Medical Officer Health remembers, *"His approach made facility staff feel that he is assisting them; not directing them to do things. When the staff realized that the DIC is there to help and guide them, they started co-operating with him."*

Initial Organization of the Improvement Work

The process of setting objectives went through several iterations. First, a broad set of aims was taken up with the district officials. Project staff and district officials discussed the level of quality they would like to achieve for antenatal care (ANC), delivery, postnatal care (PNC), and essential newborn care (ENC) services. The parties then agreed on a set of specific aims to reach the expected level of quality, such as ensuring that hemoglobin and blood pressure are measured and patient history is taken during antenatal care to identify, refer, or manage high-risk pregnancies; administering oxytocin to women within one minute of delivery; monitoring postnatal vitals per protocol (11 times in 6 hours); and providing vitamin K to all newborns.

The DIC then worked with the facility staff to collect baseline data about these initial aims from the previous 6 months (going back to July 2013). At the same time, the CMO, Medical Officer Health, and the BMO validated each of these aims for their consistency with the government RMNCH+A guidelines of the National Health Mission.

After the district leaders and project staff finalized the general set of aims, the project team organized an initial training for the facility staff at the government training facility. Over the span of 2 days, the State Improvement Coordinator and DIC trained 45 government staff in seven basic steps to improve care (see Box 6.1). Training participants were invited through a letter from the CMO and included senior staff from the district, block, and each of the five facilities, as well as clinical staff involved in care for infants and pregnant and delivering women.

Box 6.1 Seven Steps to Improve Care
1. Decide what you are trying to achieve
2. Get a team together to work on this goal
3. Think about why you are not currently reaching your goal
4. Come up with a simple measurement plan
5. Come up with some possible solutions
6. Test these ideas on a small scale (a few patients or a few hours)
7. Apply the successful ideas to your whole ward or clinic

During the workshop, the facilitators introduced the aims from which the facility staff could choose to work. As the participants were choosing aims, they expressed concerns about how feasible it would be to meet some of these aims given their workload. For example, they flatly refused to work on increasing the number of times a woman was assessed after delivery to the 11 times in the first 6 hours as stipulated in government guidelines. The State Improvement Coordinator and DIC did not emphasize these contentious areas. Instead, they asked the participants to focus initially on the specific aims that had less resistance from the group, such as giving oxytocin after delivery and improving antenatal care.

After the initial training, the facility staff were asked to go back to their facilities and follow the seven steps to improve care. One of the first things that the participants did upon returning to their facilities was to form one QI team per facility. To do this, the senior staff who participated in the training appointed the team members and outlined the aims of the improvement project to the QI team members. Thereafter, the DIC visited each team every 2–4 weeks and spent, on average, half a day helping them learn how to practically apply improvement methods to achieve their chosen aim. During these coaching visits, the DIC would review how they were doing on the steps and help them strengthen their skills for each step. For example, one coaching visit might focus on how to better use different QI tools, such as flowcharts and fishbone diagrams, to analyze systems to understand why the facility was not currently reaching their goal; another visit might involve helping the team plan how to use small-scale tests to see if one of their ideas was feasible and effective.

When asked how these coaching visits helped them, the QI teams responded:

- *"It made the staff comfortable with the DIC. Due to the frequency of meetings and the kind of facilitation they provided, they created an environment where staff felt comfortable discussing evidence and their experience and felt involved in the process of improving the quality of services."* Medical Officer, Primary Health Center
- *"During the meetings, we used to brainstorm a lot, analyzing causes to the problem, what can be done to solve them, and how to implement them."* Block Medical Officer
- *"The coaching visits by the project DIC played a critical role in making the facility staff comfortable with the process and integrating it into their practice."* Medical Officer Health.

In addition to the coaching visits, the project provided support through bimonthly learning sessions where the teams came together to discuss what they had been working on for the past 2 months. The QI meetings and learning sessions not only built an environment of reflection and learning, it created a sense of teamwork. One staff nurse at the regional hospital remembered, *"The exchange of lessons and experiences not only helped us learn, but also made us feel connected as one team, all working to address one problem. We were exchanging experiences beyond the aims we had undertaken!"*

Teams shared learning in many different ways. For example, nurses at PHC Pukhri shot short video clips on their mobile phones to share how they had changed care to make it easier for staff to give vitamin K and oxytocin. These clips helped communicate the details of how the labor room was organized and how care was provided, making it easier for staff from other facilities to understand the specific changes.

A third component of support was clinical trainings. Whenever the QI teams and the DIC identified additional training needs, trainings independent of learning sessions were conducted. Initially, the project provided training on technical issues for the staff, like testing of hemoglobin, injection of vitamin K in newborns, and the use of oxytocin for managing the risk of postpartum hemorrhage. Later, they coordi-nated with state officials to conduct training on safe delivery and newborn care and resuscitation. For these trainings, the government would provide their trainers, either from the regional hospital or from the state level, and the project would pro-vide logistic support. This arrangement improved district participation in and own-ership of the QI work.

Measurement and Results

In initiating the improvement project, one of the first steps for teams was to set up data systems, with the help of the project staff, to support the work. In most cases, the existing government data systems were insufficient since they had limited detail on processes of care and had data quality issues. Often, health workers submitted inaccurate data to avoid getting in trouble – for example, recording that a woman had her hemoglobin measured in the antenatal period even if that was not true – and thus, problems were hidden.

The project staff helped the facility staff design simple tools to measure perfor-mance on the indicators related to their chosen aims. For example, they added new columns or rows into existing data collection sheets to record data that was relevant to their aims. The teams kept the data for their QI projects with themselves initially. Because they were not sharing them and because they were using them for their own purposes, the quality and validity of the data were substantially better than the data that they reported to the district.

Within a few months of starting the improvement work, the teams started to see evidence of substantial improvements in processes of care. Figure 6.1 shows improvement in the percentage of women receiving correct diagnostic care and an increase in the percentage of women being identified with high-risk conditions.

Institutionalizing and Spreading QI from 5 to 43 Facilities

In May 2014, after 5 months of work, key stakeholders and QI team members met to share experiences and results. At this learning session, the CMO was impressed that all five facilities had achieved their stated aims and were sustaining their results. These results generated a lot of interest among the BMOs from blocks outside of Pukhri. The BMO from Pukhri, who was originally skeptical of this work and upset that the CMO had selected Pukhri as the pilot block, recounts that after seeing the results of the intervention in Pukhri, some of the other BMOs complained to the CMO of preferential treatment to Pukhri Block and requested the inclusion of their blocks as well in interventions to improve quality of maternal and newborn health services.

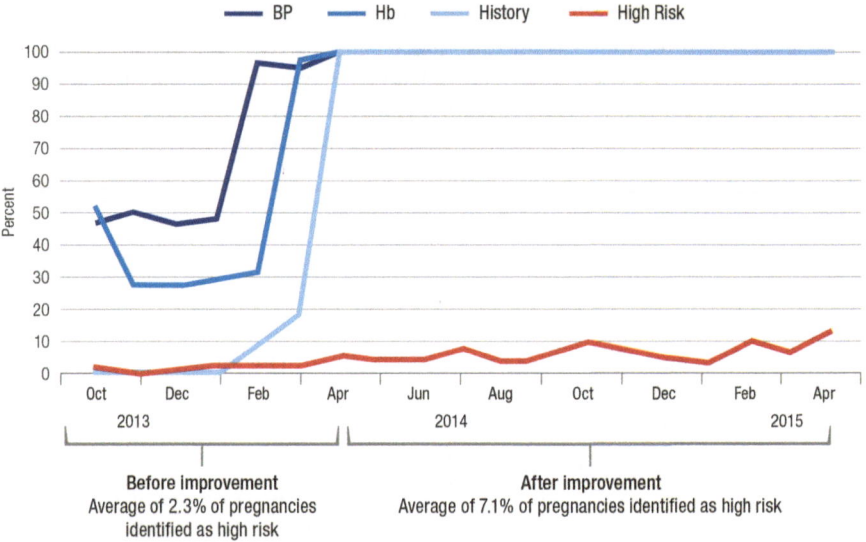

Fig. 6.1 Percentage of women coming to the antenatal clinics in five facilities having a full history taken and hemoglobin and blood pressure measured and the percentage of women being identified with high-risk conditions

Inspired by the results, the BMOs in the other blocks started telling their staff to work on the same aims as the facilities in Pukhri. The ward sister from the civil hospital shared her experience working at one of the facilities that was told to replicate Pukhri's success: *"On the instructions of our medical officer, we started checking hemoglobin and blood pressure levels more frequently during antenatal care check-ups, giving an injection of oxytocin to mothers after delivery, and giving an injection of vitamin K to newborns. There was a lot of improvement, but for some reason we were unable to achieve and sustain the high level of results as in the QI project-supported facilities. Therefore, the SMO was keen to get the QI project working with us."*

At this point, the district leadership realized that simply setting specific aims and telling people to do better was not leading to results. They realized that the QI project must be providing a different type of support, so they asked the project to help them spread the QI model to two new blocks. The focus was more ambitious than simply improving the specific elements of care addressed in the previously supported facilities. Instead, the government wanted their own staff to be able to use QI approaches for any clinical area.

The leadership selected Choori Block because of its proximity to the district headquarters and Samote Block because of its distance from the district headquarters. District leadership also decided that existing Health Supervisors would take over the coaching role previously carried out by the DIC. *"We wanted to see whether or not these interventions will work as effectively without active oversight from the external project,"* recalled the Medical Officer Health. They also wanted to see how well the Health Supervisors could perform the role of the DIC, so they included more health sub-centers (HSCs) in the spread facilities.

Between May and September 2014, the QI project staff supported the Chamba District government to develop a QI guideline detailing the roles and responsibilities of staff involved in the QI work. The guideline was based on how the project had supported the initial five facilities and highlighted three main organizational structures required to implement a QI project: facility-based QI teams, a managerial structure within and outside the facilities to support these teams, and a leadership structure that provides a clear direction for improvement as well as oversight and support during implementation. The guideline outlined key roles and responsibilities within these structures:

- QI Teams.

  - The leaders of each facility were each expected to form a QI team that would select initial aims of importance to them and then follow the other seven steps for improvement. The teams were expected to report on the progress of their improvement projects and share learning.

- Managerial Structure.

  - The managerial structure was composed of the BMO, who would support the larger facilities in each block, and the health supervisors, who would support the sub-centers. These staff assumed the role of the QI coach and visited each facility at least once a month to help the staff learn and implement QI projects. They were also asked to communicate with senior managers to help address issues, such as logistics, which were not always addressable at the facility level. The QI project provided 2 days of QI training to these staff, similar to the training that they provided to their own DIC.

- Leadership Structure.

  - The leadership structure was formed by block and district leaders. They ensured that all facilities understood their improvement priorities and also assigned time during all block and district meetings to discuss the QI work at the facilities. This structure also ensured that government funds were made available for QI activities, including QI training, coaching, and learning sessions.

With the structures in place and key actors informed of their roles, QI projects started in the 38 new facilities in September 2014. Leading up to the spread of the QI intervention, the district leadership had taken other steps to improve care in the scale-up or spread facilities, beyond the initial action of simply telling the sites that they needed to provide basic care at the same level as the sites with improvement teams. For example, in May 2014, the district provided the new sites with classroom training from government trainers on intrapartum care and the standards they were

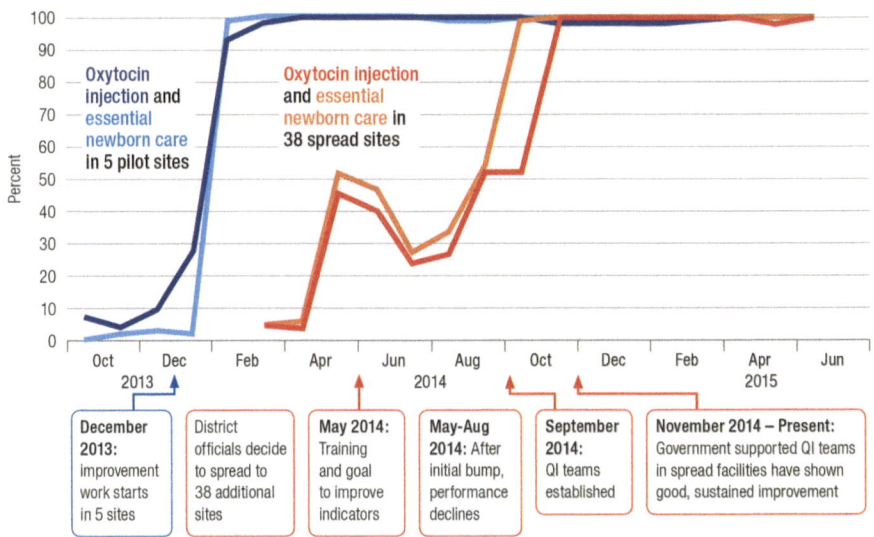

Fig. 6.2 Percentage increase in oxytocin injection and essential newborn care in 5 pilot sites and 38 spread sites, Chamba District, Himachal Pradesh, India (Oct 2013–Jun 2015)

supposed to follow. They also asked the spread sites to send monthly reports on their progress. However, as the nurse at the start of this section observed (and the data in Fig. 6.2 confirm), these interventions led to some moderate, short-term improvement, which facilities struggled to sustain. It was only when the new sites started using QI methods in September 2014 to address the poor processes at the root of these outcomes that they saw sustained improvement.

Figure 6.2 shows the data for oxytocin administration and delivery of components of essential newborn care in the 5 original QI sites and 38 spread sites.

Sustainability

The project ended support to Chamba District in December 2015 due to changes in funding. During 2016, the State Government of Himachal Pradesh developed a plan to scale up QI support in all districts based on the experiences in Chamba. In January 2017, more than a year after the project had withdrawn support, the State Improvement Coordinator revisited Chamba while working with the government on their statewide plan.

He visited two sites that had been supported directly by the project and one spread facility. All facilities had sustained improvement on the original aims and were continuing data collection related to these aims. However, they had not picked new aims nor trained new staff on QI approaches. Speaking with a Health Supervisor who had been supporting spread facilities, he learned that the Health Supervisor had continued coaching for around 4 months after the project left, but then stopped when the CMO, who had led this initiative, was transferred to another district and the new leaders did not ask for updates on the QI work.

The statewide plan has incorporated the learning from the initial QI work, the spread through the government, and what happened after the project closed and has a strong emphasis on setting up and supporting formal structures and systems to support QI at all levels of the health system.

Reflection

The work in Chamba highlights six important features of improvement work:

- First, it is possible to get rapid results. In the sites supported by the QI project directly, new improvement teams were able to achieve dramatic improvements in routine antenatal and intrapartum care within weeks.
- Second, results are critical to getting buy-in from leaders and other stakeholders. There was considerable skepticism to QI at the beginning in Chamba. This was partly because people thought that they had too few resources to provide better care and partly because there was reluctance to having external people provide help. Getting results early changed this perception. The impression in the district within months was that the QI methods were relevant to Chamba and that it was worth working with the external group to learn this new approach.
- Third, leadership is essential. The key figure in this case study is the Chief Medical Officer who was impressed by results and pushed the rest of the health team in the district to start to use this approach in other blocks and facilities. Without such leadership, it is unlikely that such rapid improvement would have occurred. After he and the project left, structures to support improvement were no longer maintained.
- Fourth, government staff were quickly able to pick up QI methods and use them to improve care. Helping the district develop strategies to integrate QI methods in existing systems at the facility, management, and leadership levels was critical to this success.
- Fifth, some problems require the use of improvement methods to fix. The unsustainable improvement in oxytocin and essential newborn care in spread sites after the training, introduction of standards, and supervision interventions, and the subsequent rapid improvement with the spread of improvement methods are evidence of this.
- Sixth, some elements of QI are more sustainable than others. The facilities visited more than a year after the end of external support continued to have data showing good performance on the aims that the QI teams had worked on. These improvements were sustained even in the facilities with extensive staff turnover. The systems to support new and ongoing QI, however, were no longer active.

Acknowledgments The QI technical assistance to Chamba District described in this case was supported by the USAID Office of Health Systems through the USAID Applying Science to Strengthen and Improve Systems Project, implemented by University Research Co., LLC under Cooperative Agreement Number AID-OAA-A-12-00101.

Chapter 7
The Business Case for Quality in Health Care

Nicole Spieker

Abstract The Constitution of Kenya gives the government an oversight role in setting and enforcing quality standards for health services. While the Kenyan Ministry of Health has numerous policy documents and legal frameworks to enforce quality care, its capacity to perform inspection visits and enforce licensing requirements has been limited. To help support the institutionalization of a regulatory framework to promote quality health care, PharmAccess, a Dutch nongovernmental organization, launched a strategic collaboration with the Kenya Ministry of Health and the National Hospital Insurance Fund (NHIF) to embed accredited clinical and business quality standards into a national quality assurance system and to introduce the standards and quality improvement methodology into the contracting process of health-care providers by the NHIF. This case focuses on the introduction of medical and business quality standards at St. Patrick Health Care Center, a private provider in Nairobi. The program has helped the facility to attract financial loans to improve the scale, scope, and quality of their services and to generate extra income by securing a contract with the NHIF to provide health-care services to NHIF members in addition to other private insurers.

Keywords Accreditation · Kenya · National Hospital Insurance Fund · Quality improvement plan · Quality standards · Stepwise certification

Background and Regulatory Framework

The Constitution of Kenya gives the government the responsibility for ensuring the realization of the right to health—meaning equitable, affordable and quality health services for all citizens—as well as an oversight role in setting and enforcing quality standards for health services. Kenya has numerous policy documents and legal

N. Spieker (✉)
PharmAccess Foundation, Amsterdam, The Netherlands
e-mail: n.spieker@pharmaccess.org

© University Research Co., LLC 2020

L. R. Marquez (ed.), *Improving Health Care in Low- and Middle-Income Countries*, https://doi.org/10.1007/978-3-030-43112-9_7

frameworks to support the national goal of health for all.[1] Although quality of health services is implied in all these documents, as of 2019, they are still being reviewed to clarify how these policies should be implemented and are therefore not fully operationalized. Despite national and county governments motivated to make a difference, as in many low- and middle-income countries, ensuring quality health care in Kenya remains a major challenge. The capacity of government to perform inspection visits and enforce licensing requirements has been limited, and inspectors are often faced with the risk of having to close down facilities that are perhaps the only possibility for patients to receive care in a region. Importantly, the same enforcement mechanisms do not always apply to both public and private facilities, creating disparities in the health sector.

With weak enforcement of a regulatory framework to measure and enforce adherence to quality standards, patients and funders of health care face uncertainty regarding the availability and quality of services in the health sector (Ruelas et al. 2012; Das and Gertler 2007; Das and Hammer 2014; Øvretveit 2004; Peabody et al. 2006; Smits et al. 2014; Mate et al. 2013). This uncertainty hampers investments in the health sector, since patients are not willing to prepay for health care through risk pooling. Low utilization of health services and a lack of reliable income refrains health-care providers from investing in the quality, scope, and scale of their services. This results in a vicious cycle of poor supply of and poor demand for health care.

Transparency about the quality of care and care delivery is crucial to break this vicious cycle. Patients need to know what quality of care they can expect at a certain facility. Funders need data on quality and risk to assess the medical, financial, and accountability risks when considering long-term investments. Insurance companies need data to determine which providers their customers can use and to assure value for money. At a policy level, data on quality and risks assist governments and donors in their choices about how to best allocate their scarce resources to improve quality and lay the groundwork for a regulatory framework (Scott and Jha 2014). Data collected during facility inspections on size, scope, and quality of health-care services can support all these objectives across the sector and stakeholders.

To help create transparency of care provision and lay the basis for institutionalizing a regulatory framework, in June 2013, PharmAccess, a Dutch nongovernmental organization (NGO) dedicated to improving access to better health care in Africa, launched a formal, strategic collaboration with the Kenya Ministry of Health, the National Hospital Insurance Fund (NHIF) and the Health in Africa Initiative of the International Finance Corporation. The key objectives of the collaboration are to

---

[1] Including the Kenya Health Policy 2012–2030, the Kenya Vision 2030, the Kenya Quality Model for Health, the draft Health Bill 2012, the draft health financing strategy, and the Kenya National Health Sector Strategic Plan III for 2013–17.

embed accredited[2] clinical and business quality standards into a national quality assurance system and to introduce the standards and quality improvement methodology into the contracting process of health-care providers by the NHIF. Use of uniform quality standards will create transparency on the size, scope, and quality of care of health-care facilities in Kenya and allow for benchmarking between facilities and regions. The results could be used to guide improvement within a facility but also for decision-making on NHIF insurance contracting, pay for performance, reimbursement based on quality of care, health system management, policy development, and access to credit.

PharmAccess' approach for this initiative has focused on public and private health-care facilities at the "bottom of the pyramid," such as dispensaries and health centers, which are the primary health-care distribution channel in low-income settings and often struggle with patient safety and quality demands. The program offers a stepwise certification process complemented by technical assistance whereby a facility pursues explicit levels of quality based on explicit criteria by implementing improvement plans to work toward the next level. Where financing for improvement is needed, facilities, through the Medical Credit Fund, can get access to affordable loans with local banks (PharmAccess Group). The Medical Credit Fund facilitates loans to clinics to stimulate growth and encourage new ways of financing health care.

Each quality level is recognized by a formal certificate. This creates an improvement path that offers positive incentives for health-care providers to enhance quality and ultimately qualify for accreditation when the highest level has been achieved. Whereas the latter objective might remain out of reach for many providers for some time to come, a pathway to work toward that objective can boost client, investor, and regulator confidence in the motivation and capacity of health-care providers to steadily enhance their performance.

Designing and Organizing the Improvement Effort

Universal Health Coverage, one of the Sustainable Development Goals, has been adopted as an important national priority in the Constitution of Kenya in 2010 and part of the "Big Four" agenda of President Kenyatta. One of the drivers for Universal Health Coverage in Kenya is the National Hospital Insurance Fund (NHIF). The

---

[2] The PharmAccess health-care quality standards program, known as *SafeCare*, has been accredited by the International Society for Quality in Health Care. SafeCare (http://www.safe-care.org/index.php?page=safecare-standards) is a collaboration between PharmAccess and the accreditation bodies Joint Commission International (United States) and the Council for Health Service Accreditation of Southern Africa (South Africa) designed to apply International Society for Quality in Health Care-recognized clinical standards that are realistic for resource-restricted settings. SafeCare dissects the improvement process of health-care providers in surveyable, measurable steps (Johnson et al. 2016).

NHIF is a publicly owned insurance corporation that provides insurance to adults in Kenya working in the formal sector but also offers the so-called SupaCover for the informal sector. For the NHIF to expand its insurance packages to all Kenyans, improving and ensuring the quality of care delivered by hospitals and clinics contracted by NHIF are critical. In order to expand coverage for its members, the NHIF developed and implemented an accreditation system for contracting providers. The management of NHIF, however, wished to have a system more aligned with international accreditation standards used by other countries, such as South Africa, Australia, the United States, Canada, and the Netherlands, based on International Society for Quality in Health Care-accredited clinical standards and evaluation processes. The system should also be part of a continuous improvement process for the facility and not just contracting. However, international accreditation standards such as those set by the Joint Commission International—globally considered the gold standard of health-care accreditation—are generally acknowledged as difficult to implement and maintain in settings where resource constraints hamper compliance. Few health-care facilities in low- and middle-income countries can afford the accreditation process, and once achieved, there are not enough incentives for facilities to make the investment worth it. In Kenya, as of 2019, only the Aga Khan Hospital and Gertrude's Children's Hospital in Nairobi have achieved Joint Commission International accreditation. For NHIF, therefore, the stepwise approach offered by PharmAccess was a better match as a basis to introduce international standards and yet support facilities to meet those standards by making structured, incremental improvements in quality.

PharmAccess built the capacity of the NHIF for a more structured quality system and to incorporate internationally recognized health-care quality and business standards into the NHIF's health-care facility contracting structure. For sustainable quality improvement, having the certification methodology embedded within the NHIF and used for contracting provides much-needed financial incentives for providers, as it provides them a regular income through the capitation system for outpatient services and fee-for-service for inpatient services the NHIF uses.

Inception of the Collaboration

The quality improvement (QI) program began with the formation of a Steering Committee—consisting of the senior NHIF managers (the Chief Executive Officer and the Manager for Benefits and Quality Assurance), the Kenya program lead of the Health in Africa Initiative, and PharmAccess leadership—convened to discuss the strategic direction of the engagement and to draft a Memorandum of Understanding that described the overall objectives of the partnership. Against this framework, more detailed operational plans were designed to achieve the agreed objectives. The Steering Committee was also responsible for overseeing the implementation of the operational plans. Progress was discussed during regular meetings.

Drafting and implementing the operational work plan were the responsibility of the Technical Working Group, which organized monthly meetings. These meetings were attended by quality managers and assessors from each organization (NHIF, International Finance Corporation, and PharmAccess) who could steer the process of developing an operational plan and report back to the Steering Committee as well as their own staff when further input was needed. The Technical Working Group addressed capacity building of NHIF quality assessors, planning of the quality assessments, the quality and business standards that would be applied in the assessments, and embedding the assessments in the overall NHIF structure of contracting health-care providers. They developed an annual training schedule, list of training participants, meeting dates, plans for software implementation, and the organizational structure to support standards-based quality assessments and stepwise certification by the NHIF through its regional managers, who were responsible for implementation. The Technical Working Group provided the implementers with practical details about how the implementation of the standards and certification process should take place.

Capacity Building at the National Hospital Insurance Fund

The NHIF, the Council for Health Service Accreditation of Southern Africa, and PharmAccess Foundation organized several five-day quality assessor trainings for NHIF Quality Assurance Officers from the 15 NHIF regions. The Quality Assurance Officers, drawn from various medical professions, including clinical officers, nurses, laboratory technologists, and public health officers, would be responsible for doing the actual assessments using the standards. The NHIF selected them based on their performance regarding quality assurance and their motivation and ability to drive quality improvement in each region and champion the process. The selection of the top performers in each region to serve as quality assessors would ensure that there would be adequate buy-in at the regional level. Pre- and post-tests were done to establish participants' knowledge and understanding of the standards and assessment process prior to and after the training. In addition to presentations and training materials, the participants discussed case studies, conducted a mock survey using the standards at three facilities, and developed a quality improvement plan using the supporting software system.

To become a qualified quality assessor, participants also needed to successfully complete two mentored quality assessments. Experienced assessors from PharmAccess accompanied the trainees to a health facility to evaluate their work during an assessment. This entailed conducting a full assessment in which the experienced assessor and the trainee both gathered data independently and then cross-checked their scores, incorporating peer-to-peer learning. Through discussion and comparison of his or her assessment with that of one of the surveyors, the trainee would identify areas of scoring that were not clear. These topics were then discussed between trainee and mentor, consulting scoring guidelines.

Next, five NHIF regions (Nairobi, Rift Valley, Nyanza, Eastern, and Central) were selected to start rolling out the quality assessments in their area. These regions conduct two assessments per month with the support of PharmAccess staff, resulting in 30 assessments in 3 months. By working together in assessment teams of two people to conduct assessments and review data at the regional level, the regions built internal capacity and became more efficient at conducting assessments and providing quality improvement support. Quality officers from the Ministry of Health joined several of the training sessions and field visits to ensure that they were involved in these activities and that the activities were aligned with national policies.

Improving Care at a Nairobi Health-Care Provider

St. Patrick Health Care Center, located on a commercial road in Nairobi's densely populated Kayole area, is one of the go-to health-care facilities for the mainly poor and low-income population residing in the area. The facility is owned and managed by a woman who is a trained nurse by profession. The private, for-profit facility has 17 staff members and 26 beds and is open 24 hours a day, 7 days a week. The patients visiting the facility are mostly self-employed in retail activities, handicrafts, or personal services, like barbers and taxi drivers.

St. Patrick joined the stepwise certification program in early 2012. At the start of the QI program in March 2012, the facility signed a participation agreement and received a one-day, on-site training for the key staff (managing director, matron, and department leaders). This was done to ensure that the team understood the quality and business standards. An external assessment was then conducted by PharmAccess staff, which resulted in the development of a quality improvement plan outlining areas for improvement. The program provided quarterly monitoring and support visits to help St. Patrick's quality team and follow-up assessments in 2013 and 2016 to evaluate overall improvement. A short overview of the process is depicted in Fig. 7.1.

Assessment Standards, Scoring, and Certification

The health-care quality and business standards included in the quality assessment cover the full range of clinical services and management functions, divided into 13 service elements grouped in four areas:

- *Health-care organization*: (1) Management and leadership, (2) human resource management, (3) patient and family rights and access to care, (4) management of information, (5) risk management
- *Patient care*: (6) Primary health-care services (Outpatient care), (7) inpatient care
- *Specialized services*: (8) Operating theater and anesthetic services, (9) laboratory services, (10) diagnostic imaging services, (11) medication management
- *Ancillary services*: (12) Facility management services, (13) support services

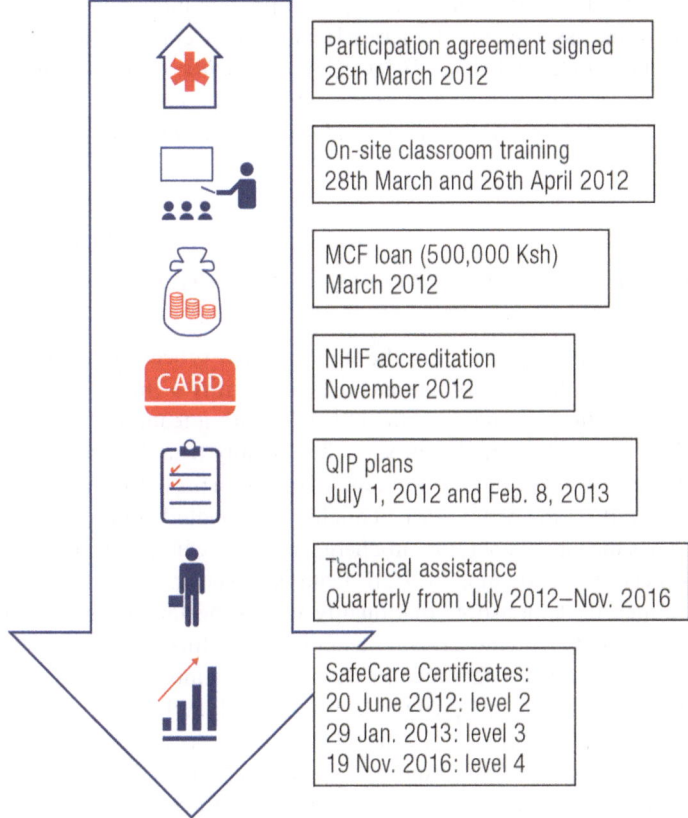

Fig. 7.1 Timeline of SafeCare program activities at St. Patrick

Adherence to standards is measured by assessing each service element against a number of scoring criteria, which are measurable elements that define specific requirements. Each criterion is marked as "not compliant," "partially compliant," or "fully compliant"; a mark of "not applicable" is given if the service measured by the criterion is not provided at a given facility. PharmAccess experts then review the results and scores and assign a certification level based on a proprietary algorithm. This certificate is awarded to acknowledge the provider's progress on the quality journey. The program recognizes five levels of improvement, with the highest (Level 5) indicating a provider's readiness to apply for international accreditation.

The first quality assessment at St. Patrick was conducted in June 2012 to measure the level of quality of health services delivered by the facility and identify priorities for quality improvement. The assessment team, who had all successfully completed the assessor training, included a nurse, a laboratory technician, a pharmaceutical technician, and a business advisor. The assessment exercise took a day to complete. The data were reviewed by PharmAccess reviewers who discussed discrepancies identified, unclear comments, and ambiguous scores in the assessment data with the team leader, who then made the necessary adjustments to improve the quality of the assessment data. The data review and approval process took 2 weeks to complete. After the baseline assessment, St. Patrick Health Care Center achieved Level 2 certification, which indicated that "*The facility is starting to operate according to structured processes and procedures, some of which are captured in written guidelines and standard operating procedures. However, health care quality is still likely to fluctuate.*"

Initiating the Improvement Process at St. Patrick

An essential part of implementing the improvement process is the creation of a quality team within the facility that includes the facility's clinical leadership, usually the medical director and department heads, with a team lead among the staff spearheading the implementation process. The quality team lead at St. Patrick was a nurse who had attended various trainings on infection prevention and risk management. Other staff on the newly formed quality team included the human resources manager, sales manager, laboratory in-charge, pharmacy in-charge, nurse in-charge, kitchen supervisor, and support staff team supervisor. This multidisciplinary approach aimed to demonstrate that quality within the facility was every department's responsibility. Having a quality team is also in line with the national policy in Kenya that requires all facilities to have one. A simple policy and procedure document was drafted and adopted by the team, which outlined management of the team and general expectations of the team, to facilitate its effectiveness.

The health facility received a quality management training by the quality officers of PharmAccess, both in a classroom setting and at their workstations. The team leader presented a draft quality improvement plan (QIP) developed by PharmAccess to the facility's quality team to discuss the proposed activities and their distribution across the implementation period as well as assigning responsible persons for each activity. The draft QIP was developed based on a proprietary algorithm of PharmAccess that identifies noncompliant areas that are either high risk to patients, to staff, or to the business performance of the provider. During the meeting, inputs and activities suggested by the facility management and staff were incorporated. The team leader made subsequent adjustments and presented the revised QIP to the PharmAccess quality officer for review and approval. The purpose of this process is to ensure both local ownership of the plan and that essential gaps in quality are addressed and that the QIP is ambitious enough.

The team leader then proceeded to share the findings of the approved assessment and the QIP with the entire facility to encourage adoption of all the actions in the QIP. The facility-wide meeting provided an opportunity for all staff to hear the findings of the assessment and discuss the proposed activities as presented in the QIP. Slides highlighting departmental performance drew particular attention. The use of pictures taken during the assessment to show gaps and emphasize good practices resonated well with the staff, causing those present to accept and own the report. The approach that was taken was nonpunitive, to stimulate an open, learning environment.

Table 7.1   Detailed improvements made at St. Patrick in human resources, pharmacy, laboratory services, and patient records management

Human resource management: High health-care staff turnover is a challenge in Kenya, and St. Patrick's situation is no different. On average, over one-third of their personnel leaves every year, although staff retention has now improved. The owner has completed and updated their personnel files, drafted job descriptions, and now facilitates continuous medical education every week
Medication management: Improvements to the pharmacy included privacy, efficiency, and inventory management. The dispensing window was moved so that clients can consult the pharmacist out of earshot of the waiting room, and there is a separate room for sensitive cases. Medicines are now stored in a locked cabinet. Hazardous and flammable materials are stored separately. The pharmacy now serves up to 200 people a day
Laboratory services: St. Patrick upgraded the lab 2 years ago, moving it to a larger room, installing separate sinks for staining and handwashing, and purchasing more equipment, such as TB and HIV testing kits. They monitor services with performance reports and have installed a standard operating procedure for every test, a tracking chart for expiration dates, and guidelines for the maintenance of lab equipment. There is also a visible price list with the expected report time for results. The number of lab tests has more than doubled, from 400 to about 850 per month. The lab generates a lot of income and has become the financial backbone of the facility
Patient records management: The facility management team procured computers and installed a hospital management system in all relevant areas. Digitalization of this key function not only improved management of records by providing privacy of patient information, but it also increased efficiency in storage of patient's data and overall communication across departments An important aspect of this development is the ability of the facility to utilize the collected data by conducting monthly data analysis, hence making key decisions based on informed analysis

Each of the members of the quality team then coached the implementation process in their respective departments. Activities varied from the introduction of stock management tools and job descriptions to redesigning the patient flow process (see Table 7.1). Thereafter, the quality team met on a monthly basis to discuss progress on improvement activities in the different departments. The team lead kept the facility manager informed about progress and funding needs. All meeting discussions were documented in the quality team file. As a result of this consultative process, the staff at St. Patrick quickly embraced the quality improvement process.

The facility received technical assistance from PharmAccess quality officers, who visited the facility approximately every quarter to measure the extent to which the quality improvement plan was being implemented. These visits aimed to assist the facility quality team to identify bottlenecks and provided support to find solutions. The facility also had access to an online library with guidelines, checklists, protocols, and other materials developed by PharmAccess to help meet the program's quality standards.

Addressing quality gaps is not only about improving structures and procedures; financial investments in equipment and infrastructure are needed. The program has helped providers to unlock investments as they help the owners think about their work as a business. Shortly after joining the program, St. Patrick obtained a loan, as well as business training, through the PharmAccess Medical Credit Fund. With a Kenya shilling (Ksh) 500,000 (USD 5000) loan, they purchased computers, installed a computerized management system, internal phone lines, and a closed-circuit television system (a TV system primarily used for surveillance and security purposes). They also invested in having an external auditor check their financial accounts and made minor infrastructural improvements. The business training helped the facility to prepare for a larger loan qualification, draft a business plan, and prioritize its investments.

The initial assessment report was an eye-opener for them. "*We were not running the facility in the right way,*" the owner explained. "*We had no administration office, no systems. We used to work from our pockets, writing on patient cards, and counting the shillings at the end of the day. SafeCare helped us to establish our gaps and set in motion interventions to improve ourselves. Now, our record keeping is accurate, and we have audited accounts and a digital client history that can be accessed at any time. The system has also helped minimize fraud and track the expiration dates of drugs in our pharmacy.*"

The experience they gained in qualifying for their first loan through the Medical Credit Fund was instrumental in building a financially sound organization. Through the training and on-site support, they learned how to draft a business plan and which documents to deliver to the bank. Financial records were now neatly in place. They repaid their first loan within 6 months. Their track record and improved financial management enabled them to secure a Ksh. five million (USD 50,000) loan from a bank to invest in their laboratory and expand the facility.

"*It was difficult sometimes in the beginning because SafeCare requires a new way of thinking, both for us and for our staff,*" the owner says. "*It's about accountability, transparency, and establishing procedures – in all departments, from the cleaners to the medical personnel. But now that our staff has seen what the program can do, they are fully on board and committed to continue to improve our quality.*"

For instance, in the beginning, St. Patrick's quality team felt that improving the facility's documentation required additional work for which they did not have time. After some initial encouragement, they realized the benefits of their time investments; fewer insurance claims (both NHIF and commercial) were rejected, thanks to the improved documentation. The facility also implemented some very visible, patient-focused improvements; for example, the renovation of the waiting room, previously a crowded room that was the cause of complaints. The redesign process was easy to implement; it involved various departments and was considered "low hanging fruit," as it did not involve complex processes, training sessions, or issues that could be considered political, such as nonperforming staff. The renovation not only resulted in better patient flow but also elicited positive responses and compliments from the patients, which encouraged the staff members to continue on their improvement journey and experience pride in the results. Table 7.1 provides illustrative examples of improvement activities instigated at St. Patrick that contributed to overall better performance of the facility and compliance with the certification standards.

Technical Support for Improvement

During the implementation process, one quality assurance officer from PharmAccess visited St. Patrick quarterly to monitor progress, identify bottlenecks, and support the quality team in finding appropriate solutions. The NHIF quality assurance manager accompanied the PharmAccess officer on two visits but had too many other responsibilities to provide regular support to specific facilities. St. Patrick Health Care Center was also encouraged to call the PharmAccess quality officer anytime if they needed specific assistance with any of their improvement activities.

During one quality team meeting, facility staff expressed the need to improve on the level of waste management and infection control in the facility. The main challenges in the facility included lack of color-coded bags for waste bins, lack of proper waste segregation at the point of generation, lack of proper storage of generated waste in the facility, and lack of a documented policy to guide staff on waste management and infection prevention. In addition, the facility was struggling with providing clean running water, soap, and hand-drying towels in key areas, such as the laboratory.

The quality team lead prepared a short presentation on waste management practices in the facility, using pictures and demonstrations (e.g., on proper hand washing techniques and waste management). This was then followed up by drafting of a quick plan of action that detailed what was required for improvement (e.g., procurement of coded bins, procurement of hand-drying towels, documentation of policies and procedures) and indicated the respective staff assigned to complete each activity, the budget required (if any), and finally, the period of completion for each specified activity.

Results

St. Patrick Health Care Center began the improvement work at Level 2 certification (based on their baseline assessment scores), but achieved Level 3 certification within 6 months through changes implemented to improve quality of care. St. Patrick's significant progress in implementing their QIP qualified the facility for a third follow-up quality assessment in November 2016.

After the third assessment, the facility achieved a Level 4 certificate, making it one of the highest-performing facilities in terms of quality in Kenya. Level 4 certification means that "*The facility is regularly monitoring the implementation of treatment guidelines and standard operating procedures through internal record reviews and (clinical) audits. Most high-risk processes and procedures are controlled.*" After the third assessment, a new QIP was prepared to guide the facility in continuing to improve quality to advance to an even higher certification level.

Figure 7.2 shows the improvement in assessment scores achieved by St. Patrick over the three assessments. While the facility demonstrated an increase in most

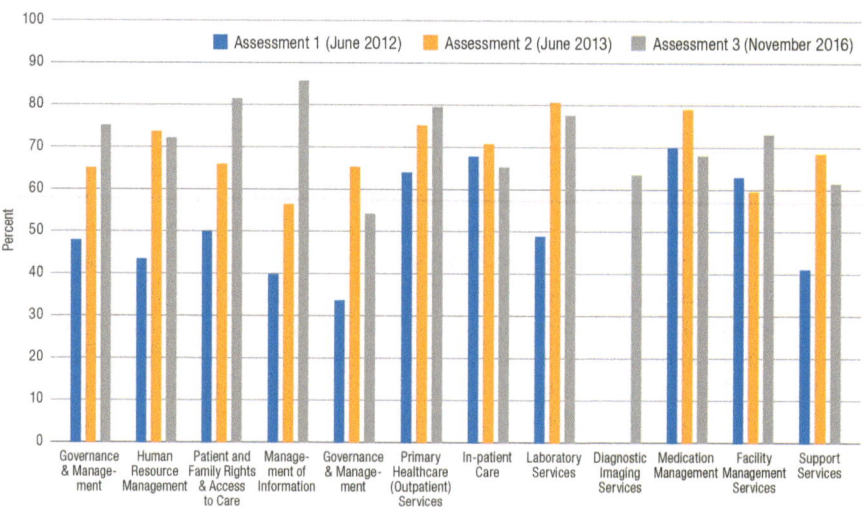

Fig. 7.2 St. Patrick quality assessment scores by service element. Note: Diagnostic imaging was introduced only before the third assessment

service elements, as is common with improvement trajectories, scores fluctuated somewhat with an overall positive trend. As St. Patrick does not have surgery services, this service element was not scored.

The next step is installing an operating theater. The facility is eager to continue improving quality of care to reach Level 5. "*SafeCare needs a lot of commitment, but you feel like you're in another world. It makes you feel like a professional,*" said the owner.

Achieving National Hospital Insurance Fund Contracting

During previous inspections by the NHIF of St. Patrick, the facility was unsure what was expected of them and what were the standards against which they were evaluated; as a result, St. Patrick failed to meet the criteria for NHIF accreditation. There was no manual or checklist used by the NHIF assessor, and St. Patrick was not offered advice on how to improve on shortcomings that prevented their NHIF accreditation. After the introduction of the program, the facility received a clear overview of what they were evaluated against and how to introduce the necessary changes to adhere to these standards. As a result, St. Patrick became NHIF-accredited in November 2012, ensuring a larger client base and income flow. Patient visits have risen, and the facility has also managed to contract with corporate clients and private medical insurance companies. In turn, the more regular income and client base from serving insured patients have been key to financing and sustaining the quality improvement work, apart from PharmAccess technical support.

Scaling Up and Sustaining the Certification Program

Introducing international standards, stepwise certification, and a transparent rating and improvement program to health-care providers in Kenya has proven to be a successful approach toward sustainable quality assurance. The combination of using this approach in conjunction with NHIF contracting and embedding it in the framework of the national quality policy of the Ministry of Health offers both the incentive and the enforcement mechanism to encourage providers to participate in quality improvement initiatives. The case study of St. Patrick Health Care Center gives insights into the actual activities that are needed within a facility to meet adherence to the standards. These activities require both committed management and committed staff. In addition, financial means/access to credit, such as through the Medical Credit Fund, are also helpful.

Data on the overall effectiveness of the program in Kenya show that 84% of the participating facilities have improved their quality scores between the initial and second assessments, suggesting that the stepwise approach is, for many facilities, an efficient and effective approach.

In 2017 and onward, quality system coverage continues scaling up under NHIF ownership. Scaling up has also come with challenges and exposed gaps in the system. The NHIF Senior Manager for Benefits and Quality Assurance at the national office states, *"The national office led the discussions for the strategic partnership and involved the regional managers through internal strategic meetings. These discussions were held in the wider context of the NHIF quality assurance program and the proper integration in the NHIF annual work plans implemented by the regions. Some of the challenges the regional mid-level Claims and Quality Managers face are competing priorities within the NHIF, compounded by staff who perform both claims and quality. These issues have influenced our decision to start with a few regions with selected staff to get results and learn lessons that can be used to scale up."*

A key learning during implementation of the program is that much more engagement with facilities on issues of quality is needed. The providers need supportive supervision and guidance, rather than just inspections and enforcement. Facilities which have been contracted by the NHIF recently need to be regularly visited because they need to be taken through NHIF processes as well as be guided on how to carry out their quality improvement meetings. It is recognized that for the NHIF, this need can compete with other needs and demands, and policy discussions should be encouraged to determine whether in the future this role should remain with NHIF, or whether an independent quality improvement and assurance institute should take up this role.

In the beginning, facilities find the quality improvement process very demanding, but as they go along, they find it easier to work with the process. Most of the facilities which have fully embraced the quality improvement process find a lot of benefit in it, since they are able to plan and budget well for the facility, monitor goods and supplies, have good bookkeeping allowing them to track their finances, and have a structured patient management process which improves client satisfaction. Another key motivator for facilities is that the NHIF can pay out their claims much faster as a result of improved bookkeeping and patient documentation. As the NHIF Regional Benefits and Quality Assurance Officer states, *"Our regional Claims and Quality Assurance Managers appreciate the stepwise accreditation standards and quality improvement methodology, since it makes their work easier, and they receive fewer complaints. Before the introduction of the stepwise accreditation standards, our work consisted of conducting inspections to see whether facilities complied with our quality and financial regulations. At the time, the NHIF concentrated more on fraud management than on quality issues."* He also advises that in order to introduce a quality program in an institution like the NHIF, it is important to study the organization well and understand its internal structures and how it relates externally. Such programs should always aim to build the capacity to develop home-grown strategies, and the process should be long term. Quality improvement programs must be institutionalized and driven by the facilities.

Reflection

A main barrier to large-scale adoption of any quality program is the relatively high cost of quality assurance, currently funded primarily by donors. First, the focus should be on how to build sufficient local capacity to ensure local ownership and low costs; next, on how to embed the methodology within the health-care system to provide both enforcement and incentive strategies that guide facilities toward improvement.

"Although quality improvement is seen as important, more work needs to be done to convince facility owners to bear some of these costs," adds the PharmAccess Country Director for Kenya. One way of promoting co-financing is to strengthen for health facilities the linkage between achieving a higher accreditation certificate and benefitting both financially (more patients and better contracts) as well as socially (awards and recognition among peers). For example, facilities in the neighborhood of St. Patrick have also asked to be in the program, and the owner of St. Patrick has been invited to talk about their experience and results at conferences and stakeholder meetings.

By requiring a minimum level (for example, Level 2) to participate in NHIF contracting and rewarding facilities that continuously show improvement with higher medical pay-outs, both enforcement and incentive mechanisms can be in place to sustain improvement. NHIF, PharmAccess, and the International Finance Corporation continue discussing possibilities of linking quality to the reimbursement of claims. A proposal has been made in the Health Financing Bill of Kenya to link quality to financing.

"It takes time for quality to improve, and for those improvements to be sustained," says a policy officer at the Health in Africa Initiative of the International Finance Corporation. *"It involves behavioral change in addition to increased motivation,*

knowledge, resources, and organizational management. Long-term strategies need to be deployed for quality improvement, designed to go beyond the project life cycle. It should be ensured so that the results achieved are not lost. Linking quality improvement to pay-for-performance mechanisms motivates the health facilities to invest in improvement and sustain this work."

Establishment of an independent accreditation body has now been endorsed in the health improvement policy, the draft health bill, and in the health financing strategy (currently under development). With policy implementation and regulation, quality improvement can be further encouraged in both the private and public sectors. The standards presented in this case study have been recognized as a key methodology for accreditation, and with franchises, private clinics, and the NHIF adopting parts of the methodology, a firm basis has been laid for institutionalization.

Author's Reflection

To strengthen health systems in low- and middle-income countries, it is important that national governments step up their role as supervisor. They need to integrate licensing, transparent quality standards and benchmarks, and accreditation into health policies and to enforce compliance. Better data will help governments to allocate their scarce resources more efficiently to invest in quality improvement. Improvements in health-care quality can yield numerous benefits to populations, bringing increased access to health services that are safe, effective, and patient-centered.

The adoption and incorporation of the SafeCare standards by the NHIF and various other health system actors in Kenya build a platform to support increased trust and transparency in the system. The SafeCare methodology is embedded in a health-financing model that aligns incentives and gives regulators and insurers leverage to ensure sufficient quality in the health-care services that are procured. The partners in this program have developed and implemented a set of quality standards and a scalable assessment and scoring methodology that assist in laying the foundation for a sustainable, Kenya-owned quality monitoring system.

–Nicole Spieker, Director Quality, PharmAccess Foundation, August 2017

Acknowledgments The author thanks the following individuals for their contributions to the SafeCare application in Kenya:

Millicent Olulo, Regional Director for Advocacy and Partnerships, Former Country Director, Kenya, PharmAccess

Kasmil Masheti, Quality Manager, PharmAccess

Mary Njoki, Quality Manager, PharmAccess

Simeon Kirgotty, Former Chief Executive Officer, National Hospital Insurance Fund

Joseph Githinji, Former Manager, National Hospital Insurance Fund

Frank Wafula, Policy Officer, International Finance Corporation

Njeri Mwaura, Policy Officer, International Finance Corporation

Ann Maira, owner, St. Patrick Health Care Center

References

Das J, Gertler PJ (2007) Variations in practice quality in five low-income countries: a conceptual overview. Health Aff (Millwood) 26(3):w296–w309

Das J, Hammer J (2014) Quality of primary care in low-income countries: facts and economics. Annu Rev Econ 1(1):1–41

Johnson MC, Schellekens O, Stewart J, van Ostenberg P, de Wit TR, Spieker N (2016) SafeCare: an innovative approach for improving quality through standards, benchmarking, and improvement in low- and middle-income countries. Jt Comm J Qual Patient Saf 42(8):350–371

Mate KS, Sifrim ZK, Chalkidou K, Cluzeau F, Cutler D, Kimball M et al (2013) Improving health system quality in low- and middle-income countries that are expanding health coverage: a framework for insurance. Int J Qual Health Care 25(5):497–504

Øvretveit J (2004) Formulating a health quality improvement strategy for a developing country. Int J Health Care Qual Assur 17(7):368–376

Peabody JW, Taguiwalo MM, Robalino DA, Frenk J (2006) Chapter 70. Improving the quality of care in developing countries. In: Disease control priorities in developing countries. Second Edition. Washington, DC: The World Bank and Oxford University Press

PharmAccess Group. Medical Credit Fund Africa. https://www.medicalcreditfund.org/

Ruelas E, Gómez-Dantés O, Leatherman S, Fortune T, Gay-Molina JG (2012) Strengthening the quality agenda in health care in low- and middle-income countries: questions to consider. Int J Qual Health Care 24(6):553–557

Scott KW, Jha AK (2014) Putting quality on the global agenda. N Engl J Med 371:3–5

Smits H, Supachutikul A, Mate KS (2014) Hospital accreditation: lessons from low- and middle-income countries. Glob Health 10(1):65

Chapter 8
Promoting Rational Use of Antibiotics in the Kyrgyz Republic

Barton Smith

Abstract Antimicrobial resistance (AMR)—the resistance of disease-causing microbes to treatment with antibiotics and other antimicrobial drugs—is a growing global health threat worldwide, making it more difficult and more expensive to treat common infections such as pneumonia, bladder infections, and skin infections. The World Health Organization's global strategy for containment of AMR calls for provision of evidence-based clinical guidelines on diagnostic and treatment strategies for common infections; the education of providers on AMR and prescribing guidelines; and institutionalization of regular audits of prescribing practices, providing feedback to clinicians using comparison with peer groups or external standards. AMR is a serious problem in the Kyrgyz Republic, which has one of the highest rates of multidrug-resistant tuberculosis (TB) in the world (25% among new cases of TB; 56% among previously treated cases). In 2012, a United States Agency for International Development (USAID) project for improving health-care quality in the Central Asian Republics began working with partners in the Kyrgyz Republic to promote the rational use of antibiotics among prescribers by using principles of quality improvement. This case describes how these actors conducted baseline audits of use of antibiotics and then developed clinical protocols, training, and job aids to change prescribing practices of providers in pilot districts and how they introduced a database to track audit indicators and feed back the results to providers.

Keywords Antibiotics · Antimicrobial resistance · Audit and feedback · Clinical protocols · Evidence-based medicine · Kyrgyz Republic · Quality improvement · Rational use of antibiotics

Background

In 2012, a US Agency for International Development (USAID)-funded project for improving health-care quality in the Central Asian Republics began working with partners in the Kyrgyz Republic to promote the rational use of antibiotics (RUA)

B. Smith (✉)
Virginia Mason Edmonds Family Medicine (Formerly with Abt Associates), Edmonds, WA, USA

© University Research Co., LLC 2020   105
L. R. Marquez (ed.), *Improving Health Care in Low- and Middle-Income Countries*, https://doi.org/10.1007/978-3-030-43112-9_8

among prescribers by using principles of quality improvement. Antibiotic resistance among disease-causing bacteria is a worsening global health threat, making it more difficult and more expensive to treat common infections such as pneumonia, bladder infections, and skin infections. The World Health Organization (WHO) developed a global strategy for the containment of antimicrobial resistance (AMR) in 2001, which included promoting RUA as a key component of national strategies on AMR, knowing that indiscriminate use of antibiotics is strongly correlated with high levels of antibiotic resistance. Promoting RUA among clinicians involves provision of evidence-based guidelines on diagnostic and treatment strategies for common infections; the education of providers on AMR and prescribing guidelines; and institutionalization of regular audits of prescribing practices, providing feedback to clinicians using comparison with peer groups or external standards.

When the RUA initiative began in 2012, no routine surveillance of antibiotic resistance levels for common infections was conducted in the Kyrgyz Republic; therefore, only limited data were available to characterize the scope of the problem. However, the rate of multidrug-resistant tuberculosis (TB) in Kyrgyz Republic is one of the highest in the world (25% among new cases of TB; 56% among previously treated cases). Likewise, no routine auditing of antibiotic prescribing practices was conducted in the country prior to this initiative, but a survey of antibiotic prescribing patterns conducted by CitiHope International in one Kyrgyz hospital in 2007 showed that antibiotics were inappropriately prescribed in 73% of cases, were not indicated in 48% of cases where prescribed, and indicated but incorrectly selected in 25% of cases.

Although containment of AMR was not prioritized in the Kyrgyz national health strategy in effect from 2012 to 2015, the RUA initiative was strongly supported by the Ministry of Health (MOH), local partners, and international development partners, including the World Health Organization and the Medicines Transparency Alliance. In fact, a national working group on AMR was established shortly after the initiative began. While the national working group was informed of the activities, they were not directly involved in overseeing the RUA initiative.

One of the first activities under the RUA initiative of the project was to identify and characterize gaps in knowledge, attitudes, and practices (KAP) through a survey related to antibiotic use among consumers and prescribers to help establish the need for intervention and to ensure that planned activities were appropriately focused. The KAP survey showed that adult consumers take, on average, over two courses of antibiotics per year and identified many misconceptions about the usefulness of and indications for antibiotics among both consumers and physicians.

Figure 8.1 shows the key stakeholders in the RUA initiative in the Kyrgyz Republic. In addition to the MOH and project staff, two professional associations—the Hospital Association of the Kyrgyz Republic (HAKR) and the Family Group Practice and Nurses Association (FGPNA)—played a central role. Both associations were created in the late 1990s to provide advocacy and support for their constituents. Both organizations began to coordinate quality improvement initiatives

USAID
- Funding and project oversight

Ministry of Health, Quality Unit (evidence-based medicine consultant)
- Facilitation of desk review of existing protocols
- Facilitation of clinical protocol development, review, and approval
- Issuance of MOH orders needed to conduct training, audits, and use of database
- Revision of orders governing the roles and duties of facility-level quality committees

Project (Regional Quality Advisor)
- Design and coordination of RUA initiative
- Provision of close technical support to FGPNA, HAKR, MOH and other local partners
- Oversight of clinical content of protocols and educational programs; training
- Design and development of database to track results

Family Group Practice and Nurses Association (FGPNA) and Hospital Association of Kyrgyz Republic (HAKR)
- Forming and facilitating focus groups
- Participation in developing of audit instruments
- Conducting baseline audit
- Training and support of facility-based QI curators
- Coordinating data entry into database
- Presenting audit results and facilitating development of improvement plans in study sites
- Review of draft clinical protocols
- Liaising with the Ministry of Health to inform them of results of the initiative and plan for scale-up

Kyrgyz State Medical Institute for Retraining and Continuing Education (KSMIRCE), Department of Family Medicine
- Drafting of clinical protocols for the primary health care (PHC) level
- Development of training curricula (lectures, clinical cases, course material)
- Training

Leading clinical specialists
- Clinical protocol development
- Training

Fig. 8.1 Key stakeholders and their roles

through previous health reform projects funded by USAID between 1996 and 2009, which focused broadly on health system strengthening with a focus on improving primary care and reforming health financing. This project included a component on "Other Public Health Threats," under which the project launched the initiative to promote the rational use of antibiotics.

Located in the heart of Central Asia, the Kyrgyz Republic is a mountainous country with a population of nearly six million and is one of the poorest of the former Soviet Republics. The socialized health-care system includes an extensive network of primary health-care (PHC) facilities and hospitals, which are managed and financed independently from one another at the district and regional levels. Regional (*oblast*) Family Medicine Centers (FMCs) represent the highest administrative level of service delivery at the ambulatory level; district (*rayon*) FMCs are financed and managed independently from regional FMCs but are under the leadership of the regional FMC director, who also serves as the regional health coordinator. Health facilities are managed by physician directors; deputy directors are tasked with ensuring the quality of clinical services, including the coordination of continuing professional development of their health-care staff through the Kyrgyz State Medical Institute for Retraining and Continuing Education (KSMIRCE). The KSMIRCE is a State institute responsible for providing continuing medical education (CME) to all physicians and nurses throughout the country and has a network of regional-level family medicine training centers, each with at least two full-time family medicine physician and nurse trainers. The Family Medicine Department of the KSMIRCE has worked closely with the FGPNA since its inception to respond to training needs voiced by FGPNA members and to coordinate continuing medical education topics with QI initiatives.

Organizing the Improvement Effort

Foundational Work with Implementing Partners

The project's first task was to meet with local partners, who would serve as the primary implementers, to outline a general strategy and assign specific roles and responsibilities. The FGPNA and the HAKR were natural choices for key implementing partners: they were recipients of grants under the project, had worked on previous QI initiatives, and had institutionalized roles in supporting their constituents at the PHC and hospital levels to provide quality care. Within each organization were two or more individuals who had worked as external quality advisors on previous quality initiatives supported by USAID. During these first meetings, the FGPNA and the HAKR, together with the regional quality advisor (who was also a physician), agreed upon the strategic approach that would be used in the RUA initiative (see Fig. 8.2).

The project's regional quality advisor also met with family medicine trainers from the KSMIRCE to solicit their help in developing the training materials. As the KSMIRCE is responsible for approval of continuing medical education (CME) and annual CME training calendars, working through them was important for institutionalization and future scale-up of training. Figure 8.3 shows the overall timeline of the initiative to rationalize the use of antibiotics in Kyrgyz Republic.

Fig. 8.2 Strategic approach used in the RUA initiative

1. Conduct a KAP survey to define the problem and inform interventions

2. Select "index conditions" as proxies for all conditions requiring antibiotics

3. Develop audit instruments for each condition based on standards of care contained in MOH-approved clinical protocols (if available) or international guidelines (if local protocols not available)

4. Select study sites

5. Conduct a baseline audit in study sites

6. Develop a training program covering index conditions

7. Conduct training for physicians and managers from study sites and present baseline audit data

8. Support study sites to conduct improvement cycles after training (conduct audits, analyze results, make improvement plans, implement plans)

9. Analyze effectiveness of interventions at district, regional, and national level and present to MOH for consideration of national scale-up

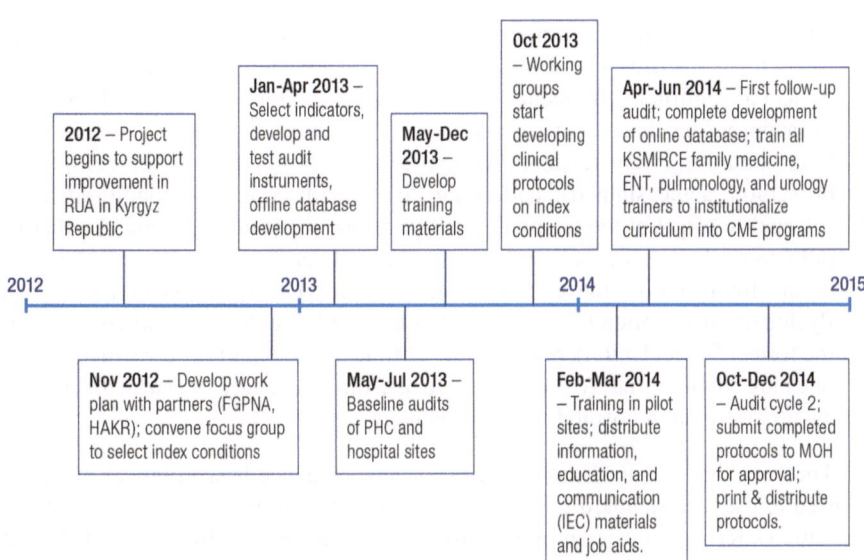

Fig. 8.3 Rational use of antibiotics initiative timeline

Choosing Improvement Priorities: Selecting Index Conditions

Focus groups of clinicians were then organized by the FGPNA and the HAKR to define a list of "index" conditions for which antibiotics were often unnecessarily or incorrectly prescribed. This was done at the national level rather than the facility level for two reasons: first, all key stakeholders agreed that these conditions were unlikely to vary significantly between facilities; second, using one common set of conditions would allow the project to use the same audit instruments and training curriculum for all participants, compare results between facilities (peer comparisons), and collate data at district, regional, and national levels. The FGPNA gathered 14 physicians representing both urban (nine) and rural (five) PHC facilities, while the HAKR gathered 9 hospital-based physicians from the Bishkek facilities.

- Brainstorming was used to develop a list of conditions that group participants viewed as significant with regard to unnecessary or incorrect use of antibiotics.
- General voting was used at the PHC level to narrow down the list to approximately four conditions, based on frequency of disease and frequency of incorrect prescription/selection of antibiotics.
- At the hospital level, conditions were selected using a prioritization matrix that included the condition frequency based on the experts' experience, frequency of incorrect use of antibiotics, problems with over- or underdiagnosis, and likelihood of changing providers' behaviors. No attempt was made to verify the frequency of the selected conditions, as there was general consensus among focus group members. Baseline data collection on the selected conditions allowed the project to confirm the frequency of inappropriate antibiotic prescriptions and use of inappropriate diagnostic criteria.
- Four conditions were selected to target at the PHC level: common cold, acute bronchitis, acute sinusitis, and acute diarrheal disease; five conditions were selected to target at the hospital level: pneumonia, asthma, chronic obstructive pulmonary disease, cystitis, and pyelonephritis. Pneumonia was selected because of the frequency of the condition and inappropriate selection of antibiotics. Pyelonephritis is often overdiagnosed in Kyrgyz Republic (as in all countries of the former Soviet Union), particularly "chronic pyelonephritis" for which antibiotics are inappropriately prescribed. At the time the study began, women with cystitis were often hospitalized for treatment.

The next step was to determine what, if any, evidence-based clinical guidance existed to use as a standard for the development of audit instruments on the index conditions. Kyrgyz physicians are accustomed to using nationally approved clinical protocols (CPs) to guide their practice decisions following a broad initiative to develop CPs in 2000–2001; however, the number of approved CPs was limited, and principles of evidence-based medicine (EBM) were not known or widely applied to CP development prior to 2004, so there was concern that CPs on the index conditions might not be available or, if available, might not be evidence-based. For this reason, a desk review of existing CPs on index conditions was conducted by the regional quality advisor in conjunction with the EBM unit within the Kyrgyz Ministry of Health. No protocols existed on the four topics targeted at the PHC level. Of the five conditions targeted at the hospital level, evidence-based guidelines had been approved for three (pneumonia, asthma, and chronic obstructive pulmonary disease). No guidance was available for cystitis, and the CP available on pyelonephritis from 2003 contained many non-evidence-based recommendations on risk factors, diagnosis, and treatment. A decision was made at that point that the needed clinical protocols would be developed simultaneously with the training curriculum for the initiative, as evidence-based source materials were needed for both. CP development teams were composed of KSMIRCE family medicine trainers (for PHC protocols) and clinical specialists, with technical support from the regional quality advisor and with methodological support from the MOH EBM consultant.

Developing Audit Instruments

The regional quality advisor worked with the QI coordinators from the professional associations to develop audit instruments (checklists), from which QI indicators would be taken for each index condition. The intended use of the audit instruments was that they would be applied quarterly by facility-level curators (FMC deputy directors) in "audit cycles" and that feedback would be provided to health-care providers after each audit with assistance from the FGPNA QI coordinators.

No information on antibiotic prescription was collected and reported in the existing health information system, nor was it retrievable from the database of the mandatory health insurance fund, the State single-payer entity that regularly conducted quality assurance reviews. This was, in part, because antibiotics were widely available in pharmacies without a prescription, so doctors rarely wrote prescriptions for them, making it difficult to track their use without conducting chart reviews. Although the use of checklists like the ones created was not routine in Kyrgyz Republic and no MOH-approved process existed for their creation, the FGPNA and the HAKR had experience developing such audit instruments from previous national continuous quality improvement efforts in antenatal care and asthma, so the format was familiar to them.

For conditions with existing evidence-based guidance in the form of a national CP, the national CP was used as the source of standards on which audit instruments were developed. For conditions without an existing CP (e.g., cystitis) or if the existing CP was considered non-evidence-based (e.g., pyelonephritis), the regional quality advisor and QI coordinators collected evidence-based recommendations by reviewing clinical guidelines from other countries. For conditions where the decision to prescribe antibiotics is based on a set of clinical rules (e.g., sinusitis), the project included documentation of pertinent clinical findings in the audit instrument. The checklists did not exceed one page per condition, and about half of the included questions were common to all checklists. Examples of checklist items common to each index condition included:

- Were antibiotics prescribed? If so, how many, types, doses, route (oral, intramuscular, intravenous), frequency, and duration of each.
- Were medications prescribed for symptomatic care? If so, please list.
- Were non-pharmacologic measures recommended? If so, please list.

QI coordinators from the FGPNA and the HAKR tested the draft audit instruments in urban facilities prior to general use by reviewing 10–20 clinical records for each condition. This allowed the coordinators to identify data that were not feasible to collect, ambiguities in the instruments, and problems with identifying and finding records based on a specific diagnosis. For example, they found that patients with presumed viral "sinusitis" were sometimes diagnosed with "viral upper respiratory infection," as clinicians often reserved the diagnosis of sinusitis for patients with signs of a bacterial sinus infection.

Selecting Quality Indicators

Selection of the indicators (see examples in Fig. 8.4) was largely based on the original discussions that took place between QI coordinators from the professional associations and the regional quality advisor to develop the disease-specific audit instruments. Given that the overall aim was to reduce unnecessary antibiotic prescription, the percent of patients treated with antibiotics was included as an indicator for each index condition. Some of the index conditions required treatment with antibiotics (e.g., pneumonia), but a known problem with overdiagnosis prompted the project to include indicators related to establishing the diagnosis based on well-defined diagnostic criteria. For example, in all the study sites, chronic pyelonephritis (kidney infection) was diagnosed much more often than acute pyelonephritis and was likely to be treated with antibiotics despite an absence of clinical signs or symptoms suggesting an active infection (diagnosis was typically based on the presence of back pain and an "abnormal" renal ultrasound). For this reason, the percent of

Acute bronchitis
- % of reviewed charts with documentation of cough duration
- % of reviewed charts with cough persisting > 2 weeks with documentation that sputum was sent for tuberculosis diagnosis
- % of reviewed charts where antibiotics were prescribed
- % or reviewed charts with notation of smoking status

Acute diarrheal disease
- % of reviewed charts where antibiotics were prescribed
- % of charts with indication for antibiotic (blood in stool, high fever, tenesmus)
- % of reviewed charts with documentation of recommendation to use oral rehydration solution

Fig. 8.4 Examples of audit indicators

patients hospitalized with a diagnosis of pyelonephritis that had documented signs of infection, such as pyuria (defined as over 10 white blood cells per high-power field on urinalysis), fever, or bacterial growth on a urine culture, was included as an indicator. Similarly, the percent of patients diagnosed with sinusitis who were assessed using recommended criteria suggesting bacterial infections that would justify antibiotic use was included as an indicator. Such indicators related to diagnosis were likewise included for sinusitis, cystitis, and pneumonia.

Other indicators were included based on regional disease patterns and priorities. For example, the percentage of patients diagnosed with bronchitis who were asked about smoking status was included since addressing high mortality from noncommunicable diseases was a national priority in Kyrgyz Republic. Similarly, the percentage of charts of patients diagnosed with acute bronchitis with documentation of the duration of cough was included because of the prevalence of tuberculosis (referring all patients with a cough duration of greater than 2 weeks for TB testing was a standard of care). In total, facilities routinely analyzed and tracked 8 indicators on 4 conditions at the PHC level and 15 indicators on 5 conditions at the hospital level. The database-generated reports, however, included additional indicators on each condition as well as data about which antibiotics were prescribed, antibiotic dosing regimens, and medications prescribed for symptom control. Facilities had the option of using this additional data to better understand physician prescribing behaviors.

Developing a Database to Track and Analyze Quality Data

Early in the organizational stage, it was necessary to think ahead and decide how audit results would be recorded, analyzed, and tracked. Based on prior experience implementing QI initiatives, one of the main roadblocks to the improvement cycle is the limited ability of health managers and leading clinicians to analyze collected data in a way that promotes problem solving and formation of improvement plans. Large volumes of data were routinely collected by health facilities, but most often, this data was simply passed up the chain of command and summarized at the national level rather than being used by facilities for decision-making.[1] During previous QI initiatives, advisors found that they were frequently retraining managers on how to calculate and graph relatively simple indicators. On the other hand, managers and providers were usually able to interpret audit results when external QI

---

[1] The traditional management approach to perceived quality gaps in health facilities included in the study was one of "inspect and punish." This particularly applied to routinely collected health statistics submitted to higher-level managers and to external audits conducted by governmental organizations, such as health departments and the State single-payer insurance fund. Frequently, a fear of punishment (usually monetary) led to underreporting of disease burden or "cleaning" of data before it was passed up the chain of command. Facilities, in turn, paid little attention to health reports based on data combined at the regional or national level, because they knew facility-level reporting was flawed. This led to a vicious cycle characterized by the "garbage in, garbage out" axiom, resulting in negligible use of data for decision-making by facilities.

advisors presented them with time series charts (line graphs showing changes in one or more indicators over time). During previous projects, quality advisors and/or QI coordinators from professional associations entered all data into Microsoft Excel-based spreadsheets, generated graphs, and presented them to physicians during coaching visits. The Excel-based system was cumbersome, prone to data entry errors, and placed a heavy data entry and processing burden on the professional associations. Further, it did not provide flexibility with regard to the type of data analysis, making it infeasible to collate data at the district or regional level.

Therefore, to overcome these limitations for this initiative, the project developed a database that would have the following features:

- Data entry could be managed at the facility level with a user-friendly interface that minimized the risk of data-entry error.
- Data could be automatically collated at district, regional, and national levels and by selected dates.
- All indicators would be graphed automatically to facilitate analysis.
- Indicator results could be presented by provider or facility code to maintain confidentiality and avoid the risk of facilities being penalized through traditional lines of reporting.
- Results could be presented by QI coordinators or coaches with relative ease (either using a projector or printing hard copies of graphs for distribution during QI meetings).
- The database could be used on computers without the latest versions of operating systems or productivity programs such as Microsoft Word, Excel, or Internet Explorer.

An information technology specialist and systems analyst working on the project developed the database based on a detailed list of specifications submitted by the project's regional quality advisor. This included a list of indicators and detailed definition of each indicator; the numerator and denominator of each indicator; and a description of how the results should be displayed, depending on whether the desired report contained data from a single audit or from multiple audits over time.

The original version was created for offline use out of concern that some PHC facilities might not have Internet access. However, as collation of data from multiple facilities and districts was essential, the information technology specialist included a feature that would allow QI coordinators at the regional or national level to import updated database files from facilities, allowing them to keep a "master" database.

To facilitate data entry, the user interface looked almost identical to the paper-based audit instruments developed for each index condition. Once data from the audit instruments was entered, reports could be generated by selecting the condition, audit cycle (baseline, first follow-up, second follow-up, etc., or any combination), and the level of data analysis (provider, facility, district, region, country). The database also generated lists of antibiotics and medications prescribed for symptom control, displayed by frequency of their use, from the most recent audit cycle included in the report.

Selection of Study Sites

The FGPNA and the HAKR selected study sites to pilot the audit instruments in consultation with the regional quality advisor. The following issues were considered in the selection of pilot facilities:

- Selected sites should represent both rural and urban facilities due to potential variations in practice patterns.
- Selected sites should represent the northern and southern regions of the country due to potential variations in practice patterns.
- If possible, selected facilities would be from districts in which the FGPNA and the HAKR already conduct monitoring (for cost containment and efficiency).
- Selected hospitals and PHC facilities should be from the same districts. In addition, the regional "parent" hospital, often located outside of the district, would be included to ensure consistency of practice patterns between regional and district facilities.

Three pilot districts were selected for the PHC-level interventions (one rural district from the north; one rural from the south; and three Family Medicine Centers in Bishkek, the capital). The hospitals in each of these rural districts were selected, along with their respective regional hospitals and four Bishkek facilities, for the hospital-level initiative. The MOH concurred with and approved the facilities proposed for the initiative.

Representatives from the HAKR and the FGPNA conducted baseline monitoring in all study facilities. This monitoring occurred prior to any educational intervention and provided verification that gaps in quality existed for each index condition, helped to better focus the content of the educational intervention, and allowed each facility to see the "starting point" from which they could later measure improvement. At the PHC level, at least five patient records on each index condition were reviewed from each Family Group Practice. (See "Audit and Feedback" section below for details.) There are 10–15 Family Group Practices in each district, and the aim was for no less than 30 records per condition per district. At the hospital level, the data collectors attempted to review 30 records per condition in each facility.

Developing Training Materials

In parallel to the development of the audit instruments and database, family medicine trainers from the KSMIRCE, the MOH chief pulmonologist, and two urologists with academic appointments began to develop training materials and clinical protocols on the index conditions with a focus on appropriate antibiotic use. Those involved in this QI initiative were convinced that an educational intervention would be necessary to effect change in the antibiotic prescribing practices of target physicians based on awareness of existing practice patterns (verified by the results of the baseline audit), results of the KAP survey, and the lack of approved, evidence-based guidance on the selected index conditions. The project aimed to develop a training program that was focused and effective, relying heavily on the practical application of knowledge to solve clinical vignettes. A 2-day training for PHC providers and a separate 2-day training for hospital providers on the selected conditions were developed with a mixture of didactic presentations and case-based, small group activities. The lectures focused on clinical features, diagnosis, and the evidence for or against the prescription of antibiotics. Clinical vignettes were developed to be discussed in small groups where participants would be asked to make a diagnosis and treatment plan and to defend their answers using information from the lectures. The regional quality advisor helped coordinate these efforts and gave ongoing technical support by providing evidence-based source materials, reviewing draft versions of all training materials (schedules, handouts, lectures, clinical vignettes, and written knowledge assessments), and providing feedback to the developers. All partners working on the educational materials had previously been trained in principles of evidence-based medicine under USAID health reform projects and were encouraged and supported by the regional quality advisor to ensure that all clinical recommendations included in training materials were supported by evidence. Once developed, the training materials were approved through the KSMIRCE, which enabled the project to offer CME credit to all training participants.

Carrying Out the Improvement Effort

The basic design of this improvement effort was to train family medicine providers from pilot districts on evidence-based standards of diagnosis and management of the index conditions, followed by regular use of audit and feedback, combined with facility-level discussion of results and formation of improvement plans, to promote adherence to the standards. Feedback was based on the previously described set of indicators that was common to all study sites at the PHC or hospital level, which allowed results to be collated at the district, regional, and national levels. In addition to training, the educational intervention included a set of job aids that served as reminders of key standards of care.

Training

Training was conducted in all target districts over a period of 3 months, with KSMIRCE family medicine trainers, the MOH chief pulmonologist, and the regional quality advisor serving as trainers. At the end of each 2-day training session, QI coordinators from the FGPNA or the HAKR presented results of baseline monitoring. Participants from the hospitals and PHC facilities were asked to critique their own prescribing patterns and, where indicators showed a need for improvement, to discuss how to implement recommendations presented during the training. Each district was able to see results from other districts, which seemed to be a particularly strong motivator for change when providers saw that their diagnostic or prescribing patterns were further out of compliance with standards than those of providers in other districts.

Job Aids

In preparing for this initiative on reducing unnecessary antibiotic prescriptions, the project studied similar initiatives carried out in other countries, including the United States, United Kingdom, and Italy. One practice common to most initiatives was the use of a job aid that allowed providers to give something to patients in place of an antibiotic prescription. The project developed a non-antibiotic prescription pad for common respiratory illnesses that allowed doctors to simply check one of the several common diagnoses, check one or more recommended non-pharmacologic approaches for symptom control, and make a recommendation for non-prescription pain medicine or fever reducers. Space was also provided to indicate when the patient should return should symptoms not improve. This "prescription" incorporated key messages to reduce the amount of time physicians spent counseling patients.

"How to take antibiotics correctly" was another job aid printed on a prescription-sized pad that informed patients how to properly take antibiotics (take as prescribed, finish course, don't share, don't save for future use). Both job aids were distributed to all study facilities along with posters containing key messages on antibiotic use for consumers targeting knowledge gaps that were identified through the previously mentioned KAP survey. The posters and leaflets were approved by the MOH, but facilities were not mandated to use them. The project found that the pilot facilities were universally eager to use these materials.

"When to prescribe antibiotics," a one-sided, letter-sized sheet with antibiotic prescribing indications for pharyngitis, otitis, and sinusitis was a job reminder borne out of the first seminar the trainers delivered to PHC providers on index conditions. When reviewing key points with the participants at the end of the second day, the trainers realized it would be helpful for busy providers to have the commonly used clinical scoring systems and criteria for starting antibiotics summarized on a page that could be kept on the desktop or at arm's reach. As these criteria were new to the providers, it did not seem realistic that they would remember them, and the trainers wanted to do everything possible to ease the translation of this new knowledge into practice.

Audit and Feedback

QI coordinators from the HAKR and the FGPNA conducted a follow-up audit visit approximately 2 months after training. During visits to each participating facility, the QI coordinator worked side by side with either the deputy director of an FMC (PHC level) or the chief physician (hospitals) to identify and review medical records. These particular positions were chosen to act as "QI curators" because they were, by decree, responsible for ensuring the quality of clinical services in their respective facilities.

As part of the country's routine health information system, physicians complete a "clinical information form" for all PHC visits and hospital admissions, assigning one or more diagnoses with corresponding International Classification of Diseases, tenth revision (ICD-10) codes, which are subsequently entered into a database by a data entry clerk. The QI coordinator and QI curator used this database to identify medical records for audit by the ICD-10 code of index conditions. Depending on the number of patients diagnosed during the audit period with the condition of interest, either all applicable charts were reviewed (if less than five for a PHC facility or 30 for a hospital) or an appropriate subset. The QI coordinator and QI curator would then complete audit instruments (checklists) for each condition. Data from the review of five medical records could be entered on a one-page checklist. At the hospital level, the QI coordinator helped the QI curator enter data into the database; at the PHC level, the audit instruments were collected and entered into the database by the FGPNA's QI coordinators after returning to their national office. External coaches informed facility QI curators of their visits in advance so that an internal QI meeting could be scheduled with all relevant clinicians immediately after the audit.

During these feedback meetings, the external QI coordinator and facility QI curator presented indicator results to facility providers using time series charts and tables automatically generated from the database during the same visit (hospital level) or a subsequent visit (PHC level). After displaying the result of a quality indicator, the coach would ask clinicians to recall the standard of care and evaluate their facility's performance based on the indicator result. Typically, the providers would be asked to comment on each indicator result, noting where improvements had been made and pointing out where there were persistent problems with adherence to clinical standards and offering an explanation as to why (barriers to improvement), followed by a discussion of potential steps to improve adherence to standards. QI coordinators also showed comparison data for neighboring districts and regions.

Data Collection and Analysis

Although installation of the offline database described above was quite simple using a self-extracting file, it had to be done in each facility by the QI coordinators from the professional associations. In addition, there were occasional problems with exporting audit report data to save in document or spreadsheet format, depending on the end user's software. A more significant problem was maintaining a "master" database at the national level and getting results to the facilities in a timely manner. Theoretically, database files updated at the facility level could be e-mailed to the QI coordinator to import into the master database. However, this rarely happened, either because end users had difficulty locating the database file or were not skilled enough at sending e-mail with file attachments. In reality, the QI coordinators gathered audit data in the field using paper forms and then returned to their central offices where they would update the master database file. They would then provide facilities with the updated database files during their next planned visit. As a result, the QI discussions that occurred during visits by the QI coordinators were always focused on results from the prior audit cycle rather than "real-time" data. This was not universally true at the hospital level, where the QI coordinators occasionally had time to help the facility QI curators enter data and generate reports that were discussed during the same visit.

These problems prompted the project to move to an online database in year two. The transition to using an online database was fairly seamless and resolved all of these issues, while creating a few unexpected challenges. Computer and Internet access was often limited to one office within each facility, but this did not pose a significant barrier to utilization. Most users were trained in person on how to find and log on to the database and were able to use it well afterward. Although not an issue in the Kyrgyz Republic, other countries where the project implemented identical initiatives were hesitant to have their QI data stored on a server outside the country (the project rented server space from a company based in the United States for the online database). In the Kyrgyz Republic, there remain challenges with transferring the database to an MOH-based server, as they have limited capacity to provide 24-hour server support and maintenance.

The online database was designed to assign various roles to users, each with a customizable set of privileges. For example, a national-level QI coordinator from a professional association or the Ministry of Health might have full privileges to enter, edit, and view data from any district, while a facility-level QI curator would be allowed to enter and edit data only for their facility, but could view data from any facility or district. Facility- and provider-level data were always displayed by code to maintain confidentiality.

Support for Improvement Coaching

QI coordinators from the FGPNA (three) and the HAKR (two) were trained in QI and gained QI coaching experience under previous USAID projects and other QI initiatives during the first 2 years of the project. The regional quality advisor provided support and supervision to each of them during the RUA initiative through frequent face-to-face meetings, phone conversations, and electronic communication. Because the regional quality advisor lived in the Kyrgyz Republic, it was possible for the QI coordinators to discuss issues with him on an "as-needed" basis, even during on-site monitoring visits.

In turn, QI coordinators from the FGPNA and the HAKR trained facility-based QI curators on the following topics:

- QI methodologies
- How to select charts for audit
- How to use the audit instruments (checklists)
- Use of the database (enrollment, data entry, generation of reports)
- Facilitation of feedback sessions

Training/coaching was tailored to the needs and skills of each QI curator, as some of the curators had participated in QI training and audits organized under previous USAID projects. During each monitoring visit made by the QI coordinators, several hours were spent supporting the QI curators in conducting audits, entering results into the database, and conducting feedback sessions so that they could eventually conduct these QI cycles without outside support.

One deficiency identified during monitoring and support visits conducted by the FGPNA and the HAKR was the absence of a clinical specialist to answer questions posed by the physician participants. While skilled in QI methodologies, the QI coordinators were not necessarily competent to answer clinical questions that might not have been addressed in the training materials. When possible, experienced clinicians involved in the development of the CPs and/or training materials traveled with the QI coordinators to participate in the feedback decisions (e.g., the chief pulmonologist or the quality project's regional QI advisor).

Financial Support

The FGPNA and the HAKR received USAID-funded grants through the project for their work on the RUA QI initiative. These grants covered travel expenses and some salary support for staff members, including the QI coordinators. The project made individual consulting agreements with trainers and leading specialists to develop training materials, conduct the seminars, and develop the clinical protocols. Per diems were provided, at rates set by the Kyrgyz Republic Government, for training participants who had to travel more than 25 kilometers, and transportation expenses were reimbursed by receipt. Financial support was not provided to the study facilities or their clinicians to participate in the initiative, to conduct chart audits, or to participate in feedback sessions.

Results

QI coordinators collected baseline data from 26 PHC facilities and 7 hospitals in three districts/municipalities between April and June of 2013. They collected follow-up data 3 and 6 months after the initial training, which was conducted in February 2014. At the PHC level, the FGPNA could collect only 3-month follow-up data.

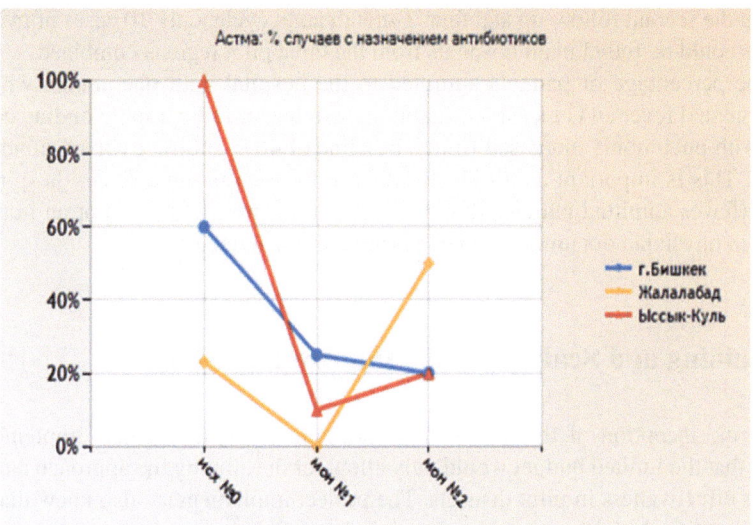

Fig. 8.5 Example of graph from database

Following training in pilot sites, fewer patients seeking care for common viral illnesses received unnecessary prescriptions for antibiotics. Compared with baseline prescription rates, the percent of patients receiving antibiotics for the common cold dropped from 31% to 0% (193 and 103 records, respectively); for acute bronchitis, from 89% to 1% (195 and 76 records, respectively); for acute diarrheal disease, from 46% to 0% (126 and 8 records, respectively); and for asthma, from 43% to 25% (41 and 24 records, respectively). Figure 8.5 presents an example of a graph generated from the database on the percentage of patients with asthma for whom antibiotics were prescribed.

Providing facility-specific feedback and comparing performance between districts were powerful motivators of change. For example, acute pyelonephritis (kidney infection), a condition that requires antibiotics, was often overdiagnosed and always treated in the hospital. Baseline monitoring showed that the diagnosis could be confirmed by clinical and laboratory criteria in only 68% of total patients hospitalized with acute pyelonephritis; this indicator ranged from 47% to 98% among pilot regions. During training, the trainers emphasized the typical clinical presentation of acute pyelonephritis and the diagnostic criteria. A QI coordinator from the HAKR then showed the results of baseline monitoring. When the lowest-performing region saw that another pilot region outperformed them (98% versus 47%), there were many gasps and a bit of nervous laughter among participants. During the next two audit cycles (approximately 2 and 5 months after training), this same low-performing region achieved a 100% result on this indicator (the countrywide result increased to 90%). At baseline, physicians were ordering urine cultures for only 17% of patients admitted with the diagnosis of pyelonephritis; during the second audit cycle conducted after training, cultures were ordered in 80% of cases. Not only did the quality of diagnosis improve, but the number of cases being admitted to the hospital dropped dramatically so that during the second follow-up and final 3-month audit cycle, only 10 cases of pyelone-phritis could be found in all hospitals from the three pilot regions combined.

The percentage of patients admitted to the hospital with pneumonia who had documented fever and at least one additional clinical or radiographic finding consis-tent with pneumonia increased from a baseline of 46% to 86% by the second audit cycle. This is important as it reflects either a decrease in unnecessary hospitaliza-tions (fewer admitted patients that do not meet diagnostic criteria) or an improve-ment in physician documentation of essential clinical data.

Sustaining and Scaling Up the Improvement Effort

From the inception of this initiative to promote RUA, the project implementers knew that the limited budget would only allow for developing the approach and test-ing its effectiveness in pilot districts. The project implementers also knew that suc-cessful national scale-up could only take place after the project ended and would have to rely on institutionalized processes that were supported by the State budget. The following activities were considered prerequisites for future scale-up:

- MOH approval of clinical protocols that contained evidence-based recommenda-tions on antibiotic use for the index conditions and dissemination of the proto-cols to end users
- Integration of the training on index conditions into the curriculum and training calendar of the KSMIRCE
- Institutionalization of the antibiotic prescription audits and feedback mechanisms

Clinical Protocols

Over the course of this initiative, clinical protocols were developed and approved by the MOH, covering all index conditions for which MOH-approved, evidence-based guidance did not previously exist as well as the following conditions or syndromes, which were identified as high priority by the initiative:

- Structured approach to the diagnosis and treatment of patients with cough
- Acute viral infections of the upper respiratory tract
- Acute bronchitis
- Acute otitis media
- Acute sinusitis
- Acute tonsillopharyngitis
- Acute cystitis in nonpregnant women
- Acute pyelonephritis
- Chronic pyelonephritis
- Prostatitis

The project implementers prioritized the development and approval of clinical protocols for several reasons. First, physicians in the Kyrgyz Republic are hesitant to follow recommendations made in training (even MOH-approved trainings) if they are not consistent with standards of care in existing CPs, even if those CPs are outdated. Second, physicians in the Kyrgyz Republic know that they can be held to standards of care contained in MOH-approved CPs through external quality assurance audits conducted by The Mandatory Health Insurance Fund. Noncompliance with standards discovered through such audits can result in monetary penalties. Finally, USAID had promoted evidence-based medicine in the Kyrgyz Republic for over 10 years; support and promotion of the development and use of evidence-based CPs were foundational to those efforts.

In fact, the successful development of these CPs was possible only because of groundbreaking work accomplished under previous USAID health reform projects. As a result of those efforts, an evidence-based medicine unit led by a well-trained local EBM consultant existed within the MOH, an approved CP development methodology was in place, EBM training programs were developed for CP developers, and a clear process existed to coordinate CP development from the first steps to final MOH approval. Near the beginning of the initiative to promote RUA, the project implementers proposed a list of topics to the EBM unit to prioritize for development, offered to provide close technical support to the guideline developers, and committed to finance the printing and distribution of finalized CPs. The MOH's EBM consultant subsequently coordinated the necessary steps to develop and approve the CPs.

The six respiratory conditions were grouped into one collection of protocols; the four urologic conditions into another. The project funded the printing of over 3000 copies of each collection, and they were distributed to all PHC physicians and relevant hospital physicians (urologist, pulmonologists, internists) throughout the country by the FGPNA and the HAKR.

Institutionalization and Scale-Up of Training

Although not originally planned, the KSMIRCE family medicine trainers involved in developing and conducting the seminars on RUA requested that the project implementers organize a "training of trainers" so that all family medicine trainers from the KSMIRCE's affiliate family medicine training centers in the regions could be trained, which would allow them to scale-up training throughout the country. The national family medicine trainers, with support from the regional quality advisor, decided to combine relevant portions of the hospital-level seminar into the PHC seminar, lengthening the final training to 3 days; trainings on pneumonia, chronic obstructive pulmonary disease, asthma, cystitis, pyelonephritis, and prostatitis were added. Thirty trainers were trained using this combined curriculum, which was approved by the KSMIRCE and added to the following year's national CME calendar.

Institutionalization of Audit and Feedback Mechanisms

Development of the online database was considered to be a key step toward sustainability of the audit and feedback process, as it reduced the time and skill level required to analyze results. This database was made available to all pilot health facilities and was coordinated by the FGPNA and the HAKR. The project's regional quality advisor held a number of meetings with the MOH, the FGPNA, and the HAKR to determine where the database should "sit" in the Kyrgyz Republic. It was decided that the Republican Health Information Center would be the most logical choice for long-term sustainability, as they already had information technology specialists trained to manage databases and had available space on hosting servers. The project coordinated training of local information technology specialists from the Republic Health Information Center on technical specifications needed to host the database on a local server, how to troubleshoot problems with the database, and how to create templates for index conditions should local partners wish to audit additional conditions in the future. In the process of training, however, the project's information technology specialist discovered that the Republic Health Information Center probably did not have the hardware or people with the necessary technical skills to host and maintain the database. It was, therefore, recommended that arrangements be made to continue to pay a small annual fee to maintain the database on the server of hosting company based in the United States.

Since the first quality improvement initiatives were implemented through the professional associations (FGPNA and HAKR) in 2005, there were many national-level discussions about the need to institutionalize QI approaches in all health facilities and how best to approach institutionalization. The selection of professional associations to coordinate QI efforts was a step in that direction. As monitoring conducted by the MOH had traditionally been punitive in nature, mechanisms existed at the facility level to ensure audit results were "satisfactory" (i.e., not always reflecting actual practice). It was important, then, to have QI promoted by organizations that were trusted by health facilities and disconnected, as it were, from disciplinary measures so that facilities felt safe to identify and address gaps in quality of care. Having been founded to advocate for and represent their respective members, the FGPNA and the HAKR were well connected with and respected by health facilities. As NGOs, the FGPNA and the HAKR were also able to receive grants from international organizations, such as USAID, that were interested in promoting QI.

The FGPNA and the HAKR were originally trained in QI principles by personnel from the USAID-funded health reform project ZdravPlus II (2005–2009). As they became more familiar with the principles and practice of QI, the professional associations took on increasingly greater responsibility with training, conducting QI audits, and leading feedback sessions.

The intent of the USAID projects had always been to institutionalize QI efforts at both the PHC and hospital levels. The professional associations were advised to support facilities to conduct the key steps in the QI cycle themselves rather than having the professional associations conduct audits, which carried the risk of turning QI activities into "external monitoring and feedback." In fact, the project never reached the goal of having PHC facilities independently conduct QI cycles. Through many discussions with FGPNA and project quality advisors, the project identified a number of factors that may have acted as barriers to institutionalization of QI at the PHC level:

1. The FGPNA did not have the personnel and the USAID project did not have funding to conduct QI audit cycle visits to each PHC facility more often than once a quarter. The number and geographic spread of PHC facilities in each district contributed to this challenge, as most districts were served by 15–50 PHC facilities, and the FGPNA might be able to visit only two or three facilities in 1 day. If in-person visits to each facility were not required, medical records could be sent to the district-level family medicine center for review, but this created another set of challenges, as FMC personnel rarely made visits to daughter facilities, and personnel from the daughter facilities typically traveled to the district center only monthly. The FGPNA did its best to coordinate audit cycle visits at the time when routine district-level health meetings were conducted so that results of monitoring could be discussed without personnel having to make additional trips to/from their facilities.
2. The time between visits (typically 3 months) seemed too long for participants to "internalize" steps in the audit cycle. In other words, the QI approach did not become habitual, and FGPNA personnel often felt like they were starting from square one during follow-up visits. This primarily applied to the mechanics of auditing medical records and calculating indicator results. There was not such a problem with facilities forgetting the goals of the QI efforts, their results, or the clinical standards on which the indicators were based.
3. Many of the rural PHC facilities had only one or two physicians, making it impractical for them to conduct their own audits. Successful monitoring of charts from these facilities required a new organizational process of getting the appropriate charts to the district FMC and back. On the surface, this may sound simple enough, but success depended on a number of conditions:

   (a) Medical records of patients with particular (target) conditions are not easily identifiable. In fact, in the Kyrgyz Republic there is no electronic or paper record of patient visits below the district FMC level. A paper "clinical information form" is completed for each patient visit (or visits, if more than one visit is required to manage the same complaint or condition), which is then sent to the district level and entered in a database, but this often occurs weeks after the visit, and only the district FMC has access to the information. So, in order to select medical records for audit, either an additional journal must be kept at each facility to record the names of patients seen with a target condition or a list of patients seen with the target condition must be generated from the database at the district FMC level and daughter facilities notified by phone of which charts to select for review.
   (b) Charts selected for audit are physically located in the target facility. Quite often, patients take their medical record from the PHC facility, either because

it is needed during a visit to a consulting physician or simply because they are afraid their record will be lost by the PHC facility. The FGPNA raised this issue at the level of the MOH, and an order was issued restricting facilities from releasing the original copies of medical records to patients. However, given the absence of electronic health records and photocopying capabilities in facilities, the order was never fully implemented.

(c) Charts selected for audit by one of the processes listed above should be reliable, meaning they are not "enriched" by the treating physician prior to being delivered to the district facility for review.

(d) Personnel from the target facility actually travel to the district facility for the monthly meeting. Costs of such travel were typically not reimbursed by the district FMC, leaving nurses and physicians from daughter facilities to pay for the travel themselves.

4. Health-care workers were not comfortable with nurses reviewing physicians' notes in medical records, effectively eliminating this as a monitoring option in smaller PHC facilities. This resistance was likely due to the limited scope of clinical responsibilities traditionally designated to nurses and a historical approach to clinical audits that was rather subjective and dependent on the clinical expertise of the reviewer (rather than using objective checklists with clearly defined quality indicators).

5. The deputy directors of FMCs and hospitals were responsible for quality of care but often overburdened with administrative and clinical responsibilities, leaving them little time or mental space for conducting quality audits and quality meetings between visits of the FGPNA QI coordinators.

At the hospital level, significant effort was made during the initiative to develop the capacity of personnel to conduct the quality audits without external support. During all follow-up visits after training, the HAKR representative worked side by side with the hospital's deputy director (responsible for quality) to select and review charts and complete the audit instruments. Beginning with the second follow-up visit, deputy directors entered audit data into the database.

An order was issued by the MOH to task all pilot hospitals to continue with at least quarterly monitoring of antibiotic prescription patterns and to enter results into the database after the closing of the project. In fact, since the close of the project, further audits have been completed (without external funding) and entered into the online database.

The HAKR attempted to activate hospital quality committees that existed by MOH decree, hoping that audit tasks could be shared among committee members rather than falling to one person (the deputy director); however, the project has yet to see that these efforts will lead to sustainable institutionalization of this approach. For the most part, the quality committees in hospitals exist on paper only, and most of the members do not have a vision of what their role should/could be. In 2015, the MOH revised the national QI strategy and scope of work of quality committees, incorporating many of the principles of QI that had been introduced by USAID and other international development partners over the past 10 years, which is seen as a positive development for institutionalization of QI.

Reflection

Specific to the RUA QI Initiative

Many factors that contributed to the success of this QI initiative are important to keep in mind if one is hoping to apply a similar approach in other contexts. First, the project's approach must be understood as a "next step" in a series of QI initiatives that were undertaken over a period of more than 10 years. Although the topic was new, the key players had worked together on a number of previous QI initiatives, and there was political support from the MOH for facility-level QI work as a result of prior successes. The FGPNA had over 7 years of experience coordinating QI projects when this work on RUA began, and the HAKR had just completed a 2-year QI initiative on cardiovascular disease. Also, the same international and local partners had worked together closely on previous QI initiatives, so all participants benefited from mutual trust, respect, and a knowledge of one another's strengths and limitations. The project's regional quality advisor, who coordinated the initiative, had lived in the Kyrgyz Republic for 10 years, spoke the local language, and was very familiar with the local health system and medical practices.

> *I liked the methodology of continuous quality improvement: clear; detailed; understandable for training; transparent in regards to monitoring; and a universal approach that can be used to solve many different types of quality problems. Secondly, quality improvement involves all levels of hospital services, making this experience unique.*
>
> –Staff member, HAKR

Some features of this QI initiative evolved from lessons learned through prior initiatives. The most significant was the development of the online database that simplified data entry, automatically generated user-friendly and customizable reports of indicators, and allowed coordinators to collate data at any level. The database was regarded positively among all users, from rural facilities to the national-level coordinators and MOH. Importantly, it continues to be used in the same pilot hospitals as of 1 year after the close of the project.

> *The main challenge we faced was physicians' resistance to implement new recommendations. New clinical protocols were published at the end of the project, which became the basis for subsequent training of hospital providers.*
>
> –Official, Issyk-Kul Oblast Merged Hospital

The project also learned lessons to guide future QI initiatives. In the past, the FGPNA selected QI topics taking into consideration whether evidence-based guidance was already available in the form of MOH-approved clinical protocols and/or practice guidelines. In most cases, target providers had already been trained on the new guidelines through CME programs led by KSMIRCE trainers. Because the goal of this particular initiative was to promote RUA, the project needed to select conditions where antibiotics were being overprescribed rather than conditions for which MOH-approved CPs already existed. Developing a new CP and getting it approved in the Kyrgyz Republic is a lengthy process, typically taking 12–18 months. Because of the time limitations, the project did not have the liberty to wait for approved CPs to be published before starting to train physicians in the study sites. This resulted in physicians being trained in new approaches without an official protocol with which they could justify or defend their practice. The project handled this by working through the postgraduate institute (KSMIRCE) to develop the training curriculum, which was then approved by the MOH, providing legitimacy to the content. Trainers informed participants that content of the training would be reflected in new clinical protocols that were currently in the development stage.

Introducing and Institutionalizing QI Methodologies

Workplace culture is largely determined by the larger cultural context in which it exists and can be counter to some of the foundational principles of QI. QI principles have their roots in a Western culture that highly values democracy, teamwork, and problem-solving. Individuals contributing their ideas for the betterment of an organization and achievement of its goals are valued and often rewarded. Different values exist within the cultural context of Central Asia: respect for strong, authoritarian leaders who give clear direction on how things are to be done (the "why" is often secondary); respect for workers who strictly adhere to orders; and disdain for workers who are critical of existing processes (this is typically equated with being critical of leaders, which is not acceptable). Often, those who show too much initiative in changing the status quo in the workplace are looked upon with suspicion or contempt. It is not difficult to imagine the challenge of introducing standard QI approaches in such a context. Almost each step in the QI process demands a willingness on the part of participants to be counterculture:

- *Problem identification.* This requires being willing to admit that there are problems with resources, organization, and/or content of care. Health-care workers did not always feel safe or comfortable volunteering their thoughts about quality gaps and, in some countries of the Central Asian Republics, seemingly could not see such gaps. QI approaches to selecting problems are, in the Western context, very democratic, often involving brainstorming and voting. Workers in the Central Asian Republics were not accustomed to participating in such a process and had no reason to think their opinions would be valued by leadership. Likewise, health managers were not always ready to accept a decision made by a group.

- *Problem analysis.* As with problem identification, there was no cultural context for team-based activities such as brainstorming or an open discussion with all members of a process about quality gaps. With rare exception, the project found that brainstorming sessions were rarely productive if a health facility director participated, as health-care workers were simply too reluctant to share their true opinions openly.

- *Planning for improvement.* Within a cultural context that valued adherence to top-down standards and subtly or overtly discouraged individual initiative, the project found that health-care workers had a very difficult time thinking "outside the box." Such thinking is not easily taught. Rather, it is, at least partly, a learned ability that grows only when rewarded within a cultural context that values creativity and initiative.

- *Implementation of improvement plans.* The project encountered little resistance to implementing audits, likely because some form of chart auditing had been institutionalized for many years, although its effectiveness in improving quality might be questioned. Because of the challenge of soliciting improvement plans that involved anything more than "improving adherence to the standard of care" or purchasing a needed resource, there was often very little to implement in regard to changing the organization of services.

Giving visual feedback in the form of time series charts showing change in performance over time was a significant motivator of change, particularly when providers could see their performance in comparison to the performance of other facilities. Improving the approach to audits included defining standards of care and clearly defining a feasible number of reliable and valid quality indicators that could be tracked over time. The project found that improving the approach to audits and facilitating feedback and discussion of audit results had a measurable impact on quality, even if all steps of QI had not been institutionalized.

Acknowledgments The project described in this case study was the USAID-funded Quality Health Care Project implemented by Abt Associates. The following individuals contributed to the activities described in this case:
- Suyumjan Mukeeva, Director, Family Group Practice and Nurses Association
- Nurgul Usenbaeva, Quality Improvement Specialist, Family Group Practice and Nurses Association
- Kubanychbek Dzhemuratov, Director, Hospital Association of the Kyrgyz Republic
- Gulmira Saadakbaeva, Quality Improvement Specialist, Hospital Association of the Kyrgyz Republic

- Bermet Baryktabasova, EBM consultant, Ministry of Health of the Kyrgyz Republic
- Saltanat Moldoisaeva, Chief Specialist on Pharmaceutical Policy, Quality Unit of the Ministry of Health of the Kyrgyz Republic
- Talantbek Sooronbaev, Professor and Chief Pulmonologist, Ministry of Health of the Kyrgyz Republic

Chapter 9
Applying a Standards-Based Approach to Reduce Maternal Mortality and Improve Maternal and Neonatal Services in Mozambique

Edgar Necochea, Maria da Luz Vaz, Ernestina David, and Jim Ricca

Abstract This case demonstrates how a Quality Improvement (QI) initiative systematically improved the delivery of maternal and newborn health services at a large number of health-care facilities in Mozambique, with limited external assistance (e.g., external supervision or technical assistance after the initial 6 months), despite facing the challenges common to many low-income settings. In particular, this case examines the organization of a QI effort, including the formation of QI teams, enhancement of data collection to document QI activities, and national scale-up of a QI intervention. The QI intervention applied relied on provider training provider training on evidence-based standards, assessment of compliance with the performance standards, strengthening of the health management information system to enable tracking of selected quality-of-care indicators, and formation of facility-level QI teams to lead the implementation of the standards through performance assessments and action plans to address performance gaps, followed by recognition ceremonies if the facility achieved a high level of compliance with the standards based on an external assessment.

Keywords Antenatal Care · Emergency Obstetric Care · Labor and Delivery · Maternal and Neonatal Care · Maternal and Neonatal Mortality · Mozambique · Postnatal Care · Standards-Based Management and Recognition

E. Necochea (✉)
Jhpiego, Baltimore, MD, USA
e-mail: Edgar.Necochea@jhpiego.org

M. da Luz Vaz · E. David
Jhpiego, Maputo, Mozambique

J. Ricca
Jhpiego/Maternal and Child Survival Project, Baltimore, MD, USA

© University Research Co., LLC 2020
L. R. Marquez (ed.), *Improving Health Care in Low- and Middle-Income Countries*, https://doi.org/10.1007/978-3-030-43112-9_9

131

Background and Setting

Although more than 50% of deliveries in Mozambique occur at health facilities, high maternal mortality rates – an estimated 506 deaths per 100,000 live births in 2014 – have persisted as a public health issue. To address concerns about the quality of public health services, the Mozambique Ministry of Health (MOH), in partnership with a USAID-funded project, launched in 2009 a maternal mortality reduction initiative intended to reduce high mortality rates and improve facility-based maternal and neonatal care. Known as the Model Maternities Initiative (MMI), the initiative began with 34 maternities. The main criteria for the selection of the initial maternities, made jointly by the MOH and the supporting partner, were high volume of deliveries and being the practice sites for midwifery students. After 5 years, by 2014, the initiative had expanded to 120 maternities, about half of all maternities in the country. Approximately one-third of all the institutional deliveries take place in these facilities.

The MMI draws on the Standards-Based Management and Recognition® (SBM-R®) approach to quality improvement (QI), which uses practical and educational assessment tools to embed the evidence-based service delivery standards (Necochea and Bossemeyer 2005). The tools drive a systematic process to spearhead, roll out, and scale up a QI process at the facility and national levels.

Since 2004, the approach has been applied in Mozambique in areas such as infection prevention and inpatient care, to promote adoption of evidence-based care. Because of its national scope, the infection prevention initiative was previously implemented in all the participating maternities, while the inpatient care one was conducted in the medical and surgical wards in some of the hospitals where the maternities are located. The provincial- and district-level MOH staff had supported both experiences through supervision and resource allocation and were familiar with the SBM-R®. The MOH officials' and facility health-care providers' familiarity with SBM-R® helped to pave the way for the introduction of the maternal mortality reduction effort.

At the start of the MMI, the major obstacles to the quality of maternal and newborn care in Mozambique included a severe shortage of the doctors and nurses who provide support during the antenatal, labor and delivery, and postnatal care at the health facilities, as well as the variable competence of these providers. Other constraints on the quality of care included infrastructure inadequacies and shortcomings (e.g., limited space for labor and delivery rooms), lack of material resources and equipment, and weak preservice training and supervision systems (MOH 2008, 2016). These challenges had to be considered by the MOH and supporting partner when the MMI intervention was designed and implemented so that it could eventually be scaled up nationwide. For instance, the method and tools were simplified as much as possible to make them less time consuming to apply by the staff already overloaded with patient care; the content was organized to serve as a job aid; and emphasis was placed on resource mobilization skills.

Designing and Organizing the Improvement Effort

Approach and Strategy

Following the SBM-R® process, the MMI took a four-step approach, as depicted in Fig. 9.1:

1. Development of performance standards
2. Implementation of the standards through facility assessments and improvement actions
3. Measurement of progress through review of the repeated assessments and tracking of selected indicators
4. Recognition of achievements

The design of the improvement effort is focused on the development of the performance standards, the training of the health-care providers in the standards, the implementation of assessments and correction of gaps, and strengthening the health management information system to support measuring progress.

Development of the Performance Standards

In one of the initiative's first steps, a group of technical experts comprised of leaders from the MOH and the USAID-funded project convened to develop assessment tools intended to operationalize performance standards. The group reviewed the evidence for the good practices in the four areas of the maternal and newborn care: antenatal care, normal labor and delivery, emergency obstetric care, and postnatal care. The technical experts consulted the recommendations and materials issued by the World Health Organization (WHO) and the guides on the Integrated Management of Pregnancy and Childbirth (IMPAC), as well as the national guidelines and

Fig. 9.1 The MMI method model

protocols. They also considered other factors that affect the implementation of these kinds of evidence-based practices, including the available resources; facility management; community information, education, and involvement; and the instruction of the student health-care workers who do practical rotations at the maternities. For instance, standards on the resources needed for the provision of clinical care, the basic management support functions, and the teaching process and involvement of midwifery students were developed specifically to strengthen these areas. All the standards were consistent with the Mozambique national guidelines for maternal and neonatal care. Table 9.1 lists some examples of the key evidence-based practices identified and considered by the group.

The technical group used this information to develop the performance standards and organized them into nine areas, listed in Table 9.2. Reflecting a holistic view of quality, the final standards included high-impact, effective, evidence-based practices, as well as guidelines, to ensure safety for the patients and providers, respectful and humanized care, and facility readiness. The group developed a list of specific measurable tasks – verification criteria –intended to be used in a checklist format. As illustrated by the example in Fig. 9.2, the group developed a form to assess whether the performance standards in each area were being met. To successfully achieve a performance standard, a health facility had to meet *all* of the verification criteria for that standard. Across the nine areas, 81 standards and a total of 511 verification criteria were defined.

Table 9.1 Evidence-based practices promoted by the MMI

Service area	Evidence-based practices
Antenatal care	• Minimum of four antenatal care visits • Services should include provision of iron folate supplements, prevention of mother-to-child transmission of HIV, and preparedness and planning for obstetric complications
Normal labor and delivery	• Consistent use of partograph • Active management of the third stage of labor (AMTSL) • Skin-to-skin contact with mother immediately after delivery • Breastfeeding within 1 hour of delivery • Immediate postpartum family planning
Emergency obstetric care	• Provision of the basic emergency obstetric and neonatal care[a] • Timely referral for comprehensive emergency obstetric and neonatal care[b]
Postnatal care	• Three postnatal care visits for the mother and newborn at 2–3 days, 7 days, and 21–28 days postpartum • Promotion of long-acting family planning methods

[a]Basic emergency obstetric and neonatal care includes parenteral treatment of infection with antibiotics, parenteral treatment of severe preeclampsia or eclampsia (e.g., magnesium sulfate), treatment of postpartum hemorrhage (e.g., uterotonics), manual vacuum aspiration of the retained products of conception, assisted vaginal delivery (e.g., vacuum-assisted delivery), manual removal of placenta, and newborn resuscitation
[b]In addition to the elements included in the basic emergency obstetric and neonatal care, comprehensive emergency obstetric and neonatal care includes surgical capability, such as, anesthesia (e.g., cesarean section) and blood transfusion

Table 9.2 The MMI performance standards, by area

	Area	Number of standards	Number of verification criteria
1	Management of maternal and neonatal services	8	27
2	Information, monitoring, and evaluation	5	20
3	Resources: human, infrastructure, and commodities	4	24
4	Working conditions and safety	8	18
5	Health education and community involvement	4	35
6	Antenatal and postnatal care	14	96
7	Care during normal labor, delivery, and the immediate postpartum period	24	188
8	Management of obstetric and newborn complications	10	86
9	Teaching process	4	17
	Total	81	511

Performance Standards	Score	Verification Criteria	Yes	No	N/A	Comments
1. The facility manager ensures the minimum supportive environment for ANC service.		Ensures in the examination area the existence of: a door that can be closed and good illumination and ventilation (fan/heating)	☐	☐	☐	
		Ensures the existence of clients' and staff washroom in or near the ANC clinic with available water, soap and paper towels and with a functioning toilet	☐	☐	☐	
		Ensures the existence of working washbasin with faucet or bucket with lid in the examination room	☐	☐	☐	
		Ensures that the essential furniture and minimum required equipment are available	☐	☐	☐	
		Ensures that the minimum required infection prevention materials are available	☐	☐	☐	
2. The provider prepares and checks the ANC clinic/ examination areas before starting daily consultations.		Ensures that the floors, walls, furniture, equipment, surfaces of the waiting area, consultation rooms and clients' washroom are clean	☐	☐	☐	
		Ensures that the essential tests, drugs and vaccines are available	☐	☐	☐	
3. The person who receives the pregnant woman conducts a rapid initial evaluation at the first contact.		Ensures that the minimum required disposable materials, forms and registers are available	☐	☐	☐	
		Asks about or observes if the woman has or has had: vaginal bleeding, breathing problem, fever, severe headache/blurred vision, severe abdominal pain and/or convulsions/loss of consciousness	☐	☐	☐	
		Assures immediate attention by a skilled provider in the event of any of the above signs	☐	☐	☐	

Fig. 9.2 Excerpt from the assessment tool for the antenatal care performance standards

The project and MOH technical teams, which included national and provincial officials and frontline providers, discussed the proposed standards in two national-level workshops, which also included representatives from the Mozambican Association of Obstetricians and Gynaecologists. The tools were then pretested in a few settings, and additional input was collected from frontline providers and managers. The Maternal and Child Health Directorate at the MOH reviewed and approved the final MMI assessment tool with the 81 performance standards.

The Provider Training

The USAID-funded project recognized that the evidence-based standards and rationale for the newly developed standards had to be disseminated and discussed with the providers in order to facilitate their adoption at the facility level. Updating providers' technical knowledge and skills was essential because many were unfamiliar with the recommended clinical practices, and their level of training and technical skills varied.

Competency-based training served as a critical component of the initiative. The project and MOH technical staff conducted a series of 10-day competency-based training workshops for two to four providers from each participating facility. These workshops were implemented at the provincial level at the beginning of the year every time a new group of maternities was incorporated into the initiative. Facility managers selected these providers, who were usually maternal and child nurses (the equivalent of midwives). The course covered basic maternal and neonatal care practices with an emphasis on deliveries and management of complications.

During the last day of each workshop, trainers introduced the initiative assessment tool and explained the QI process. They instructed the providers on the following:

- How to use the tool to conduct a facility assessment
- How to analyze the results to identify gaps in performance (standards/criteria not met)
- How to identify and design corrective measures addressing issues of competency, lack of resources, and lack of motivation
- How to implement an action plan with corrective measures including all members of the team
- How to measure progress through periodic internal assessments and tracking of selected indicators
- How to implement recognition activities for partial and comprehensive achievements

Over 5 years, the project trained close to 1560 health professionals in maternal and neonatal care. Provincial health offices often decided to also implement the clinical training in facilities not participating in the initiative. In these facilities, representing around 15% of all the staff trained, the workshop excluded the QI portion. Coaches also participated in the trainings for their provinces and, in addition, held quarterly meetings to review the implementation process and discuss approaches to overcome the challenges and foster change.

Strengthening the Health Management Information System

The USAID-funded project worked with the MOH and partners (WHO, UNICEF) to enhance and strengthen the Mozambique's Health Management Information System (HMIS), so that it would be possible to track the selected quality-of-care indicators relevant to the MMI. In 2011, the MOH revised the reproductive, maternal, newborn, and child health component of the HMIS to collect the additional data on quality of care, respectful care, and direct and indirect obstetric complications and maternal deaths. New maternity registers were created to collect information on the key clinical practices promoted by the MMI, including the active management of the third stage of labor, treatment of eclampsia with magnesium sulfate, use of partograph, family companions present at delivery, immediate skin-to-skin contact with the mother after delivery, and breastfeeding within the first hour after birth. During the initial 10-day workshops, the MMI facility staff were trained on the modified registries and asked to track the newly recorded quality indicators (as well as, institutional maternal deaths) and to provide routine reports to the Maternal and Child Health Directorate at the MOH. The MOH and project provincial supervisors checked the data for quality and consistency.

Carrying Out the Improvement Effort

The Formation of the QI Teams

The QI process took place at the facility level with the participation of health-care providers, as well as, the facility managers. In Mozambique, the providers who attended the MMI training workshops became the core members of the facility QI team, along with the other providers and key managers. The number of members of each team varied, but in general, they included 5–10 facility staff. These teams, which were responsible for overseeing the entire QI process at their facilities through periodic monthly meetings, operated with limited external assistance. In each of the Mozambique's 10 provinces, one coach – a midwife hired by the USAID-funded project – supervised and supported the facility QI teams, making quarterly visits to the facilities and involving the MOH provincial technical staff as much as possible. Distant support was also provided through telephone.

Each of the provincial coaches oversaw approximately 10–12 maternities. The most important duty of a provincial coach was to help the facility QI team with the improvement process, including participating in the assessments when possible, reviewing progress with the teams, providing guidance on the gap analysis and improvement tasks, reinforcing the training on the evidence-based practices, facilitating support from the facility managers, conducting quality assurance of the data collected on the indicators, and promoting learning exchanges through the involvement of the facility team members in the external assessments of the other facilities. The provincial coaches, in turn, received support from the five MMI regional coaches, also midwives. Often, but not always, the provincial coaches provided support for the baseline service assessment and regularly reported on the activities in their provinces, including the progress on assessments and evolution of the selected indicators. One national coordinator of the initiative, a medical doctor specialist in obstetrics and gynecology, provided support to the regional coaches working in coordination with the MOH Maternal and Child Health Directorate.

Implementing the Standards Through Facility Assessments, Action Plans, and Change Management

Figure 9.3 depicts the facility-level improvement process. The facility QI teams began the process by conducting a baseline assessment on the maternal and newborn health services using the MMI assessment tool (an excerpt of which is provided for antenatal care performance standards in Table 9.2). The assessment required the teams to record direct observations concerning the infrastructure and processes of care, review the records, and interview the staff in order to determine whether the facility met each of the verification criteria listed in the MMI

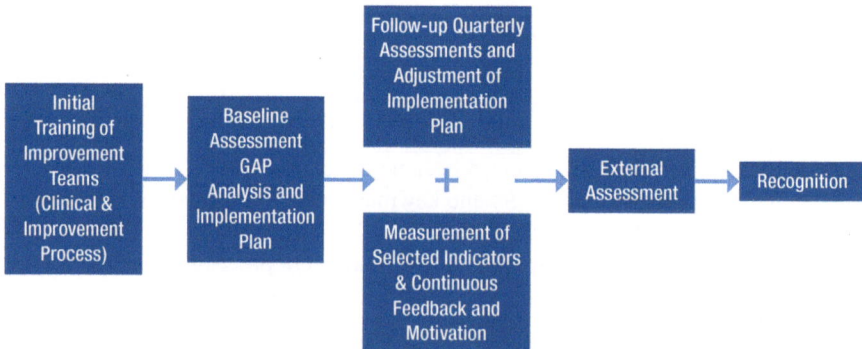

Fig. 9.3 The MMI improvement process at the facility level

assessment tool. Typically, each assessment took 2 days to complete and included observations of at least three deliveries. After collating and analyzing the results, the team identified the unmet standards as the performance gaps and developed an action plan to correct those gaps. Whenever the assessments coincided with a visit by the provincial coach, they then helped with the analysis of the results, offering guidance on feasible solutions, including those already adopted in the other maternities.

Because some performance gaps in facilities often can be addressed fairly quickly and easily, the initiative focused on implementing rapid interventions rather than on in-depth analysis of complex problems. The interventions were aimed at correcting simple and clear shortcomings in quality, for example, lack of cleanliness, failure to practice basic infection prevention, disorganized work space, and minor infrastructure disrepair. Teams were instructed to focus initially on the rapid interventions rather than on the analysis of the complex problems. A key theory underlying the approach is that promoting rapid and visible changes at the maternities quickly fosters a sense of empowerment and increases self-efficacy, preparing the facility QI teams to gradually undertake more complex tasks.

Improvements in the facilities attracted the attention and support of the managers and generated enthusiasm among the other providers, who then joined the improvement efforts. At one facility, for example, the team observed a lack of privacy in the maternity for clients accompanied by companions. The team members mobilized support for the placement of curtains between maternity beds. While pursuing the curtains (the team obtained support from the local sugar-cane plantation and refinery to finance the purchase of the curtains) for increased privacy, providers discussed the need to address other aspects of clients' rights, such as, respectful care and the right to adopt positions at birth according to cultural preferences. After the curtains were put in place, this visible improvement prompted the team to make other improvements in cleanliness and the organization of the maternity ward. The facility manager was happy with the improvements and called the maternity the "best service" in the health facility, reinforcing the positive momentum for change. To address more complex issues, the teams met and more carefully analyzed causes and potential solutions.

The facility teams repeated the assessments every 3–6 months in order to measure progress and identify additional performance gaps that needed to be addressed. Because MOH policies encouraged community involvement, several facilities shared the results of the performance assessments with the facility comanagement committees. These comanagement committees, promoted by the MOH, included traditional leaders and active community members. Their function was to provide the community perspective on health care, participate in improvement activities, and mobilize community support. The facility QI teams acted quickly to address the gaps that could be corrected through local action or with the local resources (for instance, reorganization of spaces, hygiene and cleanliness, minor repairs, and better coordination with management) and then move on to the more difficult challenges, such as, obtaining additional supplies, remodeling infrastructure, expediting the flow of care, and making behavioral changes needed to adopt recommended practices (e.g., encouraging providers to use partographs to identify danger signs during labor and encouraging women to adopt early breastfeeding). Administrators often expedited the process by offering additional support, for example, by providing cleaning and medical supplies or by initiating repairs.

When proposed solutions were outside of the facility's purview, teams could request support from the MOH provincial directorate or from the USAID-funded project to address a performance gap. For example, the project provided support for minor renovations at some facilities, such as, painting, fixing water pipes, and installing sinks.

Supported by the project, some teams organized visits to other facilities to exchange experiences, which helped motivate staff participating in the MMI. The highest-performing members of the facility QI teams were selected to join the external assessment teams that visited and rated other maternities; providers perceived this recognition as an incentive.

Facility managers, in general, favorably reviewed the QI process. They commented that it helped improved the organization of services and encouraged adoption of the best practices for deliveries and obstetric and neonatal complications. They noted that the providers spoke "the same language" after they were updated and adopted the standard practices.

The providers reported that, although they felt that they were being "observed and watched", they perceived that the actions emanated from a supportive and non-judgmental viewpoint. The standardized tools helped to improve supervision and substantiated requests for additional support from the provincial and national MOH levels. They also noted that patients' anxiety decreased as a result of the adoption of respectful care practices, such as, allowing clients to have companions present. The nursing and other medical students also are benefited because the maternities serve as clinical practice sites, and improvements in the facility practices are carried over to improve teaching.

Improvement Efforts at Xai-Xai Provincial Hospital, Mozambique

Xai Xai Provincial Hospital had been implementing the SBM-R® approach in the area of infection prevention and control for nearly 5 years, achieving successive recognition for their high level of compliance with the standards. When the MMI was launched by the MOH in 2009 using the same approach, a baseline performance assessment using the MMI standard tool was conducted in the hospital. The hospital initially had poor compliance with the standards (24.1% on baseline assessment); however, the hospital was determined to improve the maternity and immediately began to implement interventions to introduce and strengthen the high-impact practices and humanized care stipulated in the standards. Compliance

Table 9.3 Selected indicators, performance assessments, and maternal mortality, Xai-Xai Provincial Hospital, Mozambique (2009–2014)

	2009	2010	2011	2012	2013	2014	2015
Maternal deaths, all causes		15	12	10	8	12	10
Companion during birth		These indicators were not reported in the MOH HMIS as of 2010	2%	2%	6%	72%	76%
Active management of the third stage of labor			81%	85%	81%	80%	71%
Delivery in vertical or semi vertical position			<1%	<1%	1%	3%	1.4%
Mother–newborn skin-to-skin contact			86%	88%	86%	85%	80%
Immediate initiation of breastfeeding (within the first hour)			87%	89%	87%	85%	81%
Compliance with the MMI performance standards during assessment[a]	24.1%	81.7%	51.7%	72.9%	83.9%	98.4%	N/A

[a]Scores taken from performance assessment conducted in the last quarter of the year

with standards improved markedly in the subsequent performance assessments (Table 9.3).

In 2011, the MOH, with the support of the USAID-funded project, introduced modifications to the HMIS, including inclusion of the key quality-of-care indicators, which allowed for tracking of quality-related maternal and neonatal care practices. Tracking of selected indicators in the modified HMIS showed that some practices at Xai-Xai, such as, AMTSL, skin-to-skin newborn care, and early initiation of breastfeeding, had already reached high levels of compliance by 2011: these practices were not implemented before 2010.

Other practices, such as, presence of a companion during birth, required more consistent leadership, teamwork, and community involvement. The hospital considered that birth companions were a good strategy to prevent or limit abuse and promote a better client–family-provider interaction. The team concluded that critical constraints were the physical area of the maternity (too small to accommodate companions) and the attitude of clients and providers. After discussing several options, the team decided to remodel the physical space of the maternity (and got external support for this) and promoted community-provider meetings and discussions on the process of care for deliveries. After the maternity was renovated and expanded in the early part of 2014 to allow companions to be present during labor and delivery, relatives were more open to participate as companions and the providers incorporated relatives as helpers for the care of mothers. Using a similar approach, Xai-Xai also undertook other key improvements related to clinical practices.

The Role of Mid-level Managers in the Health System

The provincial MOH managers supported the initiative and its expansion. They promoted and coordinated the participation of their technical staff in supervision and assessments and were involved in training activities. The provincial managers participated in and approved the selection of the project's provincial coaches or supervisors and provided them with office space in the provincial health director-ate offices. Often, the provincial managers, in an effort to maximize the interven-tion's benefits, involved maternities that were not part of the MMI in the training activities. The snapshot from a participating hospital director (see Box 9.1) illus-trates the process from a facility perspective and highlights the relevance of respectful care.

Box 9.1 A Doctor Tells Her Story

I am Mozambican, 59 years old, and mother of three women and a girl aged 42, 39, 20, and 5 years. My country is young; it has been independent for 41 years. Particularly at the beginning, health services were scarce and inad-equate for a population with many health needs. I was also young when I got pregnant, I was 16 years old. Even when I was a child or adolescent with an unwanted pregnancy, it happened without complications. When my delivery date became near, my problem was where to deliver my baby. I was extremely afraid of the local hospital. As a child and teenager, I had heard many stories about pregnancy and deliveries: that it was very painful, that I could not eat eggs because the baby would not get out of my womb, that health providers at the hospital maternity were cold and insensitive, and that the care they pro-vided was not good. In particular, what I heard about one of the most experi-enced midwives at the hospital made me shiver. This woman was famous because of her cruelty to the women under her care: she insulted and even physically abused and mistreated them.

For this reason, when the time of my delivery came, I was so afraid of going to the hospital, that I had my baby at home, helped by my mother. My baby weighed 3.8 kg (8 lbs, 6 oz) and was born with the umbilical cord wrapped around her neck. In spite of this complication, my baby fortunately was born normally.

When I grew up and decided to become a medical doctor, I promised myself that nobody under my care would experience the same as I did. Over the years, I became director of a provincial hospital with 53 maternity beds.

That is why, when I learned about the program started by the Ministry of Health of Mozambique ... to make maternal health and deliveries safer, respectful, humanized, and successful, I decidedly embraced it and mobilized

Box 9.1 (continued)

my staff to implement it. We did not want any more abuse and fear of the hospital. We put in practice standards of care through continuous assessments, staff meetings, and supervision. ... We implemented practices, such as, allowing a companion for women in labor and delivery, respect for their preferences regarding position at birth, privacy, freedom of movement when in labor, early breastfeeding, mother and baby skin contact, and others.

We worked hard for 6 years. At the beginning, it was difficult: the population did not believe in our "sudden" change of attitude. Companions did not want to see blood and did not want to be present, in spite of the requests of their patients. So, we involved our hospital–community committee (formed by community leaders, religious leaders, traditional providers, and women's and youth organizations) to better communicate with our clients. I do not believe our work has finished, but we have made visible progress: our staff has a better and more respectful attitude and appears more motivated, there are fewer abuses, including illegal charges to patients, more satisfaction expressed by mothers and families, fewer complaints by clients and the community, and better teaching for new midwifery and nursing students. The community participates actively and reports any abuses to our joint committee. We have also reduced the number of maternal deaths from 15 in 2010 to 10 in 2015.

The Power of Recognition

Providing public recognition – the final step in the initiative's QI process – played a key role in motivating and engaging providers. Once an internal assessment showed that a maternity was complying with 80% or more of all the maternal and neonatal health standards, the facility QI team could apply for recognition. An external assessment team consisting of central- and provincial-level MOH technical staff and project representatives would visit the facility and use the initiative's tool to assess performance.

If the external assessment verified a high level of compliance with the standards, the MOH officials will formally organize a ceremony at the facility to publicly honor the achievement. The recognition ceremonies are a visit to the maternity, interactions with clients, speeches by the authorities and community leaders, stage performance by maternity staff (theater, dances), and awarding of plaque.

These ceremonies, in which all the facility staff would participate, proved to be powerful motivators. Facilities were motivated by an opportunity to gain public recognition and will strive to achieve the level required. They value the presence of high-level authorities and the community at the ceremonies. At the same time, the ceremonies helped to reinforce leaders' commitment and support for maternal and neonatal health.

The Implementation Challenges

Levels of commitment and enthusiasm varied among the teams, as did the impact of their efforts. The facility improvement teams who were proactive quickly produced visible and significant improvements in the use of evidence-based practices and respectful care. Other teams delayed the implementation of the QI and required additional guidance and support from the external supervisors and facility managers before getting started. Still other teams were reluctant to undertake improvements because they often feel their workload was already too heavy and the constraints imposed by infrastructure, supplies, and human resources were too great. Adoption of the QI process was slower and more difficult when facility staff perceived it as being promoted by an external nongovernmental organization. In contrast, when the MOH supervisors were involved, they lent more legitimacy to the process.

The facility managers noted a variety of problems during the initial implementation of the intervention. At the beginning, some providers were not inclined to adopt the evidence-based practices promoted by the initiative; in these cases, continuous on-the-job training proved important to reinforce the best practices. Human resources shortages and staff rotation also posed significant barriers to the adoption of best practices. Time constraints, aggravated by staff shortages, often made the adoption of the QI processes more difficult. Further, in what was most likely an effort to show progress, some facility improvement teams are too lenient in their maternity assessment. After the external assessment teams highlighted the inaccuracies and the providers realized that the purpose was not punitive, the teams gradually began to do more accurate assessments.

The Measurement and Results

Modifications and enhancements to the HMIS enabled the Model Maternities' Initiative to routinely collect quality-of-care data that is not accessible to most of the similar initiatives. The facility QI teams, the MMI leadership, and the MOH relied on the three types of data to measure quality improvement at participating maternities:

1. Self-reported performance, based on the facility assessments performed by the facility teams
2. Clinical practice indicators, based on the data from the facility registers
3. Maternal mortality, also from the HMIS registries

The Provider and Facility Performance

Regular internal assessments of facility performance were a core activity for the QI approach used in Mozambique. The facility QI teams conducted an assessment every 3–6 months (which took around 2 days to complete) and used the data to calculate the percentage of the performance standards achieved in each of the nine areas. The teams reported the results of these internal assessments to the project's

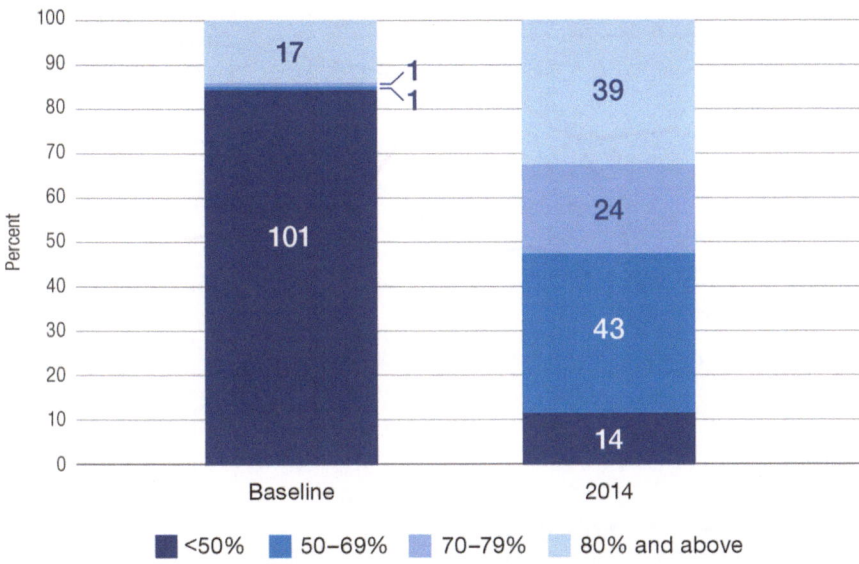

Fig. 9.4 Number of maternities ($n = 120$), by percentage of performance standards met at the baseline and at the end of the MMI process

monitoring and evaluation unit, which periodically consolidated and reported them to the MOH. The provincial coaches were responsible for reviewing the quality of the data. Provincial directorates analyzed the data from their facilities and, guided by that information, implemented the appropriate support measures.

Changes did not occur at the same pace or with the same magnitude in every facility. Some maternities excelled, most made significant improvements, while others lagged behind. Data are available for 1–13 assessments at each maternity, depending on the year they joined the initiative; a new group of 25–30 maternities was added each year. At baseline, four-fifths of maternities complied with less than 50% of the performance standards (Fig. 9.4). Toward the end of the project, the vast majority of maternities had achieved at least 50% of standards, and one-third had achieved at least 80% of standards. Compliance remained below 50% at only 12% of maternities, typically those that had only recently launched the MMI intervention. Taken as a whole, the improvements observed were sufficient to have an impact on the prevalence of evidence-based practices and ultimately on the institutional maternal mortality ratio, as shown in Fig. 9.5.

The Clinical Practice Indicators

The MMI facility QI teams monitored relevant clinical practice indicators, using data from the revised MOH facility register. Team members entered and reported monthly information on selected indicators related to preselected evidence-based and respectful care practices:

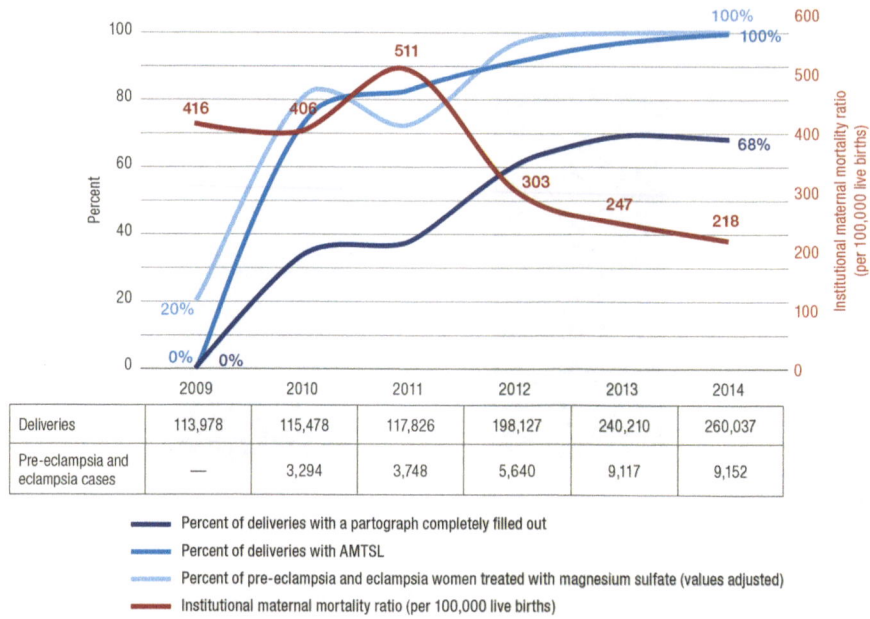

	2009	2010	2011	2012	2013	2014
Deliveries	113,978	115,478	117,826	198,127	240,210	260,037
Pre-eclampsia and eclampsia cases	—	3,294	3,748	5,640	9,117	9,152

━━━ Percent of deliveries with a partograph completely filled out
━━━ Percent of deliveries with AMTSL
━━━ Percent of pre-eclampsia and eclampsia women treated with magnesium sulfate (values adjusted)
━━━ Institutional maternal mortality ratio (per 100,000 live births)

Fig. 9.5 Improvement in selected high-impact maternal care practices and maternal mortality ratio

- Births with active management of the third stage of labor (AMTSL)
- Eclampsia cases treated with magnesium sulfate
- Deliveries with a partograph completely filled in
- Number of obstetric complications
- Deliveries with a family companion present
- Newborns with immediate skin-to-skin contact with the mother
- Newborns breastfed within the first hour

Provincial coaches or supervisors and the central monitoring and evaluation team conducted active data quality assurance at the facility level. The coaches conducted careful review of the data from the facilities, checking for inconsistencies. Any discrepancy was discussed by phone and during the periodic visits to the facilities, and if needed, additional training on how to fill the registries and report data was conducted. The information was used by the MOH (provincial and central levels) and the project to monitor progress and success of the intervention on a quarterly basis.

All of the clinical practice indicators showed marked improvement after the launch of the initiative, as shown in Figs. 9.5 and 9.6, which compared the last quarter reported data each year. Improvements were especially notable for the AMTSL, treatment of preeclampsia or eclampsia with magnesium sulfate, skin-to-skin contact with the mother after delivery, and breastfeeding in the first hour; all four of these indicators exceeded 80% in 2014.

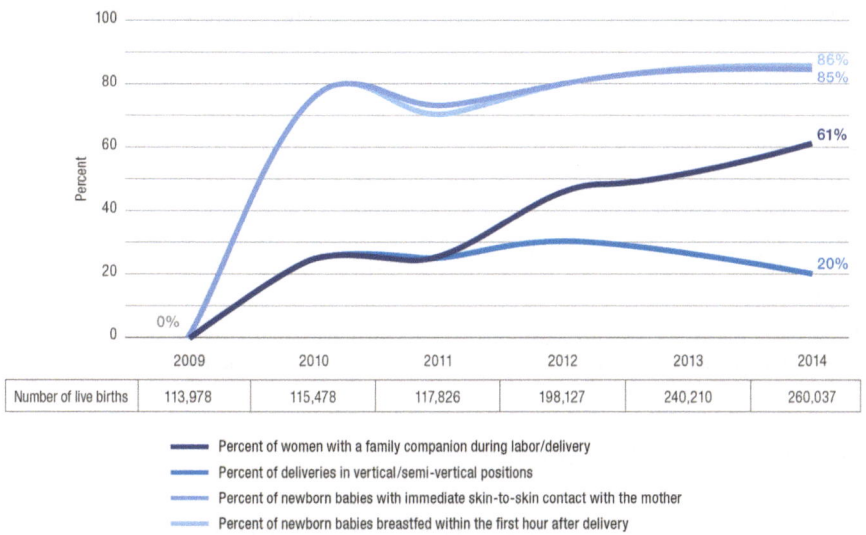

Fig. 9.6 Improvement in respectful care and humanized practices

The Maternal Mortality

The facility improvement teams used the HMIS to report maternal deaths and analyze institutional maternal mortality each quarter. The same data quality assurance mechanisms were used to verify mortality data. From 2009 to 2014, the institutional mortality ratio reported in the HMIS fell by 46% – from 416 to 218 deaths per 100,000 live births – in the participating maternities. Mozambique has a 53% institutional delivery rate, and the MMI covers about one-third of those institutional deliveries. Thus, the initiative should have made an appreciable contribution to reducing the national maternal mortality ratio, which had remained stagnant for several years.

A project technical advisor conducted an independent modeling exercise using the Lives Saved Tool (LiST) (Winfrey et al. 2011). The Lives Saved Tool exercise estimated the impact of the improved coverage of three clinical practices – AMTSL, magnesium sulfate for eclampsia, and use of partograph – on maternal mortality. This modeling exercise predicted a 26% drop in the institutional maternal mortality ratio from 2009 to 2014 (see Table 9.4). This figure is considerably less than the 46% decline in the maternal deaths reported by the HMIS, presumably because the HMIS data reflected improvements in a wider array of clinical practices. According to the Lives Saved Tool, 1139 maternal lives were saved during the 5 years of the initiative.

Table 9.4 The actual maternal deaths at the participating facilities, compared with the estimated impact of the three clinical practices on maternal mortality

	HMIS		Lives Saved Tool modeling[a]	
Year	Deaths	% reduction from 2009 baseline	Deaths	% reduction from 2009 baseline
2009	416	N/A	416	N/A
2010	406	−2%	356	−14%
2011	433	−4%	345	17%
2012	305	−27%	306	−26%
2013	258	−38%	316	−24%
2014	226	−46%	308	−26%

[a]Lives Saved Tool (LiST) was used to estimate the impact of the improved coverage of the AMTSL, magnesium sulfate for eclampsia, and use of partographs on maternal mortality

The Status of the QI Program

The MOH said it wanted to continue expanding the implementation of the evidence-based and respectful care practices to all the maternities in the country. However, a USAID independent external evaluation team recommended that follow-on activities of a new maternal and child project should be focused on the two provinces with high maternal mortality in order to accelerate the impact during the next phase. This follow-on project, now in implementation, incorporates additional components, such as, child health, nutrition, immunization, and water and sanitation. The MMI component is a critical element of the new project and expected to reach more facilities in each of the two selected provinces. The MOH continues the implementation of the MMI in the other provinces not currently covered by the project, based on the capacity developed at the provincial level.

Reflection

The approach to quality improvement used in this effort was the key to the success of the initiative. The approach focused on using the tools that define the performance expectations, placing a focus on immediate action rather than repetitive analysis, stressing formal recognition to increase motivation, and relying on the data collection to document the QI activities.

The approach offered a simple, intuitive, and systematic QI process that was easily understood and well accepted by participants and facilities. It also provided a single tool summarizing recommended practices, which could be utilized throughout the QI process – for internal and external assessments, teamwork and action planning, and for supervision. This reduced the need for external assistance. Appropriate training to disseminate the evidence-based knowledge and practices captured by the assessment tool and to strengthen provider competencies was an essential part of the initiative's foundation.

Focusing more on action and less time on problem analysis led to rapid change and visible results at the participating facilities (the "low-hanging fruit" approach). This not only empowered and motivated maternity teams but also attracted attention and support from the local and district managers. However, the extent to which facilities adopted the improvement process varied, depending on the factors, such as, local leadership and staff commitment.

The involvement of clients and communities proved to be an effective way to reinforce the change management process, creating a spirit of partnership and accountability. The involvement and support of the MOH gave legitimacy to the process and helped to mobilize resources for the maternities.

Recognition proved an effective motivator. The facility staff felt honored by the public recognition of their efforts, especially when it came from the high-level authorities, such as, the Minister of Health or Provincial Governor. The nation's First Lady participated in two recognition ceremonies for maternities in provincial hospitals. The high-level policymakers also became more engaged in the MMI through the recognition ceremonies, which offered the MOH national visibility in the mass media. Other forms of motivation and learning, such as, inter-facility benchmarking, are also proved effective.

Enhanced data collection also contributed to the success of the initiative. The modification of the MOH HMIS provided new information on the indicators of quality-of-care and evidence-based practices that were essential to monitor progress in the short term. In the long term, these indicators were able to document the impact of the QI process on health outcomes. Improvements grew more visible over time, and changes in the key indicators, such as, maternal mortality, only became evident over a period of 5 years.

The gradual expansion of the initiative over the course of 5 years allowed the facilitators and coaches to gain experience in the QI process, resulting in a better planned and organized scale-up of the initiative. The experience in Mozambique demonstrated that often overburdened and poorly motivated providers readily accepted a simple, self-explanatory improvement process. The straightforwardness of the process also helped reduce the need for external assistance, which would have been very expensive when the program reached scale. In addition, the early involvement of the MOH and having it in the "driver's seat" (e.g., the selection of coaches and the integration of the process into the provincial health directorate dynamics) accelerated the scale up of the intervention. As mentioned, on many occasions, provincial authorities expanded the process beyond the donor-supported maternities.

This experience in Mozambique highlights some of the challenges to putting QI in place and suggests potential solutions. Certain critical constraints – notably staff shortages and shortcomings in facility management – created barriers to the adoption and expansion of the MMI. Resolving these issues is important to facilitate the continuing scale up of MMI. One possibility is to develop and implement strategies to further simplify the QI process, for example, by streamlining the tools and making use of the technology-supported job aids, performance support tools, and communication mechanisms. In addition, leaders should also work on guaranteeing more human and other resources to maternities adopting the MMI, strengthening facility management, and optimizing service delivery processes.

The MMI in Mozambique shows that it is possible to implement a quality improvement initiative at scale in a low-resource setting, achieving important improvements in the adoption of evidence-based practices and outcomes, such as, institutional maternal mortality. This success was achieved in spite of the severe constraints typical of low-resource settings, including lack of staff, physical plant constraints, and scarcity of other material resources.

Acknowledgement The authors gratefully acknowledge the support of the following individuals for the Model Maternities Initiative in Mozambique: Ministers of Health, Dr. Paulo Ivo Garrido and Dr. Alexandre Manguele; Vice-Minister of Health, Dr. Nazira Abdula; National Directors of Public Health, Dr. Mouzinho Saíde and Dr. Francisco Mbofana; National Directors of Medical Care, Dr. António Mujovo and Dr. Ussene Isse; Associate National Directors of Public Health, Dr. Lidia Chongo and Dr. Quinhas Fernandes; Heads of the Department of Maternal and Child Health, Dr. Nazir Amade, Dr. Munira Abudou, and Dr. Pascoa Wate; Provincial- and District-Level Directors, Ministry of Health from 2009 to 2013; all the midwives, health professionals, and staff of the participating maternities; and staff of the USAID Mission in Mozambique: Polly Dunford, Ana Bodipo, Juno Lawrence Jaffer, Lilia Jamisse, and other officials of the Health, Population, and Nutrition unit.

References

Ministry of Health (MOH) (2008) Plano Nacional de Desenvolvimento de Recursos Humanos para a Saúde [National Plan for Health Human Resources Development] 2008–2015.

MOH (2016) Plano Nacional de Desenvolvimento de Recursos Humanos para a Saúde [National Plan for Health Human Resources Development] 2016–2025.

Necochea E, Bossemeyer D (2005) Standards-based management and recognition: a field guide. Jhpiego, Baltimore

Winfrey W, McKinnon R, Stover J (2011) Methods used in the Lives Saved Tool (LiST). BMC Public Health 11 Suppl 3:S32

Chapter 10
Strengthening Services for Most Vulnerable Children Through Quality Improvement Approaches in a Community Setting: The Case of Bagamoyo District, Tanzania

Flora Pius Nyagawa

Abstract This case describes the application of quality improvement to improve services provided at the community level to the most vulnerable children (MVC) in the community, those orphaned or affected by HIV. The case describes the experience of supporting local communities in Tanzania to implement the QI approach outlined in Tanzania's National Most Vulnerable Children QI Guidelines. In particular, the case focuses on start-up activities needed to get the initiative up and running, including gaining buy-in from community leaders, determining baseline performance, mobilizing MVC committees to serve as QI teams to test changes to care processes, and supporting shared learning across teams. The case also speaks to the particular challenges as well as benefits of implementing QI at the community level.

Keywords Collaborative Improvement · Community Health Workers · Community-Based Organizations · Most Vulnerable Children · Orphans and Vulnerable Children · Shared Learning · Tanzania

Background and Setting

In Tanzania, the Department of Social Welfare (DSW) of the Ministry of Health and Social Welfare is responsible for guiding and coordinating interventions to ensure the care, support and protection of most vulnerable children (MVC). MVC are defined as children who are 18 years old or younger, who live in high-risk circumstances, and whose prospects for continued growth and development are seriously impaired. MVC, including those who are affected by and living with HIV, are

F. P. Nyagawa (✉)
Formerly with University Research Co., LLC, Dar Es Salaam, Tanzania
e-mail: flopius@hotmail.com

© University Research Co., LLC 2020

L. R. Marquez (ed.), *Improving Health Care in Low- and Middle-Income Countries*, https://doi.org/10.1007/978-3-030-43112-9_10

vulnerable to chronic diseases, developmental delays, and reduced educational opportunities, as well as potential abuse, stigma, and discrimination from their family members, caregivers, and communities.

The 2012, the Republic of Tanzania Population and Housing Census (PHC) estimated the number of MVC in the country at 3,000,000. However, the 2012 National Indicator Survey revealed that 1.3% of children below 19 years old are HIV positive and that 9.4% had had their first sexual encounter before the age of 15. Around 37% of children in this age group reported at least one episode of sexual violence, while 23% reported an episode of physical violence. Like all vulnerable population groups, MVC struggle to access basic services, such as education, adequate food, shelter, and social and psychosocial support. To bridge the access gap, the DSW developed the National Costed Plan of Action (NCPA) for Most Vulnerable Children I (2007–2010). The Plan sought to establish a community-driven response to strengthen households' and communities' capacity to care for, protect, and support MVC who are HIV-positive or affected by HIV.

Developing and Communicating Standards for MVC Care and Support

In 2009, the DSW led development of the National Quality Improvement Guidelines for Most Vulnerable Children (National MVC QI Guidelines) to standardize and improve the quality of services provided by various stakeholders. The guidelines covered eight service areas:

- Food and nutrition
- Shelter
- Family-based care and support
- Social protection and security
- Primary health care
- Psychosocial care and support
- Education and vocational training
- Household economic strengthening

The National MVC QI Guidelines shifted MVC program priorities from distribution of commodities to ensuring an improved quality of life. Guidelines defined stakeholders' roles and responsibilities and specific standards for quality improvement (QI) of each of the eight service areas, including desired outcomes, essential actions, illustrative activities, best practice notes, and quality indicators.

The DSW sought to disseminate the National MVC QI Guidelines in a way that would ensure that stakeholders would understand and implement its principles. The department called upon a donor-funded project to develop a training package to facilitate communication of the guidelines to service providers throughout the country's health-care system, from the village to the national level.

In 2010, the DSW published the *Training Package for Improving Quality of Care, Support, and Protection for MVC in Tanzania*, which standardized training procedures to guide implementation of the national guidelines. The DSW and project staff trained 39 national facilitators, who in turn trained government representatives and implementing partners involved in care, support, and protection of MVC at regional and district councils in 19 regions.

Following the training, the DSW set up a demonstration site by focusing on intensive implementation of the guidelines in one of the districts.

Organizing the Improvement Effort

Actors at the Village Level

In Tanzania, the government administrative system is comprised of national, regional, district (council), ward, and village or hamlet levels. The village or hamlet, the closest point to the household level, is where MVC beneficiaries interact with entities and groups which provide care, support, and protection services, including community-based organizations, government social and health services, and local nongovernmental organizations (NGOs). These organizations and groups include district- and village-level MVC committees, village authorities, community health workers, support groups, and households.

MVC committees play a critical coordination role in providing services to MVC. The DSW provides guidance and criteria for the formation of MVC committees and selection of members. The community, during an open public meeting, uses a participatory approach to nominate and select MVC committee members. To support this selection process, the community development officer (CDO) or any designated government official from the ward level provides guidance on qualifications. The MVC committee's main role is to coordinate all interventions related to care, support, and protection of MVC in that community.

While the MVC committee plays a leading role in service coordination, other players at the village level also are critical to the provision of services. The village authority, a government entity, oversees all village activities, including resource mobilization for MVC to access services. Community health workers—village residents who have undergone basic health training—play key roles by monitoring the growth and general health of under-five children, including MVC. Volunteer groups, such as savings and internal lending groups, women's groups, and faith-based organizations, sometimes play a role in resource mobilization and in supporting MVC to access various services.

District Selection

The DSW was aware, as a result of observations gained from their own supervisory visits and feedback received from partners, that MVC committees had been largely ineffective in organizing and supporting MVC to access quality services. MVC committees had inadequate understanding of their role and were not effectively utilizing available local resources. The DSW requested that a United States Agency for International Development (USAID)-funded QI project provide technical support to effectively train providers at the primary service level to understand and implement the National MVC QI Guidelines.

Since improving care for MVC was a new activity, the DSW and the USAID-funded QI project decided to start by supporting improvement activities on a small scale, in three wards of one demonstration district. The main objective of the demonstration was to engage those involved in caring for MVC to understand and apply standards stipulated in the National MVC QI Guidelines.

The DSW and project staff reviewed a range of options to select the location best suited to serve as the demonstration site. Not all districts in the country had active MVC programs, so the DSW opted to choose a district where services were already being provided. Bagamoyo District, where UNICEF had already started initiatives to support MVC activities, emerged as a top choice. In addition, it was a rural district which was relatively close to Dar es Salaam, where the project office was located making it easier to monitor. Bagamoyo District was eager to expand on its current MVC activities and had a social welfare officer (SWO) committed to the effort, so it was decided to move forward with this district. At the time, there were a total of 169 districts in Tanzania; Bagamoyo was one of the six districts in the Pwani Region.

Collaborative Improvement

The project and DSW staff agreed that a collaborative improvement approach would be the most appropriate and effective way to organize teams and improvement activities for this initiative. Collaborative improvement brings together multiple teams working on the same improvement aims in order to share experiences, foster peer-to-peer learning, and spread successful changes rapidly across all participating teams.

Collaborative improvement serves as a way to organize and leverage the efforts of multiple teams. Teams use plan-do-study-act cycles to test the effectiveness of changes implemented at their sites. On a regular basis, usually every 3–5 months, all teams in a ward or district are brought together in a learning session to share the changes they have tested and their results. They compare and learn from each other's efforts, both successful and unsuccessful. Following the learning session, team members take successful ideas back to their own improvement efforts and adapt and test changes using additional plan-do-study-act cycles. Throughout this process, the

October 2010: Initial visit to Bagamoyo

January 2011: initial data collection in 3 wards

March 2011: Advocacy meetings conducted

April 2011: Learning Session 1

May 2011: Teams conducted actual Baseline data collection

June 2011: Coaching 1

August 2011: Coaching 2

September 2011: Coaching 3

October 2011: Learning Session 1 for 6 new wards (spread sites)

November 2011: Learning Session 2

February–June 2012: Coaching and mentoring to wards

July 2012: Learning session to all remaining teams within 13 wards

August 2012–to June 2015: Continuous coaching to teams based on their performance

Fig. 10.1 Timeline of activities

community's quality improvement teams are supported by coaches who provide feedback, guide data collection and analysis, and help teams carry out the steps in the plan-do-study-act cycle.

The demonstration involved all key stakeholders working in Bagamoyo on MVC services, including representatives from the DSW, the regional health management team, council staff, nongovernmental organizations, community-based organizations, ward and village authorities, and MVC committees. Start-up and implementation involved a series of steps and activities, which are summarized in Fig. 10.1 above. This case study describes each of these steps in detail.

Initial Introductory Visits

In October 2010, staff from the DSW, the USAID-funded QI project, the Regional Health Management Team in Pwani, and the implementing partner conducted an initial site visit to Bagamoyo District to hold discussions with district authorities to gain their support and to create a working relationship with key stakeholders in the district. This visit, the first of a series arranged by the DSW, provided an opportunity to learn and understand how the district's MVC program worked.

The planning group was comprised of five people, each with a specific role: two project staff provided technical assistance on how to put QI into action, the DSW gave technical guidance on policy and national guidelines, the implementing partner's representative described MVC activities, and the Regional SWO provided guidance on how to translate policy into implementation at the council level. Government standards encouraged projects and implementing partners to involve Ministry level staff in first visits.

The visit involved a series of meetings with a few representatives from targeted departments and organizations within Bagamoyo District, such as a visit to a local NGO that provided MVC services. The planning group held discussions with the district's SWO to explore the district's engagement and identify gaps in community structures and services.

Planning group members conducted an introductory visit with district authorities, including the council health management team, which plays a primary role in the coordination and supervision of all health-related activities, and the district executive director. The meeting was intended to help officials recognize where their missions and goals overlapped and to identify areas in which they were able to collaborate. The district executive director reported that the meeting shed light on how improvement activities fit within their mandate to ensure that all vulnerable groups have access to various services. This initial visit enabled them to draw up a plan and begin key activities to launch the improvement collaborative.

In addition, the planning group conducted interviews with children and guardians to informally collect qualitative information. This data collection was continued during the baseline assessment. The group interviewed not only six informants from council departments, giving priority consideration to social welfare, but also the education and community development departments. They met with two local service providers and nine ward officers, three from the Ward Executive Officers, three from community development, and three from education.

When group members compared notes, they found that concerns focused on several key areas: MVC committee functionality, MVC data quality, the role of the SWO, and budget support for MVC. At the end of visit, the planning group analyzed and employed the information and began to plan implementation of MVC improvement activities.

The planning group noted performance gaps with respect to DSW guidance, particularly pertaining to communications and relationship dynamics between the village authorities and the MVC committees. They found that the MVC committees were inadequate reporting to the village authorities, and the village authorities, in turn, were inadequate providing guidance and support. In addition, the interests of the MVC committees and village authorities appeared to conflict. The MVC committees lacked updated and consistent data and information; for example, their data registrars were incomplete and out-of-date. Further, the MVC committees did not have plans in place to provide support services to MVC and were not linking them to services. The planning group conducted a feedback meeting for the head of the Community Development Department and the district-level SWO. The information was also presented at the first district-level learning session.

Ward Selection

The planning group worked with council staff from the social welfare and community development departments to identify and select wards to participate in pilot improvement activities. In searching for pilot sites, the group took into consideration a range of criteria in order to achieve a well-rounded sample. They searched for sites that would provide a balance of rural and urban areas and that had a high concentration of MVC. They also focused on sites that had current MVC data as well as those where volunteers were actively working. They gave primary consideration to sites that had existing community structures which were supported by other implementing partners.

The SWO provided basic information about the wards, including the number of MVC and the number of MVC committees, and records of previous trainings and interventions. The planning group and council staff chose three out of the 22 wards in Bagamoyo District for the pilot improvement activities. The three wards included the Dunda Ward, with its 22 hamlets; Fukayosi Ward, located in a rural setting, with four villages; and the rural Kiwangwa Ward, with five villages. The three wards had a total of 463 MVC (Kiwangwa, 154; Fukayosi, 98; and Dunda, 211). At the time of the intervention, Bagamoyo District had 5504 MVC, of which 2904 were males and 2600 were females. The district's SWO held discussions with the ward authorities from each location, including the executive, community development, and ward education officers, all of whom agreed to participate in improvement activities.

District and Ward Start-Up

In March 2011, the DSW and project staff conducted advocacy meetings at the district and ward levels. Specifically, the DSW and project staff held a 1-day meeting in each ward to explain the project's objectives and approach to authorities. The objectives were to explain the roll-out of activities and to determine appropriate coaches at the district and ward levels.

The DSW and project staff provided district and ward leaders with guidance and made recommendations regarding selection of coaches. Coaches would support the improvement teams by providing a variety of services:

- Acting as mentors to team participants on all aspects of the improvement process (team formation, problem analysis, and conducting plan-do-study-act cycles), as well as data collection and analysis
- Providing training on MVC guidelines
- Serving as advocates and intermediaries with higher levels of government on how to address larger systemic problems

The district-level SWO and community development officer (CDO) were largely responsible for selecting district coaches. They chose representatives from the Social Welfare, Community Development, Education, Health, and Planning departments, as well from nongovernmental and faith-based organizations. In total, about 10–12 representatives served as district coaches over the course of the project. The district coaches' primary responsibilities were to coordinate and coach ward and village teams and to ensure allocation and mobilization of resources at the district level across all sectors.

In addition, the district SWO, in collaboration with the ward executive officer, selected ward-level coaches. They chose individuals from departments that had an oversight role for MVC or MVC services, such as the education or community development department. Ward-level coaches were community development officers, education coordinators, executive officers, and agriculture extension officers. These coaches were responsible for guiding MVC committees at the village level, overseeing all activities within the villages, and serving as a key link between the village and district levels. All information moving between the district and villages passed through the ward coaches.

Two of the coaches, one from an NGO and one from a faith-based organization, received funding from an implementing partner to provide MVC services. Based in the wards, the two coaches were able to work with the teams on a day-to-day basis to help them identify gaps and find ways to address them. The two coaches stayed with the project for a few years until funding for their organizations ran out.

Baseline Assessment

In January 2011, the first major activity was to conduct a baseline assessment in the three wards and associated villages and hamlets. The project staff, with input from the DSW, designed a simple questionnaire with key questions targeting services areas and indicators stipulated in the national guidelines. Baseline survey respondents included MVC parents or guardians and the children themselves. Project staff, together with Bagamoyo's Department of Social Welfare and social welfare officer, conducted a one-day orientation meeting for 13 volunteers who were identified by local implementing partners and paid to participate in the data collection. At the end of the session, each data collector was allotted, based on the number of MVC they oversee within their residential areas, a number of respondents to interview. Two project staff, the SWO, and a Ministry of Health and Social Welfare representative served as supervisors.

Questionnaires were administered to MVC beneficiaries and to parent or guardian caregivers to elicit information on the MVC and their perspectives on the quality of services provided. Project staff received information on 367 respondents (85.7% of the 428 MVC registered in the three wards) of whom 180 were female and 187 were male. Data on 340 MVC were used for analysis.

The findings were presented at the first district-level learning session to give teams an understanding of the current level of ward performance and to select improvement priorities. In May 2011, following the first learning session, village-level QI teams collected their own baseline information using a subset of the indicators.

The results of the original and QI team baseline surveys are shown in Table 10.1. The two baseline surveys showed large discrepancies. One explanation for the discrepancies is that volunteer data collectors may have been affected by a desire to portray the results in the best light possible. By the time the teams collected their own baseline numbers, they had updated registries and had perhaps better understood the

Table 10.1 Indicators and results from the baseline assessment (three wards) in January 2011 and baseline self-collected data (25 teams) in May 2011

Key indicators (taken from National Guidelines)	Baseline assessment (Jan. 2011) ($n = 3$ wards)	Team baseline (May 2011) ($n = 25$ sites/villages)
Percentage of MVC who get two or more meals a day	89%	62%
Percentage of MVC ages 0–5 whose health cards/charts reflect normal growth for age	–	35%
Percentage of MVC household living in secure, dry, and adequate shelter	69%	43%
Percentage of MVC who have birth certificates	19% (two wards)	6%
Percentage of MVC reported to be abused in last month	–	1%
Percentage of MVC who are sleeping under insecticide treated mosquito nets	60%	15%
Percentage of MVC who were sick and referred to a health facility	–	37%
Percentage of MVC in the program who are attending school regularly	88%	76%
Percentage of MVC caregivers who are able to meet their households' basic needs as a result of economic strengthening interventions	89%	12%
Percentage of MVC over 5 years of age with Community Health Fund cards/insurance	–	0%
Percentage of MVC enrolled in primary education	100%	100%
Percentage of MVC who are living with trusted male/female guardian	90%	–
Percentage of MVC who were reported to have received at least one service during the year	90%	–
Percentage of MVC under 5 years of age who are fully immunized	100%	–
Percentage of MVC who play with their age mates/peers	90%	–

improvement process and the value of honest reporting. The largest identified gaps appeared in the area of services for vulnerable children under 5 years of age, the result of many service providers focusing primarily on providing education services for older children. As a result, primary school enrollment was at 100%. Going forward, the project used the team baseline as the more reliable source of information.

Team Formation

The project staff, working together with the DSW, determined that since the MVC committees existed for coordinating MVC activities at the district, ward, and village levels; no parallel or new system should be created. Instead, project staff worked with the SWO and executive officers from each ward and village to assess how well their MVC committees were functioning. When necessary, an MVC committee added members that would bring useful skills, functions, experience, and perspective to the committee. For example, an MVC committee added as a member a home-based care provider who was able to link children to MVC services and caregivers to treatment adherence support. Also invited to join the committee was a village extension officer who oversaw agricultural development to help with issues of household economic strengthening. The criteria for adding new members included selection and acceptance by a village assembly (which occurred at open community meetings), a clean criminal record, and residence within that village or hamlet. By adding additional members and responsibilities, the MVC committee went from an entity that coordinated activities to a QI team responsible for improving the quality of care of MVC support and protection services.

Initially, the council MVC committee planned to conduct improvement activities at their own level. The council MVC committee was trained in quality improvement, but only some four or five members remained on the committee. Members served as coaches, but no district-level improvement activities took place.

A total of 25 MVC committees were strengthened to implement QI in nine villages and 16 hamlets[1] in three wards. Each village or hamlet had one MVC committee consisting of 10–12 members, including community health workers and a community justice facilitator. Members also included influential community members, such as, representatives from religious organizations (primarily Muslim and Christian), caregivers, vulnerable children aged 12 years or older (one boy and one girl), and teachers.

In villages where there was MVC committee turnover due to relocation, dropouts, or deaths, the village authority replaced them by following the selection procedures and guidance laid out by the DSW.

Capacity Building

The first learning session, held in April 2011 and organized by project, DSW, and Regional Health Management Team staff, introduced district, ward, and community MVC committees to key policy issues, offered guidance on MVC programs, and provided QI training. In addition, the session was intended to help participants reach mutual agreement on how improvement activities would be carried out. During learning sessions, MVCC reviewed topics, such as planning actions, setting aims and goals, identifying initial changes for improvement, and selecting indicators. Four learning sessions were held: one for the district level and one for each of the three wards.

---

[1] The term hamlet, *vitongoji* in Swahili, is used in small township areas and is equivalent to village.

First Learning Session at District Level

Facilitators from the project and implementing partners, the DSW, and the regional SWO conducted the first 3-day learning session for 30 members of the district-level MVC committee in Bagamoyo township. The participants were from council departments and representatives from local non-governmental organizations who were involved in supporting the district's MVC services. The session, held at participants' work stations, was cost-effective as transportation and accommodation costs were not incurred. The location also conveyed a sense of ownership among participants. The main aim was to train participants on the detailed content of the National MVC QI Guidelines and their application to planning and budgeting processes. The objectives of the learning session were to:

- Orient district staff on the national guidelines for MVC programs
- Introduce the concept of QI in MVC service delivery
- Explain the collaborative improvement approach at the community level
- Create a common understanding of roles and responsibilities in the implementation of QI activities

The facilitators trained participants on the model for improvement and plan–do–study–act cycles. Participants learned how to guide ward coaches and village MVC committees on how to identify existing quality gaps, develop and test changes, and measure for improvement. Some of the key training topics included the following:

- Identifying the factors that make services effective
- Recognizing how stakeholders can implement QI in MVC services
- Understanding QI guidelines and approaches
- Organizing QI activities
- Measuring changes in MVC wellbeing

The facilitators emphasized the use and strengthening of existing structures and systems at the community level for implementing the National QI Guidelines in MVC service delivery.

District participants were expected to provide supportive supervision to ward and village teams, as well as to develop improvements (changes to test) in their own work. For example, they chose to improve coordination between the social welfare and education departments in the use of MVC data for service support.

First Learning Session for Community Level

To build QI capacity, the DSW officer, project staff, and ward authorities, with support from the national and regional levels, organized a 3-day learning session for the MVC committees from each ward. Five members of each team participated in the learning sessions, including the chairperson, secretary, community health worker, community justice facilitator, and village executive officer. The learning session was held within the participants' ward on community premises, such as a school or ward hall.

The trainings have been very helpful because we were just doing things in our way, we had no knowledge to identify MVC needs and address them on the set standards because we didn't recognize that there were certain standards to be followed. But now we know what we are supposed to do, we can plan and also act accordingly. QI team member, Bagamoyo District

The DSW and project staff trained the MVC committees on the National MVC QI Guidelines by using the training package designed for this purpose. Facilitators focused on building participants' understanding of the MVC service standards in each of six core service areas: food and nutrition, shelter and care, education, health, protection, and household economic strengthening. In addition, they were also oriented on key national plans and existing MVC policies, such as the National Costed Plan of Action (NCPA) II, 2010–2013.

Facilitators then taught the participants how to improve their performance in achieving those standards by analyzing their own systems and processes for MVC service delivery, identifying and testing changes in the organization of care that could result in improved quality and efficiency, and using data to document and understand the effect of changes.

At the end of the learning session, each MVC committee came up with a plan to address initial issues based on their own performance gaps or problems identified through the training exercises. The plans included the key challenge/problem, activities to address the problem, responsibilities of different actors, and a timeline. Following the learning session, each team collected their own baseline for the key indicators.

Carrying Out the Improvement Work

Following the learning session, the MVC committees took the first step by updating their own community data. Most vulnerable children (MVC) data consists a range of variables: the number of MVC in a village; demographic data, such as age, sex, and location of residence; data on the needs of each child; and the caregiver's information. The MVC committees carried out visits to all MVC homes to collect this information and update their records to serve as a baseline.

Each MVC committee reviewed data for the eight improvement areas and determined which one or two areas they would start with. During the meetings, teams discussed the service areas and related key essential actions from the guidelines to determine which needed improvement. The teams compared the needs of the registered children with the essential actions to identify the biggest gaps. They used this information to develop their improvement aims. The teams then discussed the key issues and gaps and those which most significantly affected their local services. They developed several possible goals and then narrowed the list down to a few with which to begin. Each team agreed on their own aim based on the vulnerable children's priority needs. The village executive officer and ward coaches provided guidance to their teams on how to set goals based on ideas received from team members. They discussed which steps were needed to implement, essential actions, and who or which group should be involved. They then tested their plan for changes using plan-do-study-act cycles.

> *...As I am speaking we have mobilized TSH 335,000 to support children with various services ... such as paying school fees for two secondary children, and we have other four children who are doing exams this year and they have special session at their school so they don't break for lunch hours to go home rather all parents have contributed for food to be prepared at school, so we have paid that contribution for lunch for these four children ... we want them to concentrate so they can perform well and their health not to deteriorate.*
> Reported by QI team member, Bagamoyo

The team agreed to monitor their changes using indicators selected from the National MVC QI Guidelines. After indicators were selected, they tasked each team member with visiting children and providing feedback both during regular meetings and with QI team members who lived nearby. In some cases, teams created their own indicators to track and test specific changes, for example, the number of MVC visited by MVC committee members each month.

Organization of MVC Committee Meetings

MVC committees conducted regular meetings to discuss progress and goals. While most MVC committees conducted monthly meetings, some teams conducted them every 2 months or even twice per month, depending on priorities and tested changes. Each MVC committee met in a variety of venues within their village: at village authority offices, in schools, or in any available community building. Sometimes they chose informal areas to meet, such as under a tree in the village authority office area. In some cases, meetings were held at the houses of team members, depending on agreement of members, convenience, and availability of space. The MVC committee chairperson convened the meetings, and either the team secretary or village executive officer facilitated discussions. The chair was responsible for ensuring that all agenda items were discussed and that consensus was reached on next actions.

Examples of changes implemented in three service areas and their results are shown in Table 10.2.

Table 10.2 Specific tests of changes implemented by teams in three selected service areas

Improvement objective for each service area	Change ideas implemented by teams	Results
Food and nutrition: Ensuring all vulnerable children have access to adequate, quality food and nutrition services	1. MVC committee members conducted home visits to update MVC registers and prepared a list of vulnerable households which need food support 2. MVC committee mobilized faith-based organizations and community members to supply food 3. MVC committee wrote a letter to request village authorities to provide land for vulnerable families 4. MVC committee involved agriculture and nutrition extension workers	1. Community members contributed food from their harvests or money to purchase food. For example, faith-based organizations in Fukayosi Ward gave maize to support MVC living in the villages 2. Community health workers from the QI teams did monthly follow-up visits to all children including vulnerable children who are under 5 years of age to monitor their growth 3. Village authorities in Fukayosi Ward gave two acres of land, and at Masugulu village in Kiwangwe Ward, one acre to cultivate food and cash crops to support vulnerable children with food and other basic needs. However, in Fukayosi, this did not work well initially since there was a land dispute. The issue was later resolved 4. The agriculture extension officer provided technical assistance on best agriculture practices. The QI team acquired agriculture inputs, such as, fertilizer under the government's subsidized price for vulnerable families
Social protection and security: Ensuring adequate protection and security for all vulnerable children	1. MVC committee mapped location of vulnerable children without birth certificates (required for receiving other government services) 2. MVC committee supported the compilation of necessary demographic data required for each child 3. MVC committee presented estimates of resource requirements (photos, etc.) to village council and conducted community sensitization on the importance of birth certificates 4. MVC committee submitted demographic information on vulnerable children and paid required fee to district authority	1. There was an increase from 6% in May 2011 to 74% in May 2015 of vulnerable children who had birth certificates 2. There was a significant increase of awareness among community members about the importance of providing birth certificates to all children
	1. Community justice facilitator sensitized community members on abuse, neglect, discrimination, and exploitation of MVC	1. A total of 26 cases related to abuse, exploitation, violence, and neglect were identified and reported to relevant authorities

Improvement objective for each service area	Change ideas implemented by teams	Results
Primary health care: Ensure all vulnerable children have access to medical services when ill	1. MVC committee mapped location of vulnerable children who are older than 5 years 2. MVC committee prepared and shared demographic information for vulnerable children with different stakeholders 3. MVC committee mobilized resources at community level to obtain children's health insurance coverage and insecticide-treated bed nets 4. MVC committee submitted vulnerable children demographic information and paid required fee to the health facility	1. A total of 84 vulnerable children have acquired Community Health Fund insurance 2. Other QI teams have included caregivers in Community Health Fund coverage. This facilitates not only vulnerable children to have access to medical services but also the caregiver 3. A total of 246 vulnerable children are sleeping under insecticide-treated bed nets

Documentation

MVC committee secretaries kept records of all meetings, including notes on all key issues. To ensure that team members were in consensus and because not all members were literate, the secretary read the minutes aloud. The records included notes covering the committee's planned actions, as well as their accomplishments and challenges encountered. Meeting records were used to discuss plans, goals, and challenges with coaches. Teams kept their own records in notebooks and/or put information into a documentation tool provided by the project.

> *After we came from the training/learning session we agreed with teams to go and update MVC data, we were sure most of the data were not updated so even the number of MVC were not realistic hence it will be difficult to implement improvement plans without knowing how many MVC are existing and what are their specific needs. So the first aim was to support teams to review their MVC data.*
>
> Ward education coordinator, Bagamoyo

To facilitate the recording of information, the documentation tool covered key topic areas and provided as an annex, a summary of the National MVC QI Guidelines' eight core service areas for easy reference:

- MVC services
- Names of team members attending meeting
- Performance self-ranking on MVC service provision (poor, average, good, and best)
- Challenges
- Planning matrix to address challenges/gaps in QI, objectives, key changes or activities, indicators, and baseline data
- Successes to be shared

> *We are now speaking the same language and using same data source. For example, if we want to support MVC through our budget line, we don't follow our own way to get names of MVC as before, but we communicate together with the SWO to ensure consistency and get names of MVC to support through MVC registers and MVC committee but not any other source.*
>
> District staff, Bagamoyo

As copies of the documentation tool were not alwayas readily available, many teams also kept counter books (notebooks) to record meeting notes. Most of the records were kept at village authority offices or by the secretary or chairperson to be easily accessed when village offices were closed. Some teams kept records of communications with village authorities.

Data Collection

Data recorded in the MVC registers were updated by following DSW procedures. The existing reporting framework required information to travel from the village (MVC committee) level through wards to the districts. However, information was not always disseminated as the reporting framework required. The project facilitated data collection while on site visits and passed on the reports.

The DSW had provided MVC registers to keep all data updated for a particular village. Prior to initiation of the QI effort, these registers had been updated only every 6 months following a process of initial identification of new MVC and updating information for existing children. The data in a register was open for official use to any service provider who was planning to conduct an intervention in that village. The MVC committee frequently used the data to plan support, such as determining which children were eligible to have school fees paid. The teams used the register to complete their indicator matrix at the end of each month to document accomplishments and actions taken. The matrix was used by all levels to review and analyze performance in a given service area.

> *Since we have done thorough updating of data, we now know our MVC and we have the plan to support them such as starting with providing birth certificates to all 13 children ... according to previous data we had 20 MVC, but it took us long and we did not take it serious, from that we discovered some children have moved out from our village.*
>
> – Village executive officer, Bagamoyo

The introduction of QI facilitated the collection and reporting of information at the village, ward, and district levels. Team members began recording services provided to children as they took place rather than waiting for the biannual report. These records were then compiled into monthly and quarterly reports. Government reports are routinely done on quarterly basis to be sent to the ward level and then to the district. However, MVC committees updated data in the indicator matrix each month to ensure that services were accurately documented.

At the meetings at the end of each month, the teams also filled out the indicator matrix as shown in Table 10.3.

Teams also made a second copy of data records which included items, such as, the number of MVC and their names, ages, gender, school status, services received, and which organization delivered them. They kept these duplicate records as a backup and to be able to get quick access to basic information without having to go to the village office.

Table 10.3 Example of indicator matrix

Name of village_____ Ward _____ District_____Region_____			
	Indicator	January 2015	February 2015
Numerator	Number of MVC who received a birth certificate (cumulative)	10	20
Denominator	Total number of MVC in MVC village register	100	100
1. Indicator	% of MVC with birth certificates	10%	20%

Teachers or village executive officers would often help other team members, whose educational levels varied, to understand the data.

Support for Improvement Teams

Coaching visits were scheduled to allow teams time, between visits, to implement planned activities and document key successes, accomplishments, and challenges. The initial coaching visit was held 4–5 weeks after the first learning session and aimed at reminding teams of what they learned at the first learning session. The visit was also intended to support teams to revise their initial implementation in coordination with a wider group of stakeholders from the village.

The main objective of ongoing coaching was to strengthen the capacity of MVC committees to implement their planned priority actions. National and regional coaches provided policy guidance and updated district coaches and teams on national issues related to MVC programming. They also provided guidance and feedback on implementation of teams' plans and analysis of data. District coaches provided immediate, ongoing technical support and guidance through visits and calls. They linked QI team members with stakeholders, when appropriate.

> *It has been more than six months since we submitted requests for birth certificates for our children at the district office, we are following up and we are not sure what is happening, if you can find out for us since you are also coming from the district that will be great.* A QI team member, giving a message to the district coach

District coaches got ready for visits by preparing a letter, accompanied by any relevant documents, to inform ward authorities of the planned visit, including its objectives, expected attendees, date, and place. Due to time and resources, two or three QI teams met jointly and shared with coaches the challenges in implementing changes and QI action plans, as well as their achievements. Coaching sessions lasted between 2 and 3 hours. During these visits, a representative of each QI team, often the chairman or secretary, would present on which of the planned actions had been accomplished. They also presented on how challenges were addressed and their upcoming plans and strategies. Members of other teams were given an opportunity to comment and ask questions.

Coaches supported teams in the following ways:

- Reviewed accuracy of data and provided guidance on filling out data collection forms. For example, teams were initially unclear about how to read numerators and denominators so the coaches helped team members understand them.
- Explained each component of the documentation tool and reviewed how to fill it out.
- Reviewed guidelines and key actions with team members.
- Shared experiences and best practices from other Tanzanian programs to provide teams with ideas for plans and activities.
- Explained team roles and fostered teamwork.
- In order to maximize community resources, encouraged team members to create a network of providers and use it to make referrals.
- Encouraged team members to support each other.
- Suggested that teams create saving and loan groups that caregivers could also join.

One area that coaches focused on was helping team members to distinguish between which improvement work fell under the control of the MVC committee and which should be referred to other services and organizations. They reviewed, with committee members, existing support and service networks and emphasized the importance of providing referrals since MVC committees did not provide direct services. They reviewed how to link and refer children and caregivers to various services, especially those that required skilled providers, such as HIV testing and counseling and/or legal assistance. Coaches kept notes on teams' progress in order to follow up on achievements and challenges. Challenges which fell outside the team's purview sometimes needed to be brought to the attention of district-level authorities. For example, the committees would refer wide-ranging issues, such as MVC not accessing free government-provided medical services despite having community health fund cards which proved eligibility.

The coaching process empowered MVC committee members, extension workers, and district staff to improve processes by providing guidance on use of the plan-do-study-act cycle and application of National QI Guidelines. The approach of bringing two or three teams together for joint coaching allowed teams to share experiences and solutions and learn from one another. It also created a healthy competition between teams. One team member from a village in Kiwangwa Ward acknowledged that their performance was low compared to the ward's other five teams, saying: *"We can't allow other villages to be on top of us, because we can also do that and make things better. Next time you visit us you will see changes in our team".*

The first coaching visits were held in June 2011, with visits conducted each month until July 2012. Visits were then conducted only for poorly performing teams as needed through June 2015.

One example of a successful knowledge exchange occurred when the Mkenge village team presented during the second coaching visit on how they were able to obtain birth certificates for all 13 MVC in the village. The birth certificate, a document critical to MVC, is used to access and enroll in educational and other services. The Fukayosi team learned from the presentation that relationships between village authorities and community members had been key to the success of the Mkenge team. By the time the third coaching visit took place in September 2011, about 4 months after starting improvement work, the Fukayosi team reported that, by mobilizing resources together with village authorities, they had obtained birth certificates for all 55 MVC in their village.

Second Learning Sessions for MVC Committees

In November 2011, 6 months after the first learning session was held, a second round of learning sessions gave teams a chance to share their progress and experiences with other communities. National and regional coaches from the DSW, project, implementing partners, and the regional health management team facilitated the district learning session. Coaches from the district staff, with support and backup from national coaches, facilitated community-level learning sessions for the community level.

One of the learning sessions was focused on building the capacity of ward and district coaches to provide regular technical assistance to QI teams. The session offered opportunities to talk about implementation experiences, review teams' progress, and share strategies.

A 2-day learning session held at each ward for the MVC committees and ward coaches allowed teams to present on goals, actions taken, results, and challenges. The session's objectives were to engage teams in analyzing and implementing actions for change and to facilitate sharing challenges and successes according to their priority areas. Teams prepared progress reports on achievements, key changes implemented, challenges faced, and ways in which they overcame them. In addition, teams requested guidance from peers and coaches on obstacles which they had not yet surmounted.

Teams learned ways of improving care from listening and talking to each other. The friendly competition between villages (described above under Support for Improvement Teams) resulted in the Fukayosi team producing another improvement. The team became motivated to use the project's documentation tool after listening to how the Mkenge team was using it to update data and record key priorities. The Fukayosi team began to document all activities, including communication faith-based organizations and village authorities. They also started to use a counter book to record meeting activities in case they were unable to access the documentation tool.

Results

The collective results of the village teams are shown in Fig. 10.2.

Sustaining Improvements and Spread

Six months after the three initial wards started work in October 2011, MVC committees in six new wards were trained in quality improvement and began implementation. In July 2012, an additional 13 wards were added, leading to full coverage of Bagamoyo District. By the end of 2012, all 22 wards were participating in learning sessions and receiving coaching visits. These newly trained MVC committees were able to quickly adopt and implement the successful change ideas from the initial demonstration sites.

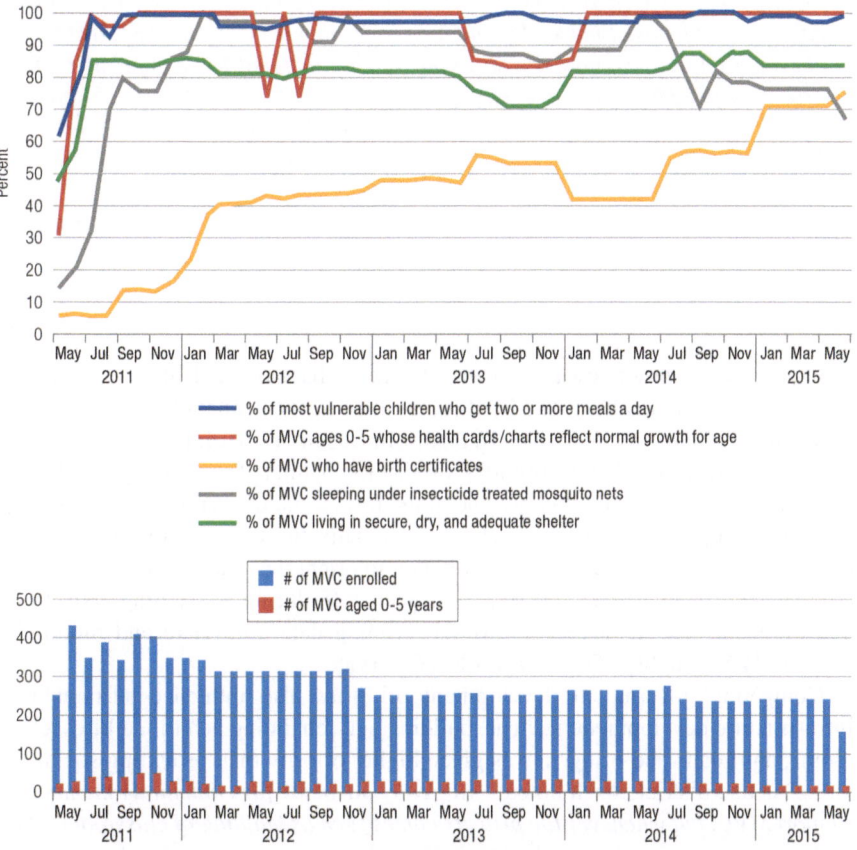

Fig. 10.2 Results from five indicators monitored by QI teams

Challenges

Coaches and MVC QI teams faced an ongoing challenge of turnover among team members. Because this work was done on a voluntary, unpaid basis, committees and coaches often found that members' own activities and work took precedence. Sometimes, team members had relocated. Some teams broke up, and the village authority had to assemble new teams. Ward coaches regularly checked on the teams' performance as part of their ongoing supervisory duties, even when they were in the village for other reasons. Three teams had to be reorganized with only one or a few of the original members remaining. Coaches and team members then faced the challenges of transferring knowledge to and developing improvement skills in new team members. These changes often happened at the same time as leadership changes at the village level, especially when new leaders were not aware of how to carry the work forward.

> *Myself I always visit villages for different work related to education, on the cause of that I make time to chat out with some members whom I will meet and checking on the progress. For example, during the visit I was informed one girl was forced to a marriage, left school at standard 6, and she was 15 years. I had two strategies with the QITs, where a visit to family was done, and we had to send the representative of QITs with the police. ... All things went well and this child is back to school. And I have assigned one teacher to continue to provide psychosocial support to this girl so that she become normal with school life.* Ward Education Coordinator, Bagamoyo

One example shows how a team was able to get back on track after losing all but one of its original members. The MVC committee in one hamlet of Dunda Ward had been rated as the most effective of 16 teams. In December 2014, the team collapsed; at the same time, new leadership took over at the hamlet. These changes led to the formation of a new team with only one of the former members remaining. The team requested support from ward coaches, specifically the Community Development Officer and the Ward Education Coordinator, to orient the new members in QI. Five months later, in June 2015, DSW and project staff, during a coaching visit, found that the team had effectively recovered: keeping data up-to-date and mobilizing 335,000 TZS (roughly 150 USD) for MVC services.

Competing government development priorities also influence sustainability. Infrastructure development, such as, building and rebuilding health facilities, class-rooms, and roads and bridges, was given higher priority than providing social ser-vices. As one district coach noted: *"We really advocate for community members to support MVC, but whenever the priority comes such as building of classroom all the directions change ... also our budget is limited compared to priorities".*

Reflection

Reflection from Team Members

Team members reported that working with community leaders and government institutions, such as village authorities and schools, helped teams reach their goals. The village chairperson successfully exercised influence to bring support through advocacy activities. The village executive officers also helped guide teams to plan and implement changes.

> *If the community is involved to know the problem facing it, it can cooperate to help to overcome that problem. For example, we are now aware of the vulnerable children, they were there before but we didn't care. But we have been empowered and sensitized. We are confident and ready to continue with what [the project] has facilitated.*
>
> QI team member, Bagamoyo

Teams acknowledged that ongoing capacity building provided through learning sessions and coaching led members to reach a consensus and share understanding about the approaches and actions to take to provide quality MVC services. Members reported that capacity building efforts were motivational. When asked for one action they would have done differently, team members shared that they would have, from the project's beginning, engaged ward councilors in meetings or coaching sessions. Although councilors had not been fully engaged in early activities, they had proven key to the improvement effort. Because they serve as decision makers and approve budgets for the district council, they provided invaluable guidance in how resources could be effectively allocated to MVC and caregivers.

Reflection from the Author

The work of this collaborative demonstrates how an MVC committee, whose members are well trained, can effectively apply service standards to improve the quality of MVC services. The introduction of improvement approaches engaged existing MVC committees to function as improvement teams and motivated and empowered them to address gaps in meeting national standards. QI activities equipped team members with the knowledge and skills needed to provide quality services to vulnerable children. In addition, MVC committees began collaborating with other stakeholders to provide services that would meet priority needs. A critical lesson the MVC committees learned was that involving families and caregivers in providing and coordinating care is critical to effective delivery of MVC services. This concept was spread to other districts beyond Bagamoyo.

Frequent external coaching, especially from district officials, motivated members to continue to be actively engaged in continuing to work to improve MVC services. Teams found that coaching and involving local leaders, teachers, and community development officers were key to supporting teams to translate standards into practice.

As teams collected data and analyzed indicators related to specific service standards, they developed a deeper understanding of the standards. Coaches encouraged MVC committees to reflect on their achievements in order to instill in them the confidence to reevaluate and modify plans when goals were not being reached. In addition, coaches found creative ways to provide guidance, such as comparing indicator performance to routine occurrences, to explain more complex QI areas. For example, they might ask: "If your child received a 0 out of 10 on an exam, would that be good? Likewise, you don't want a child to receive 0 out of 10 services". Eventually, MVC committee members were able to use indicators to assess their performance and, in turn, present data to advocate for resources. MVC committees disaggregated data by sex and age, which facilitated provision of improved services that corresponded with the needs of individual children. This approach was started in Bagamoyo and spread to all teams.

> *Services have very much improved and the QI teams are working hard to provide services to vulnerable children. They follow up vulnerable children to make sure they get all necessary services. The communities didn't recognize the importance of birth certificates but now they do. The QI teams also know the importance of data for decision making and planning. They know how many MVC they have, how many have been helped to get certain services, and how many still need services.* District Officer, Bagamoyo

Results produced by the demonstration sites showed that educating, sensitizing, and raising community awareness is a necessary first step in generating a positive response to improving the quality of programs. MVC committees led efforts to educate and sensitize other community members, including leaders, about the community's responsibility in supporting vulnerable children. Ward and district coaches needed to regularly follow up and encourage accurate and complete documentation and generate sharing of changes and best practices.

The experience of the MVC collaborative improvement initiative showed the importance of including and engaging community leaders in improvement processes. The Bagamoyo teams were at the forefront of the effort to ensure that the needs of vulnerable children were met and their rights recognized. Village chairpersons, not immediately recognizing their role and potential for contribution, were not initially involved in the effort. MVC committee members agreed that chairpersons should be included in all coaching visits in order to provide guidance on matters, such as community and resource mobilization. Thereafter, community leaders grew more active in participating in MVC committee meetings. The implementation of QI activities has facilitated the social welfare office to coordinate services with other council sectors during the planning process and to mobilize resources across sectors at the council level.

The MVC committees also enhanced public–private partnerships by engaging stakeholders, such as, shop owners, hotel owners, and farmers to support MVC to access various services. MVC committee members live in the communities they are serving, thus ensuring sustainability of improvement. The MVC committees, through learning sessions and coaching, acquired the skills and knowledge to plan and implement changes. Village authorities took active roles in supporting MVC committees, allocating resources, and involving community members in supporting vulnerable children. Coaches at the district and ward levels internalized the QI principles and guidelines which assisted them in planning technical support to MVC committees and ward and village authorities.

Acknowledgements The author expresses gratitude to Eveline Kamote, Principal Social Welfare Officer of the Ministry of Health and Social Welfare of Tanzania, and to Sayuni Hizza, District Social Welfare Officer, Bagamoyo. Jared Mussanga, QI Advisor, and Kim Stover, Senior Improvement Advisor, of University Research Co., LLC both contributed in important ways to improve the quality of services for most vulnerable children in Tanzania and the contents of this case. The activities described to improve the quality of services for most vulnerable children in Tanzania were made possible by the generous support of the American people through USAID and its Applying Science to Strengthen and Improve Systems (ASSIST) Project, managed by University Research Co., LLC under Cooperative Agreement Number AID-OAA-A-12-00101.

Chapter 11
Improving the Quality of Voluntary Medical Male Circumcision: A Case Study from Uganda

John Bekiita Byabagambi

Abstract Voluntary medical male circumcision (VMMC) is an intervention that has the potential to significantly reduce HIV transmission in Uganda. Modeling estimates suggest that if implemented to reach a coverage of 80% of males aged 15–49 years, it would prevent 300,000 new HIV infections between 2011 and 2025. But to reach such an outcome, services need to be of high quality, meeting and exceeding minimum quality standards. This case study describes the journey of 30 pilot health units in Uganda to address gaps in VMMC service delivery and the kind of support that they received. The 30 health units consisted of 29 health facilities and one mobile van, spread across all regions of Uganda. They represented high-volume sites chosen by USAID's 10 VMMC implementing partners—three sites chosen by each implementing partner. The case describes how baseline assessments were conducted to identify quality gaps and how quality improvement (QI) teams were trained and organized at each site to make changes in care processes and track their results through the review of client forms and registers. The case presents the results achieved across the 30 sites and describes how the key learning from these sites was shared with new sites which in turn improved care at an even faster rate, due the knowledge transferred about successful practices to improve VMMC service quality.

Keywords Coaching · Continuous quality improvement · Learning sessions · Quality assessment · Safe male circumcision · Scale-up · Uganda · Voluntary medical male circumcision

Background and Setting

Voluntary medical male circumcision (VMMC), also known in Uganda as safe male circumcision (SMC), was approved as one of the HIV prevention interventions by the World Health Organization (WHO) and UNAIDS in 2007 and added by the

J. B. Byabagambi (✉)
John Snow Inc., (formerly with University Research Co., LLC in Uganda),
Pretoria, South Africa

© University Research Co., LLC 2020

L. R. Marquez (ed.), *Improving Health Care in Low- and Middle-Income Countries*, https://doi.org/10.1007/978-3-030-43112-9_11

Ministry of Health (MOH) of Uganda as part of its comprehensive HIV prevention strategies in 2010. VMMC reduces by 60% the transmission of HIV from an HIV-positive female to an HIV-negative male (WHO 2007). VMMC involves removal of the foreskin along with health education of clients, especially on the need for the continued use of other HIV prevention methods, such as condom, because the procedure is not 100% protective.

VMMC has the potential to significantly reduce HIV transmission in Uganda. If implemented to reach a coverage of 80% of males aged 15–49 years (4.2 million circumcisions by the end of 2015), it would prevent 300,000 new HIV infections between 2011 and 2025 (Njeuhmeli et al. 2011). But to reach such an outcome, services need to be of high quality, meeting and exceeding minimum quality standards.

Before 2013, VMMC programming in Uganda was focused on meeting the 80% coverage target; quality issues were not given much consideration. In 2012, an external quality assessment conducted by the United States' President's Emergency Plan for AIDS Relief (PEPFAR) brought to the attention of the country quality gaps in VMMC service delivery, some of which needed immediate remediation. Among them were: use of general anesthesia as opposed to the WHO recommendation of using only local anesthesia, lack of standardized client data collection and reporting tools, and poor preparedness for management of adverse events, should they occur. Health facilities that were found to have severe deficits in meeting the expected standards were advised to suspend VMMC service delivery until the gaps that needed immediate remedies were fixed.

USAID, one of the major funders of VMMC service providers operating in Uganda, requested that a USAID improvement technical assistance project already operating in Uganda provide technical support to the MOH and to 10 implementing partners and the health units they supported with supplies and training, to address the identified gaps. USAID agreed to support a pilot collaborative improvement activity aimed at addressing the main VMMC service quality gaps initially in a selection of 30 sites and later scaled up to over 150 health units being funded by USAID to deliver VMMC services in Uganda.

This case study describes the journey of the 30 pilot health units to address gaps in VMMC service delivery and the kind of support that they received. The 30 health units consisted of 29 static health units and one mobile van, spread across all regions of the country. They represented high-volume sites chosen by USAID's 10 VMMC implementing partners—three sites chosen by each implementing partner. The static health units included three regional referral hospitals, 15 general hospitals (100–200-bed-capacity hospital), eight health center IVs (50-bed-capacity health unit with a surgical theater mainly for obstetric emergencies), two health center IIIs (10-bed capacity, with maternity services but no operating surgical theater), and two health center IIs (day care health unit). Of the 30 health units, 18 were public, six military, and six private not-for-profit.

Developing and Applying a Locally Adapted VMMC Quality Assessment Tool

After the external quality assessment, the implementing partners and health units complained that the tools used in the external assessment were for high-income countries and not appropriate for a low-income country like Uganda, and therefore they were assessed against standards which were not applicable to their sites. As such, they did not own the findings.

To address the complaint related to the assessment tools, the MOH called a meeting of VMMC stakeholders that included the implementing partners, the technical support project, and PEPFAR in-country team representatives in January 2013 to chart a way forward. The meeting reviewed the tools used and agreed to revise them and align them to existing MOH policies and guidelines.

A smaller team led by the MOH and including the technical support project and implementing partners was tasked with developing a VMMC quality assessment tool aligned to the Ugandan setting. The process of aligning the tool involved reviewing the external assessment tool section by section, identifying areas which were addressed by other existing guidelines so as to harmonize them and avoid creating new guidance and at the same time maintaining the expected standards of care. The revised tool was piloted at five sites to determine the usability and ability to collect the intended information. In January and February 2013, several meetings were convened by the MOH, involving VMMC stakeholders such as service providers, implementing partners, and MOH departments, to gain feedback on the revised tool. Comments gained through these meetings were incorporated in the drafts by the team that reviewed the tool as the drafts went through the three levels of approval at the MOH.

Owing to the fact that the process of addressing quality gaps could not be delayed, after getting and incorporating feedback from the various stakeholder meetings, the MOH agreed to go ahead and use the draft tool to conduct baseline quality assessments, while the final tool went through the full MOH approval process to adopt it as the national MOH VMMC tool. The MOH-led National VMMC Task Force eventually approved the tool with minor amendments in May 2013.

Each of the 10 implementing partners was requested to identify three sites that were high volume to be part of the improvement collaborative. The plan was that the technical assistance project would jointly work with the partners and staff at these three health units and that the implementing partner would spread the learning to the rest of their VMMC sites. A schedule for conducting baseline assessments at partner sites was agreed upon with each implementing partner to establish the baseline level of performance using the new tool developed in Uganda.

In each site, the baseline assessment was conducted by a team comprised of technical assistance project staff, implementing partner staff, a representative from the district health office, and site team members. Sometimes MOH staff were able to join the assessment teams. The implementing partners were given the responsibility of making appointments with the health facilities for onsite assessments. The

30 baseline assessments were conducted from March through May 2013 (Byabagambi et al. 2015).

On the day of the assessment, the assessment team started by meeting with the health facility in-charge and members of the VMMC team. Everyone on the assessment team introduced themselves as well as any members of the health unit present. Next, the assessment team leader explained the purpose of the visit and the format it would take. The team leader also usually gave a brief overview of the seven components of the assessment tool and explained the purpose of each section. The seven components were: (1) management systems; (2) supplies, equipment, and environment; (3) registration of clients and group education; (4) individual counseling sessions for HIV testing and for medical male circumcision; (5) VMMC surgical procedure; (6) monitoring and evaluation; and (7) infection prevention and control (including waste management). At this meeting, the team leader also mentioned that preliminary feedback would be provided to the facility and partners at the end of the assessment exercise. The leader of the assessment team made it a point to emphasize that the assessment was not a fault-finding mission but rather was an assessment conducted in good faith, aimed at identifying any gaps so that they can be jointly addressed. This information was very important because it reduced any resistance or allayed any fears that the health facility team had and thus improved their cooperation.

The facility team leader then described to the assessors the process of VMMC service delivery in that site so that they could have a clear understanding of how the service was organized and thus better plan for the assessment. The introductory meeting lasted only about 30 minutes to allow ample time for conducting the assessment, which itself could take 3–4 hours. Enough copies of the assessment tool would be prepared so that the technical assistance project, the health unit, the district health office, the implementing partner, and the MOH official each had their own copy and completed it with the same information to minimize the need for photocopying and to make the follow-up of action items easy.

During the assessment, the facility in-charge would assign a health unit staff member to guide the assessment team; this individual also actively participated in the assessment and was considered one of the assessors. In most cases, this was the technical person working with that section. Once a particular section was completed, the assessment team would give some immediate feedback to the person(s) responsible and leave them to continue with their work. This was done in such a way to ensure that respect and privacy for the client and service provider were maintained. As an example, if the service provider did not disaggregate waste at the time of generation (e.g., mixing glove wrappings with blood-soiled gauze), this feedback would be given immediately, so that the mistake is not repeated during the next surgical procedure. The assessment team would then move to assess another area. Once all sections were completed, a debriefing meeting, chaired by the site in-charge and led by the leader of the assessors, would be convened and a detailed feedback given to all the staff members who were able to attend the meeting.

For most of the baseline assessments, the assessment team assessed all sections of the clinic as one team. This was done because not many people were familiar with the use of the tool and also to avoid disagreements at the end of the assessment. The entire team would agree that the provider either met or did not meet a specific standard. This approach promoted ownership of the findings by the health facility team, the implementing partner, and the district health office. This helped to solve one of the complaints that had been raised about the external quality assessment: that some items were marked as missing yet they were present but the assessors did not see them.

At the end of each site assessment, the assessment team, together with the site staff, developed an action plan. This process lasted about 30 minutes to 1 hour and was done as part of the debriefing meeting. The action plan detailed the gaps identified, the intervention selected to fill the gap, the person responsible, and the timeline for implementing the intervention. For example, some gaps could be addressed by the site staff, such as ensuring that the team members were aware of various reference guidelines and policies. The representative from the district health office was very instrumental in addressing gaps related to missing supplies such as drugs that are supplied through the national medical stores, because the district had the power to redistribute drugs within the district, from a health unit that has excess to one that did not have enough. The district also was instrumental in supporting teams to make timely requisitions for supplies. The implementing partner was instrumental in addressing gaps that required procurement of some missing equipment for emergency preparedness and availability of other VMMC consumables such as surgical kits. The technical assistance project was instrumental in building the skills of the health facility staff in addressing gaps through training in the continuous quality improvement approach, onsite coaching and mentorship, as well as organizing learning sessions. The MOH was instrumental in supporting sites to acquire some items which are centrally procured, such as information and communication materials. Therefore, it was quite beneficial to have a team of assessors who could all contribute to addressing the gaps.

Organizing the Improvement Effort

Formation of Quality Improvement Teams

At the end of the assessment and as part of the development of the action plan, the team members were also guided through the process of forming a quality improvement (QI) team that would be at the forefront of addressing the gaps. At the debrief, the technical assistance project explained who should be on the team. The guidance for team formation mainly involved the composition, in which sites were advised to ensure all staff involved in VMMC were represented on the team. These included counsellors, data clerks, circumcisers, assistant circumcisers, community mobilizers, and cleaners.

In some instances, the site made decisions on the spot about who would make up the QI team. Others said they would meet in the next few days to decide. The team members were selected through consensus by the health unit staff. From amongst the team members, a team leader and a secretary were selected. Emphasis was made that the team leader does not necessarily have to be the health unit manager. Sites were advised that they could change the composition of the team if there was need.

During the assessments, it was noted that majority of the service providers were not familiar with the use of the continuous quality improvement approach. Therefore, after completing baseline assessments at all 30 sites, a training in the use of the continuous quality improvement approach was conducted by the technical assistance project and the MOH. Four members of each site team, including a circumciser, an assistant circumciser, a counsellor, and any other member of the team, were invited to attend the training in which they were taught how to make changes to service delivery processes using the continuous quality improvement approach to address the gaps. Owing to the large number of participants, the participants were split into three groups based on geographical location; three regional trainings were conducted, each lasting 3 days. The trainers were drawn from the MOH and the technical assistance project. The training covered the principles of QI and basic QI concepts such as identifying gaps, testing changes, and measuring improvement.

Choosing Improvement Priorities

On the third day of the QI training, the participants reviewed the findings of their baseline assessments and the action plans they had started at the baseline debrief to determine what gaps were still outstanding since the completion of the assessment, to identify priority areas of focus for improvement. The priority areas were selected based on what was in the direct control of the site team, implementing partner, or district team. For instance, gaps such as lack of a functional QI team, no waste segregation, and incomplete records were prioritized as opposed to gaps that needed external support, such as missing policy documents or equipment and the need to train staff on how to conduct circumcision. Each team was free to take on as much they could as long as they had the means to do so.

Development of Aims and Measures of Improvement

Participants selected improvement objectives both for the quality standards that mainly look at the work environment to ensure it is safe and for the processes of care that focus on individual clients. After agreeing on the improvement objectives, indicators to monitor performance on the objectives were developed.

As part of the QI training, the participants conducted a process mapping exercise in which they drew flow charts depicting the flow of events for a client who comes to the site for VMMC. Using the flow chart diagrams, they identified areas or activities in the VMMC care process where quality was likely to be compromised. Such activities included points where no uniform information was likely to be given out. For instance, some clients might not receive all the information given out during the group education session, or some clients might miss the session all together, and some clients might get to the theater without providing consent. In most cases these were points where an action needed to be taken by a service provider as a client moved from one point to another.

As part of the QI training, indicators to measure various process activities were developed, drawing on the technical assistance project's understanding of the main problem areas affecting VMMC services. These indicators included:

- HIV counseling and testing: proportion of VMMC clients who are counseled and tested and receive HIV test results.
- History taking and physical exam: proportion of VMMC clients who are screened for sexually transmitted infections prior to circumcision. Screening for sexually transmitted infections was used as a proxy for history taking and physical exam because it was a major gap at the majority of the sites.
- Provision of informed consent: proportion of circumcised clients with documented informed consent prior to circumcision.
- Surgical procedure: proportion of circumcised clients who experience moderate or severe adverse events.
- Postoperative care: proportion of circumcised clients who return for follow-up within 48 hours of circumcision.
- Postoperative care: proportion of circumcised clients who return for follow-up beyond 48 hours but within 7 days of circumcision.

The pilot sites participating in the improvement collaborative had two main ways of tracking improvement. First, improvement in compliance with quality standards (based on the assessment tool developed at the start of the activity) was measured using a color-coded dashboard that characterized performance as green (good), yellow (fair), or red (poor). After every assessment, scores were awarded to each standard, and a percentage computed based on how many standards the team got right out of the total number assessed. Along the way, the coaches noted that the scores were difficult to understand and the idea of developing a dashboard was borne. A score of less than 50% was coded red, signifying poor performance; above 50% to below 80% was coded yellow, signifying fair performance; and 80% or more was coded green, signifying good performance. A dashboard template already with preprinted colors was used to display the findings at site level. If for instance a site scored 85% in management system, a mark (X) would be made in the green section of the template. This template was used because color printing services were not available at the sites.

The second way of tracking improvement was through measuring care processes within VMMC service delivery using the indicators that were developed at the first quality improvement training. Prior to starting the collaborative, there were no indicators monitored by the teams apart from tracking the number of clients circumcised. Initial support dwelled on guiding the teams to understand how to collect the data from individual client forms and transfer it into registers. Most sites were not used to this process and often compiled reports by collecting data from individual client forms as opposed to getting it from the register. Because many sites were not used to using registers, the technical assistance project developed a standard register. Service providers at each site were mentored on the process of getting the data from client forms on days when they worked on clients and transferring it to the registers. At the end of each month, a summary of data would be made in the register for each indicator.

Various records were kept to document the quality improvement work. At each site, teams maintained documentation journals which contained all the information about their improvement work. In these journals, teams recorded the changes that were tested to improve processes of care and the results achieved. During QI team meetings, the data for each indicator was abstracted from the summary in the register and transferred to documentation journals in order to be able to track improvement using line graphs. The abstraction of data was done by the team members themselves. Each of the six indicators had a separate journal. Since the indicators were many, at some sites a specific team member was assigned the task of collecting data for a particular indicator and sharing the information with the rest of the team members during QI team meetings. At other sites this was done jointly during the QI meetings. External coaches would verify the data collected by the teams during coaching visits to ensure accuracy and completeness. For some indicators, such as client follow-up, this was done by taking a sample of some records if they were many or by looking at all the records if they were few. The coach would crosscheck the figures against the primary source documents (individual client forms). For indicators such as obtaining informed consent, this was done for all the individual records because it was easy to conduct and also because this indicator was of outmost importance.

Carrying Out the Improvement Effort

Development, Implementation, and Testing of Change Ideas

At one of the general hospitals, the team had a gap of poor client follow-up within 48 hours after circumcision. The team identified this gap through the analysis of their baseline data. The team reviewed data on the number of clients who were circumcised and compared it with how many of those returned for review within 48 hours as per the MOH guidelines. The team noted that 10/1201 (0.8%) clients circumcised in March 2013 and 8/1426 (0.6%) in April 2013 came back for review within 48 hours. The team was alarmed by these statistics.

The team discussed the reasons for this gap and noted several causes: service providers were not actually passing on information to the clients that they needed to return for review; some clients lived far away from the clinic and did not have money for transport to return 2 days later; and other clients could not afford to be away from work for another day within the same week. The team discussed these underlying causes to determine which problem affected the majority of the clients. After a thorough discussion that involved trying to understand what was the biggest cause of poor client follow-up, the team agreed that the bigger problem was inadequate information given to clients, leaving the majority of them with the option of not returning. The information given was not convincing enough to make clients who live far away or who cannot afford to be away from work for 2 days in the same week to return to the clinic. This discussion was facilitated by a coach. The main role of the coach was to ensure the discussion remained focused and logical, but the coach did not try to determine for the team the underlying cause of poor client follow-up.

The team agreed to change the information given to the clients. The team planned on how this change would be implemented. This included specifically mentioning that clients need to return as opposed to telling them to return only if they have a problem. The information would be given to all clients who are circumcised, and this was to be done at all service delivery points, starting from group education, during individual counseling, during the surgical procedure, and during postoperative care. The team tried out this change in May 2013, and when they analyzed their performance at the end of May, they had improved to having 619/1953 (32%) returning for review. The team was impressed by the result of their efforts but still they were not happy with 32%.

During the next coaching visit, the coach reviewed what the team had done and was also happy with the efforts of the team. In the same meeting, the team discussed ways of improving further. The staff member (part of the improvement team) who attended to the clients who returned for follow-up said that the majority of the clients who returned for review said it is because they want to have their bandage removed. The team agreed to add this to the information they gave to clients and changed the message from "come back if you have a problem" to "you need to come back for bandage removal and review." This led to further improvement, and by July 2013, 69% of the clients were returning for review.

Over the next 3 months, improvement leveled off. The team was invited to a learning session in August 2013, and while there, they further learned about the importance of improving documentation. They also noted that at their own site, some clients were returning for review, but this information was not recorded. The team decided to address the gap of ensuring that all clients who return are actually reviewed and their records updated to reflect that they indeed returned. A focal point for clients who return for follow-up was designated, and clients' forms for those who were recently circumcised placed at this point in a folder labeled 48-hour follow-up. When the team analyzed data for November, they noted that they had been underreporting client follow-up due to poor documentation because there was a 20% increment in performance. The team continued to monitor progress on this indicator and maintained the good performance, as shown in Fig. 11.1. Examples of changes that were tested by teams to improve this indicator are shown in Table 11.1.

Support for Improvement

After the QI training, every health unit was supported to improve the composition of the QI team they had formed at the end of the baseline assessment by building a team around the newly trained staff. The support involved working with service providers to identify who else should be on the improvement team to ensure that the team is fully functional and all sections of VMMC are well taken care of.

Since the main aim of the collaborative was improvement, the QI team members were trained on how to use the assessment tools in the absence of external coaches to conduct self-assessments on their own. Teams were encouraged to identify gaps

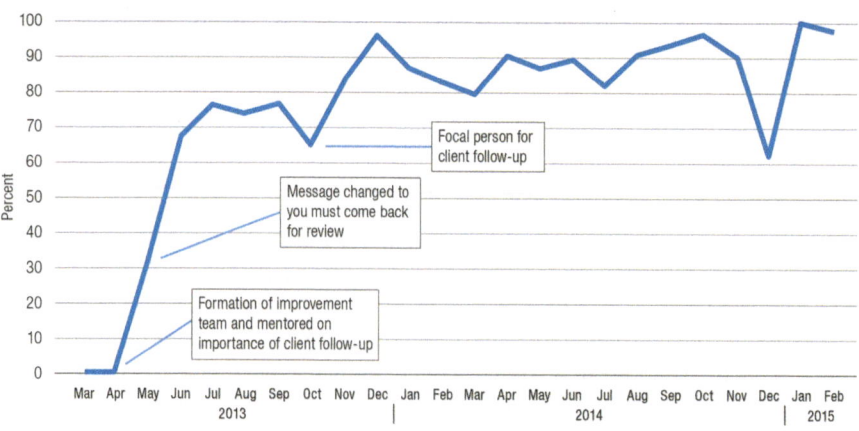

Fig. 11.1 Percentage of clients who return for follow-up within 48 hours at one general hospital

on their own and then make changes. During subsequent coaching visits, the external coaches would review the self-assessment findings, the changes being tested to establish if they are in line with the gaps identified, and then make amendments where necessary. On a quarterly basis, the coaches would conduct an objective assessment at each site.

The teams were visited once every month by a team of coaches from the technical assistance project, the district health office, and their assigned implementing partner who helped them to refine the changes that they were testing. During the coaching visits, the teams were supported to implement the interventions they had selected. The support included reviewing the changes being tested by the teams to ensure that they were aimed at addressing the identified gaps and that the teams were able to accurately measure the impact of the changes tested. For example, at one of the sites, the team had a problem of poor documentation of clients who return for review. This team was planning to use the members of the village health teams to remind clients to come for follow-up. Such a change would not solve their problem. In reality, the clients would return and be attended to, but no records were made to show that clients actually did come back. In such a situation, the coach would systematically analyze the problem with the team so as to ensure that the change being tested can logically address the gap. They were also supported to plot their data and make decisions based on this data through analyzing the trends of the graphs. The analysis was made simple by merely looking at the trend of the graph to determine whether there is improvement depending on the type of indicator. For the majority of the indicators, such as client follow-up and obtaining consent, improvement was shown by a graph that had an ascending trending toward 100%. For adverse events, improvement was shown by a trend that was descending toward 0%. This support involved providing them with documentation journals and mentoring them in their use. In addition to using the documentation journals, some sites opted to plot their performance on flip charts which would be hung on the wall, so that all team members could easily visualize the team's performance.

Table 11.1 Illustrative changes tested by pilot sites to improve client follow-up within 48 hours

Change tested and number of sites which tested	How exactly was change tested/implemented (where, who, how, when)?
Giving clients information on the importance of 48-hour follow-up and to come for bandage removal at 48 hours *Number of sites testing the change: 20*	Teams held a meeting and discussed the information package for follow-up at 48 hours using the counseling guide (key points for the importance of 48-hour follow-up were discussed and agreed upon, such as bandage removal, assessment of wound healing) and changed the information that was originally being given to clients of telling them to come back only in case of complications
	Assigned staff roles to deliver this information to clients at all services points
	Other sites agreed on task sharing by staffs to ensure all staff members give this information at all service points: At group education, at individual counseling, during physical assessment, on the operating table, and at postoperative health education
	During group education, counselors used the standardized information and education and communication materials and at immediate postoperative care used the postoperative instruction leaflet to give information
	The staff at all the service points delivered the information
	During mobilization drives in the community, information was provided by counselors on the importance of a 48-hour follow-up
	Checklist of postoperative instructions with information on follow-up at 48 hours was designed by team and is used to give information to clients
Allocating a staff member to conduct and document follow-up at 48 hours *Number of sites that tested the change: 8*	Team held a meeting and identified a staff member who was assigned the role of conducting follow-up
	Team developed a duty roster to show assigned staff on duty to conduct follow-up each clinic day
	Assigned staff were oriented on the process of follow-up and its documentation by the QI team leader
	Team scheduled the follow-up visits in the morning hours
	Team identified a place through the administration where to conduct follow-up and a staff who would conduct the follow-up from the theater and document the follow-up
Sending text messages and making telephone calls to clients to remind them to come for 48-hour follow-up *Number of sites testing the change: 5*	Client contacts or for next of kin is captured in the register by an assigned receptionist
	Team budgeted for airtime allowance with the implementing partner following discussions
	Agreed on bulk short message services by a contracted service provider who sends short messages to clients immediately after circumcision. This is done twice a day
	Telephone calls are made to clients who do not return after short messages being sent to them by the in-charge. The telephone has been provided by the implementing partner
Giving appointment date for 48-hour follow-up on the appointment card given to clients *Number of sites testing the change: 6*	During the team meeting, discussed the importance of writing the follow-up date on the appointment cards and issuing the cards to clients
	Cards are filled and issued by counselors at registration and at immediate postoperative care points at other sites
	Importance of keeping the follow-up appointments is re-enforced at the postoperative care point by staff

A coaching guide was developed to aid the on-site coaching visits. The guide was developed based on the experience gained in developing such guides for other technical areas. The guide went through various iterations, and the current version captures information about the improvement team composition, any changes in membership of the team, what actions the team took between coaching visits such as inquiring if the team met in the absence of external coaches, and, if yes, if any documentation was made. The coaching guide also gathered information on changes that the team planned to test and what impact they made on processes of care, whether the implementing partner and district health official were present during the coaching visit, and if the district health office was given a report after the coaching visit. It also summarized the key findings from the coaching visit and the action plan for addressing the identified gaps.

Three months after completion of the baseline assessment, four members of each improvement team were invited to attend the first learning session. Owing to the fact that the 30 teams were too numerous to convene in one learning session, they were grouped into three based on geographical proximity to each other. The learning session lasted 3 days, in which teams shared their performance.

On the first day of the learning session, the teams shared their performance on quality standards. This was done through summarizing their performance on flip charts that stated the gap, the changes tested, and the results achieved. The site's dashboard was also presented comparing the baseline and current performance to depict the improvement that has been achieved. Because many sites did not have access to color printers, the technical assistance project coaches gathered the dashboard information from the sites prior to the learning session and printed them.

On the second day of the learning session, the teams shared performance on client-level process indicators. Whereas every attempt was made to give each site an opportunity to present, due to the many indicators and an average of 10 teams attending the learning session, the coaches reviewed each site's presentation and identified those that should be given priority to present. These included the worst and best performers for each indicator. The worst performers were selected to present so that they share their challenges and get peer support, while the best performers were selected to present so that they share with all participants what enabled them to achieve the good results. If time allowed, other teams were given the opportunity to present after the worst and best performers. The presentation was basically a time series chart on a flip chart (very few sites had PowerPoint presentations), showing the changes tested and the impact of each tested change on each indicator.

The third day was used to conduct a refresher training in quality improvement for people who were already trained and for some new members if it was their first QI training session. Improvement areas of focus were also identified for the next implementation period. As the teams presented, the coaches took note of the common gaps with compliance with the standards and process indicators, and these were shared with the entire group. These formed the basis of selection of improvement focus areas, without forgetting site-specific gaps. Still on the third day, the coaches provided the teams with technical updates as well addressed common gaps.

Learning sessions were supposed to be conducted quarterly, but for some quarters they were not conducted because based on the coaching visits, the teams were not ready for them. Learning sessions were convened when there was a need. During their visits, if coaches noted that not many new changes had emerged during the implementation period and all the teams seemed to be at the same level of performance with no very good or very poor site, they would put off the learning session until there was value in bringing teams together. Therefore learning sessions were held when there was need as opposed to having them according to a fixed quarterly schedule.

During coaching visits and learning sessions, whenever coaches shared experiences from other sites, several team members expressed the need for having onsite exchange visits to see in person how other teams were performing and organizing processes of care. Exchange visits were therefore conducted for some teams by either taking staff from well-performing sites to struggling sites, or vice versa. The exchange visit pairing was based on identifying two teams in the same region (due to cost and time) with one of them performing well on a given indicator or standard and the other performing poorly on the same indicator or standard. In most cases it was one or two members from the well-performing site that went to the poorly performing site. This was because the one or two individuals would be able to support an entire team as opposed to transporting the entire poorly performing team to the well-performing site. This not only motivated the well-performing team but was also cheaper in terms of cost.

Not all teams participated in the exchange visits, as this was an activity based on need. The weaker teams that participated in the exchange visits reported that the visits were quite useful and helped them learn how to solve some gaps which they initially thought were unsolvable.

Results

Figure 11.2 shows the performance of the 30 pilot sites on quality standards. It shows that over time, the sites reduced the number of standards that scored poor (red) and fair (yellow). By October 2013, all the sites had no standards scored as poor. The number of standards that scored fair was also gradually reduced.

Sustaining and Scaling Up the Improvement Effort

Right from the start, institutionalizing the continuous quality improvement approach in the VMMC program was a top priority. The main plan was to transfer the skills to the frontline health workers, to the district-based public health officers whose day-to-day work was to provide support to health facilities through supervision, to regional coaches, and to implementing partner staff at the national level. At the health unit level, the establishment of QI teams was done based on the guidance in the National Quality Improvement Framework and Strategic Plan developed by the MOH. Service providers were mentored on how to collect client information using standardized tools and report it through the national system.

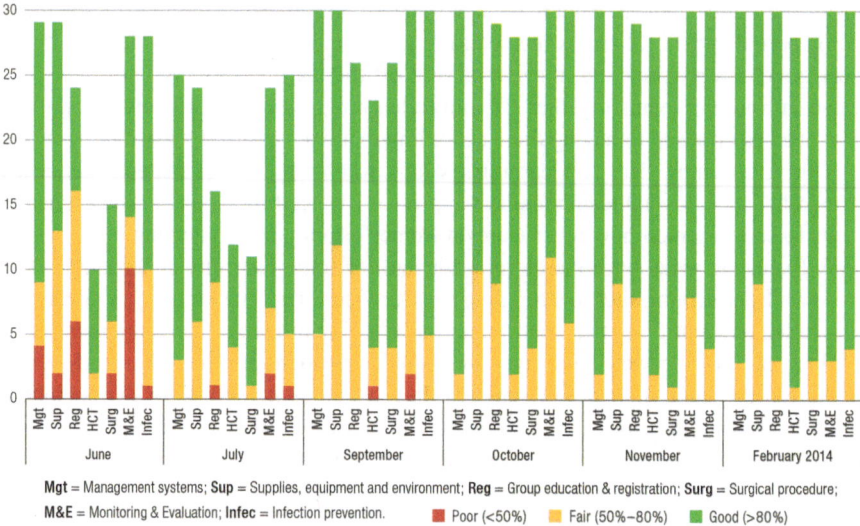

Mgt = Management systems; **Sup** = Supplies, equipment and environment; **Reg** = Group education & registration; **Surg** = Surgical procedure;
M&E = Monitoring & Evaluation; **Infec** = Infection prevention.   ■ Poor (<50%)   ■ Fair (50%–80%)   ■ Good (>80%)

Fig. 11.2 Performance of the 30 sites on the seven MOH VMMC quality areas

At the start of the VMMC QI work, sites never used to report their performance data through the MOH health management information system, but rather, the implementing partner would pick up the information from the site. This was not sustainable because in the absence of the implementing partner, there was a risk that the information might not be reported. The support involved mentoring the site teams on how to collect the data using standard MOH reporting tools and completing the tools through submission to the district.

Health units were supported to integrate requisitions for VMMC supplies into the national system. At first, the majority of the sites would not include the needs of the VMMC clinic in the health facility's drug order because they were used to the implementing partner bringing the supplies, and they would just sit back and wait for whatever amount the health unit would consume. For example, the VMMC clinics use a lot of paracetamol for pain management and, therefore, need to order for amounts that are over and above the average monthly consumption of the health facility. If this is not done, the health units will soon run out of paracetamol before its time to make the next order which for majority of health units is once every 2 months. The support involved mentoring the teams on how to estimate the required supplies, monitor supplies using the standard MOH stock cards, and integrate them into the health unit supplies. This was aimed at ensuring that the steady supply of consumables would continue beyond the period of the implementing partner's support.

At the district level, staff from the district health office were supported to join all the site-based activities so that they would acquire QI and coaching skills so that they would go to coach and where possible mentor the teams at VMMC sites. To achieve this, all planned activities were jointly conducted with the district staff, starting with the baseline assessments. The district health officer was requested to identify one person from their team who would participate in the VMMC baseline assessment. This was also aimed at promoting district ownership of the improvement activity. The district staff participated in the baseline assessments and contributed to the development of action plans. They were also invited to attend and actively participated in the monthly onsite coaching sessions. This was aimed at building their coaching skills. They also attended the QI training that was organized for service providers in addition to attending the learning sessions. The district staff welcomed the idea of the joint onsite activities because this helped them build their skills, and they also used the opportunity to look at other activities beyond VMMC. In some districts, there was a challenge of being given a new person every month which made it difficult to do the mentorship. In some districts, some of the people selected by the district health office were not popular with the site teams, and this slowed down the mentorship.

At the regional level, coaches were trained and were supported to join improvement activities. For most of the regions, the existing regional coaches were oriented on VMMC continuous quality improvement, while for other regions which had very few existing regional coaches, new ones were identified and trained. At the national level, staff of the AIDS Control Program and Quality Assurance Department were actively engaged in baseline and subsequent reassessments, onsite coaching visits, learning sessions, and QI trainings. This was aimed at building their skills and knowledge so that they would transfer the knowledge and skills to all the districts and health units which the technical assistance project was not supporting.

The VMMC national task force of the MOH was supported to convene oversight meetings in which issues related to the quality of VMMC were discussed. The support involved providing a venue for the meeting, inviting participants to the meeting, and providing stationery and supplies needed to have a successful meeting. Whereas it was the desire of the MOH to convene the task force meetings quarterly, it had taken over 1 year without a meeting prior to the support provided by the technical assistance project.

Prior to the collaborative, there was a stand-alone, implementing partner-led reporting system which would not survive if at all the implementing partners stopped supporting the health units. Moreover, not all VMMC sites were reporting through this system. With MOH leadership, standardized tools for reporting client information were developed. These included client forms, theater register, and client card; these forms were later integrated in the national health management information system. The purpose of this was to institutionalize the process supporting improvement. The VMMC quality assessment tool used to conduct the baseline assessment was adopted by the MOH as a standard tool for the assessment of VMMC quality standards and is now used to identify quality gaps within all sections of VMMC which are then addressed by the improvement teams. In July 2016, the MOH adopted all six VMMC process indicators in the District Health Information System 2, for mandatory reporting to the district level.

Scaling Up VMMC QI Activities

Throughout the period of the collaborative, the implementing partners kept requesting for support to be provided to more sites. In May 2014, 19 more sites were brought on board bringing the total number of supported sites to 49. The

implementing partners were again requested to identify two new sites to join the
second phase of the collaborative. Once again, the sites selected were high-volume
and those with gaps. The implementing partners had already conducted assessments
at these sites, so they were in a better position to identify the sites that were in most
need for this support.

Figure 11.3 shows the percentage of clients who returned for follow-up at the
pilot sites and scale-up sites. It shows that the pilot sites took more time to get 80%
of the clients returning for review, while the scale-up sites took a shorter period.
This is attributed to the spread of knowledge from the old sites to the new sites and
to the experience the coaches had gained.

Spreading the Knowledge

From the work done by the first 30 teams, several documents were developed summarizing the learning that had taken place. These included a list of changes tested to
improve the quality of SMC in Uganda. This document was shared with all the new
sites so that they could learn from what the old teams had done. The new teams were
also trained in application of the continuous quality improvement approach.

Several case studies were developed from the work done by the first 30 sites and
shared with the new teams. Improvement team members from old sites were asked to
join some coaching visits to the new sites so that they could share their experience in
starting the improvement work. A learning session was conducted in which both old and
new teams were invited to share experiences. The new teams were the first to present
their work, followed by the old teams. One of the key messages passed on by the old

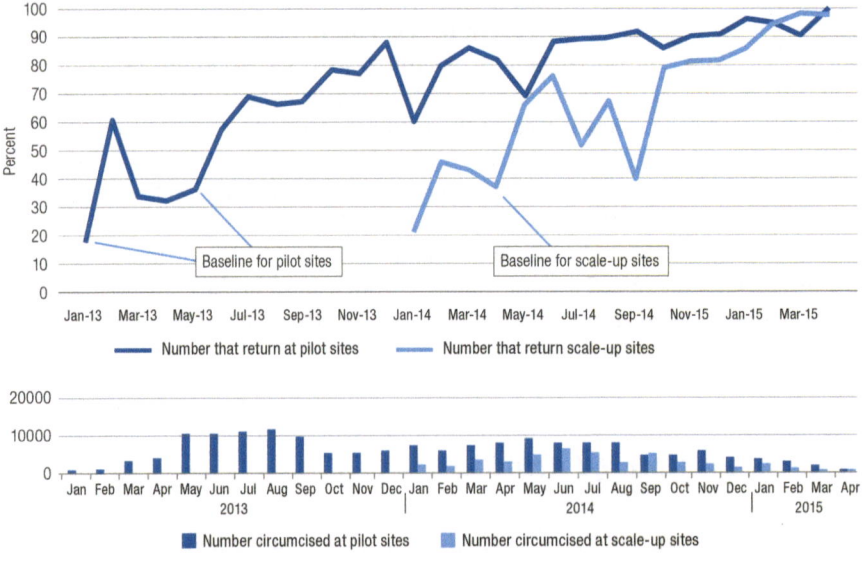

Fig. 11.3 Client follow-up at 48 hours for pilot and scale-up sites

teams to the new teams was the importance of regularly summarizing their performance data on each day of VMMC and a monthly basis to avoid a backlog. The old team members shared experiences of improving specific indicators as well as getting started.

Reflection

Author's Perspective

Looking back, I say what an interesting journey this was albeit with lots of challenges and learning on my side. The most challenging period was at the start of the collaborative when all stakeholders were skeptical of each other. Ministry of Health was alarmed by the findings from the external assessments as were the implementing partners. The implementing partners thought [the technical assistance project] had come to police them and report them to their funders and as such they did not fully cooperate at the start. My best lesson was that we need to include all key stakeholders in the planning of the improvement collaborative. The initial plan for this collaborative was done without the implementing partners, and this resulted in resistance that made us lose some time. It is important to identify key stakeholders and include them in the planning, define the roles of each, and be open and transparent. We should be prepared to change our plans as need arises.

–John Byabagambi

Implementing Partner Perspective

It gives [Ugandan faith-based organization] great joy to see the success [the hospital] has registered in providing quality SMC services despite the gaps and challenges identified at the baseline assessment. The continuous QI mentorship, support and training that was conducted by [the technical assistance project] and involving us at all stages has been an excellent learning experience that enabled us to internalize and adopt the QI approaches even beyond [the hospital]. Each site is quite unique but once the principles of QI are followed, it can create a positive change as demonstrated at [the hospital]. The mentorship and support has been continuous and allowed the actual implementers suggest and test solutions to see their results. The involvement of top leadership of both the implementing partner and the site as demonstrated by both [Ugandan faith-based organization] and [the hospital] has been invaluable. Great thanks to USAID for the funds provided to facilitate the process and to [the technical assistance project] for the QI technical support provided to [Ugandan faith-based organization]. With the lessons learnt we will continue to support [the hospital] and all other sites to improve the quality of services being provided to the clients.

–Clinical Services Specialist, [Ugandan faith-based organization]

Site Perspective

The counselor offering individual counseling admitted to hurriedly going through the post-test counseling messages and was mainly focusing on HIV test results. She was not recapping the advantages/benefits of SMC to the client because she was worried about the long waiting time for the whole SMC exercise. After the QI training, the counselor was able to develop and use a checklist to guide her during the posttest counseling session; she noted that there were a lot of issues that are not clear to the SMC clients during the group health education which she had to address in the individual session. She has also learnt that sometimes she may forget some key talking points and that's why it's important to stick to the checklist, however experienced she may be.

–HIV Counseling Program Manager at one of the supported sites

Acknowledgments The work described in this case study was supported by various individuals for whom acknowledgment is due. Thanks are due to Anna Lawino, Jude Ssensamba, and Albert Twinomugisha, Improvement Advisors with the USAID Applying Science to Strengthen and Improve Systems (ASSIST) Project in Uganda, for the direct support they provided to the sites through onsite coaching and conducting learning sessions. Appreciation is due to Esther Karamagi-Nkolo (ASSIST Chief Party), Mirwais Rahimzai (former ASSIST Chief of Party), Humphrey Megere (former ASSIST Chief of Party), Pamela Marks (former ASSIST HIV Team Lead), and Rhea Bright (formerly ASSIST Improvement Specialist) for the technical oversight they provided to the ASSIST Uganda VMMC team. Finally but not least, acknowledgments are due to Jacqueline Calnan and Sheila Kyobutungi of USAID Uganda, Emmanuel Njeuhmeli of USAID Washington, and Barbara Nanteza and Alex Opio of the Ministry of Health Uganda for the technical oversight provided to the ASSIST Uganda VMMC team.

The VMMC QI technical assistance described in this case was supported by the USAID Office of Health Systems through the USAID ASSIST Project, implemented by University Research Co., LLC under Cooperative Agreement Number AID-OAA-A-12-00101.

References

Byabagambi J, Marks P, Megere H, Karamagi E, Byakika S, Opio A et al (2015) Improving the quality of voluntary medical male circumcision through use of the continuous quality improvement approach: a pilot in 30 PEPFAR-supported sites in Uganda. PLoS One 10(7):e0133369
Njeuhmeli E, Forsythe S, Reed J, Opuni M, Bollinger L et al (2011) Voluntary medical male circumcision: modeling the impact and cost of expanding male circumcision for HIV prevention in Eastern and Southern Africa. PLoS Med 8(11):e1001132. https://doi.org/10.1371/journal.pmed.1001132
WHO (2007) WHO/UNAIDS technical consultation. Male circumcision and HIV prevention: esearch implications for policy and programming—Montreux, 6–8 March. WHO Press, Geneva

Chapter 12
Integrating Gender to Improve HIV Services in Uganda

Taroub Harb Faramand

Abstract The Partnership for HIV-Free Survival (PHFS) was a regional initiative supported by the World Health Organization (WHO), the US President's Emergency Plan for AIDS Relief (PEPFAR), the US Centers for Disease Control and Prevention (CDC), and the U.S. Agency for International Development (USAID) that applied a quality improvement (QI) approach in a select number of demonstration sites in six countries to improve the prevention of mother-to-child transmission of HIV and increase HIV-free survival of exposed infants. The Ivukula Health Center was one of the chosen demonstration sites in Uganda, one of the six PHFS focus countries. This case study describes how the Ivukula Health Center QI team improved the quality of HIV services and applied the same QI methods to integrate gender considerations into the process improvements they tested. The case illustrates how engaging male partners and community members in improving care can play a critical role in improving health outcomes and discusses a generic approach to integrating gender considerations into any development activity.

Keywords Gender integration · Prevention of mother-to-child transmission of HIV · Retention in care · Uganda

Background

Gender is a critical component of improving healthcare quality because to improve healthcare quality for all, we have to identify and address gaps in quality between women and men and girls and boys. Data and experience show that clients, family and friends, communities, and health providers are all influenced by the culture they live in and by that culture's perspective on gender. Thus, a gender-sensitive approach

T. H. Faramand (✉)
WI-HER, LLC, Vienna, VA, USA
e-mail: tfaramand@wi-her.org

takes into account the different needs, constraints, and opportunities of women, men, girls, and boys and responds to them strategically in program design, implementation, and evaluation. Box 12.1 describes the generic steps in integrating gender considerations into any development activity.

Ivukula is a rural community located in Uganda's Namutumba District, with six sub-counties and a population of 254,000 people. Agriculture is the main economic activity in Ivukula, and 80% of farmers practice subsistence agriculture. The health center in Ivukula serves a catchment population of 45,000.

In early 2013, the Partnership for HIV-Free Survival (PHFS), a regional initiative supported by the World Health Organization (WHO), the US President's Emergency Plan for AIDS Relief (PEPFAR), the US Centers for Disease Control and Prevention (CDC), and the U.S. Agency for International Development (USAID), initiated work to prevent mother-to-child transmission of HIV and increase HIV-free survival. PHFS used a quality improvement (QI) approach in a select number of demonstration sites in each country to learn how to better organize care delivery; in Uganda, the Ivukula Health Center was one of the chosen demonstration sites.

Box 12.1 Steps in Gender Integration

Gender integration refers to strategies applied in activity assessment, design, implementation, and evaluation to take gender norms into account and to compensate for gender-based inequalities. Improvement approaches provide an effective framework to identify and address the different needs, constraints, and opportunities of men, women, girls, and boys, improving outcomes for all and closing gender-related gaps.

The six-step process listed below outlines how improvement teams can integrate gender in quality improvement activities and implementation:

- *Step 1:* Conduct a gender analysis to inform program design and implementation.
- *Step 2:* Collect and analyze sex-disaggregated and gender-sensitive data.
- *Step 3:* Identify gender-related gaps and issues and develop changes to test.
- *Step 4:* Implement and monitor gender-related changes over time to determine whether desired results are achieved.
- *Step 5:* Scale up effective changes to close gender-related gaps.
- *Step 6:* Document and share learning.

For more explanation, see *A Guide to Integrating Gender in Improvement*, available at https://pdf.usaid.gov/pdf_docs/PA00TC12.pdf

Organizing the Improvement Effort

Beginning the PHFS Pilot Effort

Uganda's Ministry of Health (MOH), in partnership with USAID-funded partners, launched PHFS in April 2013 at 22 facilities, including Ivukula, in six districts in Uganda. PHFS aimed to address its goal of preventing mother-to-child transmission of HIV and increasing HIV-free survival by ensuring HIV-positive mothers were identified and retained in care and treatment, promoting optimal infant feeding practices (in accordance with WHO Guidelines on HIV and Infant Feeding), and supporting HIV-positive mothers' overall health and nutrition – in effect, integrating HIV, well-baby, and nutrition services for mother-infant pairs.

The national team leading the PHFS initiative in Uganda identified, as an integral component of the project's primary goal, developing providers' capacity to identify and respond to gender-related gaps in services or programs.

Obtaining Local Buy-in

A USAID-funded project, with decades of experience in applying quality improvement approaches to improve health outcomes, was the implementing partner for PHFS in Uganda. For this work, the USAID-funded project planned a strategy that would include gender considerations as part of the pilot effort. To support gender integration, they brought on board technical advisors with significant experience and expertise in addressing gender concerns in health using quality improvement approaches.

As a first step, the USAID-funded project's senior gender advisor sought "buy-in" from the Namutumba district health officer. The senior gender advisor was aware that to ensure the long-term success of the project, this step had to be more than routine and perfunctory. She had to begin by sparking sincere enthusiasm among key players, officials, or other stakeholders, who were able to influence and impact others.

The senior gender advisor began her meeting with the Namutumba district officer by sharing how addressing gender can improve health outcomes. In an effort to directly address topics often avoided because of cultural norms, she raised subjects that might resonate with the district officer's cultural and professional experience. In particular, the senior gender advisor pointed out that men were often concerned that they would be made to feel guilty and responsible for poor health outcomes. She talked about how, instead, awareness about gender concerns might improve interpersonal communication and increase women and men's compliance with their healthcare regimens. During the meeting, the senior gender adviser encouraged the district officer to share his own concerns about implementing gender considerations into the QI process.

Honest and open conversation yielded results: When the district officer was given an opportunity to express his own vision for integrating gender to improve the district's health services, he grew enthusiastic about the possibility of significant results.

Formation of the QI Team

Based on the district officer's familiarity with and knowledge of the district's health centers, he and the senior gender officer selected the Ivukula facility to pilot the gender interventions.

In February 2013, the district officer recruited a district coach based on leadership skills, motivation, and interest. The district coach's role included working with the project's QI advisor to assemble clinic teams and launch the QI effort, conduct training sessions for clinic staff, provide coaching support, and offer guidance and mentoring to QI team members. In February 2013, the project's QI advisor conducted a QI training for the Namutumba district coach along with coaches selected from several other pilot districts.

Improvement work in the Ivukula facility started in February 2013, 2 months prior to the official launch of PHFS at all pilot sites. Before visiting the Ivukula facility to recruit a QI team, the USAID-funded project's QI advisor and the district coach planned how they would address possible reservations and concerns from the clinic staff. During the February visit, they explained QI principles to the clinic staff and listened as staff members cited an already heavy workload and expressed reservations about gender concerns and integrating a gender component in QI interventions. The district coach and the project's QI advisor were aware that frontline healthcare workers were likely to have concerns about trying to address long-standing gender issues and social norms—issues that they saw as intractable and beyond their responsibility as clinicians. They addressed the staff's concerns by helping them envision the potential results of putting gender-sensitive QI interventions into place.

Gradually, as concerns were aired, enthusiasm for the initiative began to grow and the staff began to recruit a team. The coach and QI advisor made it clear to the clinic staff that participation was entirely voluntary and those nominated could refuse their nomination. However, they found that the staff were excited and eager to participate.

The clinic staff chose a nine-member QI team from diverse parts of the clinic, including the maternity ward, laboratory, and outpatient clinic. As their leader, team members selected a clinical officer who was widely respected for her leadership skills and commitment to her clients. In addition, the clinic staff recommended that a male expert client and a mentor mother also join the QI team, to support with outreach and ensure that community and patient perspectives were represented on the team.

The expert client was a male HIV-positive patient successfully managing his care. He encouraged men to test, enroll in care, and support their female partners and babies who were in care. The mentor mother was an HIV-positive mother who had successfully prevented transmission of HIV to her baby by enrolling and keeping herself and her baby in care. Her role was to share her personal experience and encourage women to adhere to appointments and their HIV treatment regimen. In addition, the mentor mother encouraged women to involve their male partners in care. As initial incentives to participate on the improvement team, project staff provided the mentor mother and expert client with training on health education.

Training Heightens Staff Awareness of Gender Norms

The district QI coach and project QI advisor provided training on incorporating gender in the improvement approach for the Ivukula team in March 2014. Because the facility team was being asked to pioneer gender interventions, a substantial part of the training was devoted to helping clinic staff identify and address gender-related gaps that prevented attaining the desired outcomes. The training presented a version of the model for improvement with plan-do-study-act cycles adopted to focus on gender-specific QI interventions (Fig. 12.1).

Staff were trained to adhere to the "do no harm" principle to avoid causing harm to their patients. In quality improvement, the "do no harm" principle means that the changes implemented should never intentionally or unintentionally harm participants. To do this, it is vital to consider how a change idea will affect different groups of people—and whether it might harm one group. For example, staff were trained to always ask HIV-positive women if they wanted to invite their male partners to the

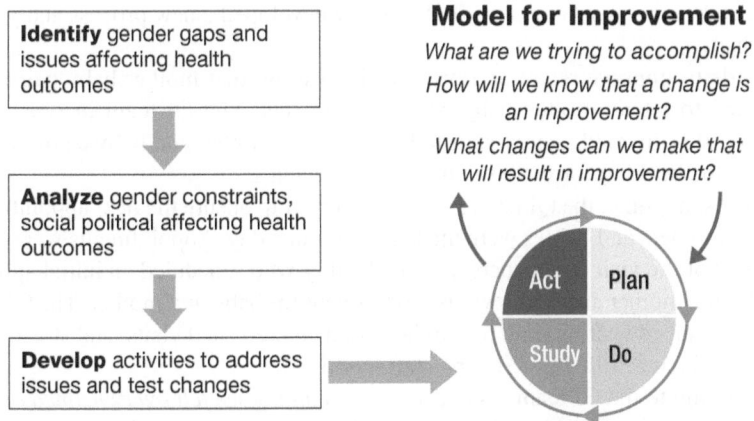

Fig. 12.1 Integrating gender within the model for improvement and plan-do-study-act cycles

facility because some women can be put at risk of partner violence if the clinic invites their male partners or discloses their HIV status against a patient's wishes.

Carrying Out the Improvement Effort

Problem Analysis

The Ivukula team initially focused on the quality of existing data on retention of mothers and their babies in care. The clinic QI team began an analysis of the services received by mothers and their infants by reviewing and analyzing the clinic's existing medical documents, which consisted primarily of "mother and baby cards" where staff recorded medical and appointment history.

The review revealed that babies and mothers were being seen separately by different providers, and their care was not linked. A large percentage of HIV-exposed infants had not been seen at the facility and were not being provided the care they should have been.

The team found logistical, operational, and administrative performance gaps that they wanted to address. One of the gaps, perhaps the most obvious, was a lack of care coordination due to the mother and baby cards being stored in separate rooms. Another issue was that appointments for mothers and babies were scheduled on different days, making compliance and follow-up more complicated for clients. The third was an issue of data quality: mother-baby cards were not being properly filled out, resulting in incomplete records and making it challenging to tell who accessed services.

The QI team set a primary goal of reaching, by January 2014, a 100% level in retention in care for mothers and babies. With support from the district QI coach, they decided to change the process of care by offering services to mothers and their babies at the same service point. To do so they developed a new process and patient flow chart.

Efforts to improve retention started with ensuring that mother-baby pairs were supported to attend mother-baby pair appointments. The QI team in Ivukula, in August 2013, directed facility staff to begin pairing mother and baby cards, storing together the health information of mothers and babies.

At the same time, the QI team also directed staff to ensure the next appointments for both mothers and babies were made for the same day. Appointments were given at the end of the visit by one person at the facility who scheduled an initial appointment for the mother and a follow-up appointment for baby and mother. The QI team reported reduced waiting time for mothers, reduced repeated visits, and streamlined services, which resulted in reducing staff workload.

According to the QI team leader, *"At the beginning we felt overwhelmed and we were worried about increased load of work, but when we saw improvements, we were so excited and became motivated to continue."*

Support for the QI Team

The USAID-funded project's Uganda staff, through monthly visits to Ivukula, supported the QI team to identify gaps in care, prioritize areas for improvement, and develop and test change ideas to address the gaps and implement these changes.

The senior gender advisor provided ongoing in-person and virtual support to project staff, including building their capacity to lead a coaching session related to gender and integrate gender into QI for staff at the health facility. In April 2013, she trained the USAID-funded project's Uganda staff on gender integration. Training included sensitizing the team to gender norms and issues, including providing general information about how gender affects people's daily lives, as well as specific information about how to integrate gender in improvement activities. This training enabled the USAID technical assistance project staff in Uganda to incorporate gender considerations affecting health outcomes as an integral component of the QI process.

The senior gender advisor supported the Ivukula QI team to document gender integration activities through development of simple tools for the QI team to use to integrate gender, including a driver diagram, which identified the contributing factors to lack of male participation in PMTCT services and to women's inability to keep appointments and remain in care due to child care responsibilities or financial constraints in addition to disclosure issues. She suggested possible activities to address gender-related drivers affecting outcomes and developed scenarios for the clinic team to use to discuss and better understand how gender gaps affected achieving their goals and improving outcomes. The senior gender advisor also provided information about best practices and activities that worked well to close gender gaps, including involving men. Table 12.1 outlines the timeline of gender support to the Ivukula QI team.

Table 12.1 Timeline of gender technical support to Ivukula Health Center

April 2013	Senior gender advisor provided an interactive training for and technical support to the Uganda project team on methods and illustrative action steps to integrate gender in all phases of improvement work
August 2013	Senior gender advisor provided a follow-up gender training for staff and technical support to adopt learning session materials to address gender issues and develop training materials to use for gender trainings
March 2014	Project staff provided a training on gender integration to Ivukula staff and met with the district health office to discuss gender integration approaches to improve outcomes
July 2014	Senior gender advisor supported project staff in supporting QI teams to integrate gender in QI activities, as well as provided direct support in gender integration to QI teams
September 2014	Senior gender advisor supported Ivukula to document gender integration activities
October 2015–August 2017	Senior gender advisor provided ongoing virtual support to project staff, including building their capacity to lead a coaching session related to gender considerations and to integrate gender into QI for staff at the health facility

Gender Interventions

Shortly after starting improvement work, midwives and other providers started to realize how much and how often their women clients talked about the role their partners and families played in making decisions about health-related matters. QI team members noted that women clients had long been raising these issues; however, without a way to address them, clients' questions and concerns went unanswered. The gender training and efforts to integrate gender considerations in QI efforts equipped service providers with a tool to begin to address the gender concerns.

During counseling sessions and in less formal conversations, women were revealing to midwives and other providers, as well as to mentor mothers and expert clients, how often and how much gender-related concerns impacted care. Mentor mothers and expert patients both reported, through informal interviews, that mothers who had not disclosed their HIV status to their partners often failed to access services because they did not want to be questioned about their whereabouts. Other mothers reported competing priorities in the household and a lack transport or other forms of family support to enable them access services in the health facility.

The clients expressed that they often feared the possibility of physical violence if they disclosed their HIV-positive status to their partners. Mothers also felt that their partners were not likely to understand the importance of HIV services and remaining in care.

After the QI team began to recognize how heavily gender concerns affected women's decisions about whether to remain in care, members decided to test whether increasing male partner involvement might mitigate the identified reasons women were not being retained in care. Change interventions to increase male partner involvement were put in place. Changes included: (1) joining with other PHFS implementing partners to reach out in the community to encourage men to accompany their female partners to the clinic regardless of the male partners' HIV status, (2) involving community leaders in encouraging men to accompany their wives or partners, (3) counseling women about the benefits of involving male partners to accompany them on clinic visits, (4) inviting male partners to attend clinic visits (per the client's wishes), and (5) offering health services to male partners at the clinic, such as measuring blood pressure and weight.

With support from the senior gender advisor, the Ivukula QI team was able to respond specifically to these gender-related issues. Male partners, the team discerned, might be motivated to attend clinic appointments because of their love and concern for their partners and children. In addition, health education and services might serve as incentives for men to come to the clinic, so efforts to involve male partners should consider such incentives. At the same time, health workers needed to be aware of an underlying concern in which men felt that efforts to address gender concerns meant that blame would be directed toward males for gender-related issues.

In August 2013, the improvement team at the Ivukula facility began an effort to raise awareness among clients and their partners, as well as in the community, about the need to involve men. They first talked about how to shape the intervention; i.e., whether men coming to the clinic was the only way that they could be considered involved. The team discussed whether male involvement could be defined as men being regularly tested for HIV or providing their female partners with nutritional, psychological, and financial support. Finally, for purposes of this initial intervention, the team decided to measure results by assessing the number of men who accompanied their female partners and babies to the facility.

The clinic improvement team encouraged community leaders to invite men to come to the facility. In addition, they initiated an effort to reach out to men by joining in ongoing community outreach efforts being conducted by two other PHFS implementing partners. The implementing partners set about raising awareness to encourage men to accompany their female partners to the clinic. Outreach representatives were usually able to talk to men about this when they came to the market. Sometimes, they were able to engage the men at religious events.

In February 2014, the clinic QI team identified a prime opportunity to further engage men in participating with their wives and children. The clinic had been offering monthly family support group meetings in which men and women came for health education and to share their own HIV experiences with others. They brought their babies below 2 years of age. During those meetings, no drug distribution took place; HIV-positive men and women had to return during the same month to receive their medications. The QI team noticed that women who attended the family support group meetings did not always return for their follow-up visits; their husbands or male partners would come to the clinic to pick up antiretroviral medications for both themselves and their wives or partners. HIV-negative men did not join these meetings as they felt they did not concern them. The improvement team identified an opportunity to utilize the meetings to engage men and keep mothers and their babies in care.

The improvement team put in place a change to synchronize family support group meetings and clinic appointments for mother-baby pairs and males. Beginning in March 2014, the Ivukula facility began to focus health talks on male partners' role in preventing mother-to-child transmission of HIV (PMTCT). The site team also offered couple's counseling during special visits when the first tests of infants were done to assess the infant's HIV status.

"Male partners are eager to know the HIV results of their exposed infants and they are motivated to support their partners when they understand their roles and responsibilities...we ensure that we always give them health talks in relation to available services for both the mother and male partner to protect the exposed infants from risk of contracting HIV infection," the team reported. Furthermore, the team leader reported that, *"Men became so engaged in their babies' health that if the nurse or the midwife would miss performing any of the follow-up items, fathers would ask why.... They demand a good service."*

Clinic staff expanded the family support group meetings to invite serodiscordant couples—where one partner is HIV negative and the other is HIV positive.

Couples became so interested in the health education sessions that they took active participation in selecting session topics. The team broadened the range of health services offered to male partners to encourage them to participate in counseling sessions. Previously, they had received services at the outpatient clinic only when they were sick or came for their medication. Clinic staff began offering blood pressure and weight measurements as well as HIV counseling and testing. In addition, the men were offered a nutritional status assessment. These incentives led to more male partners coming to the facility with their female partner. The staff shared that it contributed to driving up retention rates of mother-baby pairs in care (Fig. 12.2).

The mentor mother and expert client played key roles in implementing gender-related changes. Both had received training in gender integration and were sensitized to the gender issues and gaps that men and women might be affected by or face. Being sensitized to gender issues means they became aware that service providers might treat male or female clients differently when delivering health services and that gender issues may affect client willingness to seek services, continue to use services, and carry out the health behaviors advocated by healthcare providers.

With her knowledge and experience of the culture and mothers' issues, the mentor mother could successfully ensure that the issue of disclosure could be addressed without causing harmful consequences. She supported mothers who expressed a clear desire to disclose their status to their partner. The team members strongly adhered to a "do no harm" approach to make sure that no woman was forced to disclose status. They took a gender-sensitive approach in which members carefully

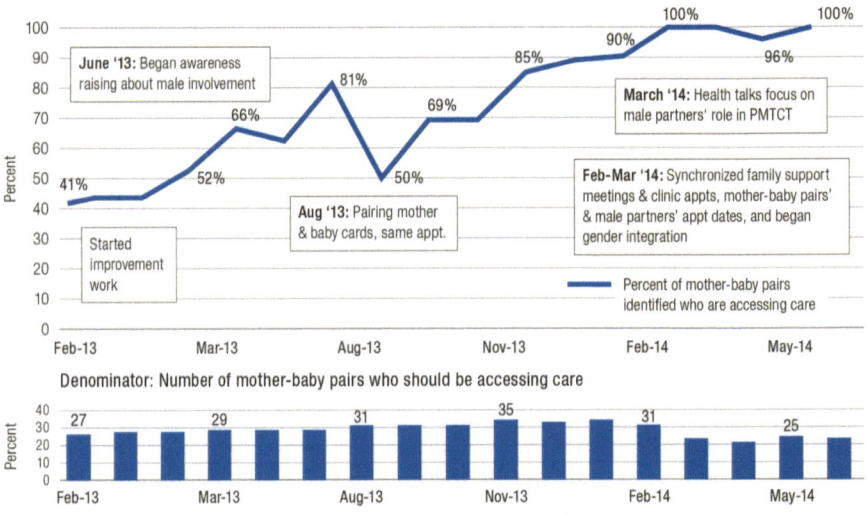

Fig. 12.2 Mother-baby pairs retained in care at Ivukula Health Center, February 2013–June 2014

made sure that male involvement and disclosure were supported, but optional, and always ultimately the decision of the female client. The team maintained a strong awareness that engaging male partners and other family members, such as mothers-in-law, should never lead to negative unintended consequences.

The expert client supported the implementation of a gender-sensitive approach by linking the QI team with the community. He helped make people in the community aware of how important it was for male partners and husbands to support their wives or female partners. The expert client and QI team members were aware that sensitization of community members would require time. The mentor mother and the expert patient visited homes and provided counseling messages to both women and men in the community. The expert client invited community members to attend clinic events. Speakers in health education sessions and clinic staff repeatedly addressed the topic of men participating in their partners' health during health talks, immunization sessions, and nutrition group counseling sessions. Team members, including the expert client, also engaged clients in person-to-person conversations, taking advantage of such times as when clients were waiting for services.

Results

Ivukula Health Center

Improvements in outcomes at Ivukula as well as all the pilot facilities came about as the result of both logistical changes, such as pairing mother-baby cards, and gender-related changes. As of January 2014, the retention rate of mother-baby pairs surpassed 85% at more than 20 of the pilot clinics, up from 22% at the baseline in April 2013. At the Ivukula facility, retention rates reached 100% for mother-baby pairs in March 2014, up from 41% in February 2013 (see Fig. 12.2). The improvement team kept coaching guides and tracked improvement on a handwritten graph as well as electronically in an Excel spreadsheet.

All Pilot Sites

By February 2014, the 22 pilot sites had all achieved strong gains in retaining mother-baby pairs in care, from 2.2% of pairs retained in care to over 60%, as seen in Fig. 12.3. The indicator used to track the retention of mother-baby pairs is the number of mother-baby pairs in postnatal care (a count of how many babies came each month and checked with whether their mothers also came in the same month) over the number of mother-baby pairs expected to be in postnatal care (calculated with the number of babies who were ever enrolled in early infant diagnosis, still under 18 months and living, as a proxy for the denominator).

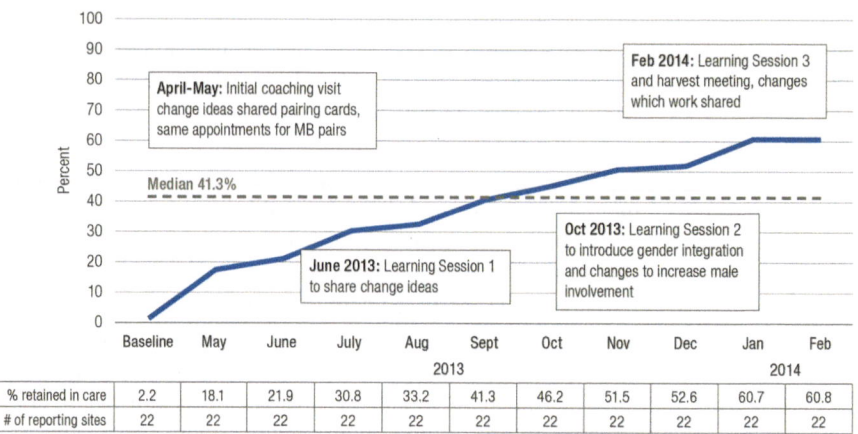

Fig. 12.3 Percentage of mother-baby pairs retained in care at 22 PHFS pilot sites, April 2013–February 2014

Team Motivation Grows as They Begin to See Results

Team members later reported that they were initially skeptical about how effective it would be to review charts and documents they knew to be inadequate. In retrospect, however, they said that were pleasantly surprised to find how much insight the analysis of the cards produced.

Before starting the improvement initiative, while the clinic staff was aware of many of the logistical inefficiencies described above, they were unable to take the time to consider changing the status quo, no matter how unworkable they all knew it to be. In addition, the staff members felt they did not have the authority or time to undertake even a basic task such as putting the cards in the same location.

By implementing a QI process that called for the analysis and identification of gaps and for regular meetings, QI team members were given an opportunity to identify inefficiencies and come up with possible solutions. They were also able to delegate responsibilities to individuals to ensure that solutions were carried out.

Institutionalization

As the Ivukula facility continued to produce tangible results, the clinic's QI team leader transferred knowledge to scale up gender integration in improvement to neighboring facilities in the Namutumba District (see Box 12.2). In addition, the USAID-funded project team based in Uganda helped to build the capacity of other implementing partners in QI and gender integration. In 2015, Uganda's MOH incorporated the gender component into the MOH's QI training curriculum.

> **Box 12.2 Ivukula QI Team's Leader Spreads Knowledge to Other Pilot Sites About Scaling Up Gender Interventions**
> In May 2015, the district health officer recognized the leadership potential of the Ivukula QI team leader and made her responsible for bringing knowledge to other clinics. She trained facilities in improvement methodologies and transferred knowledge to scale up gender integration in improvement to neighboring facilities in the Namutumba District. She presented results and challenges and how the team at the Ivukula facility addressed such challenges and achieved their goal of 100% retention. Further, she visited facilities and worked with the improvement teams to guide them on the improvement process start-up and to share changes that were tested and worked at the Ivukula Health Center. She has since been promoted, now working as an improvement coach at the district level.

Reflection

This case study illustrates how engaging male partners and community members in improving care can play a critical role in improving health outcomes. The results at Ivukula show how innovative gender integration components can dramatically improve routine care. By analyzing the causes of lack of retention of mother-baby pairs in PHFS-supported services from a gender perspective, the team was able to identify effective methods of increasing retention and improving outcomes for mothers, babies, and male partners.

When men are educated about their partner's status and the health implications of not remaining in treatment, they are more willing to support mothers by facilitating their transportation to the health center and providing nutritional needs for the family. The support of male partners, even if they are not physically able to attend clinic visits with their female partner, is important to retaining mother-baby pairs in care. Key factors that contributed to the success of the work in Ivukula included positive leadership and teamwork and passion among improvement team members.

Using a range of methods and venues to develop community relationships was critical to the team's success. Activities at the Ivukula Health Center show how empowering health workers and providing them with the tools they need can significantly improve the quality of health services. Ivukula shows how building local capacity results in institutionalization and scale-up.

The study also serves as a reminder of how important it is that those working with gender concerns be trained and sensitized to the cultural norms that underlie the issues. Throughout the QI process, technical advisors and the QI team sought to dispel the notion that paying attention to gender concerns meant blaming men for anything that goes wrong.

Ivukula's team built the capacity of healthcare providers to integrate gender issues into efforts to improve care, on the frontlines of health services. By becoming aware of social and cultural influences, the team was able to successfully engage male partners in programs focused on eliminating mother-to-child transmission and to educate them about the importance of mothers and babies accessing services, adhering to treatment, and remaining in care. This helped to create champions within families who supported mother-baby pairs to remain in care through the 18-month mark.

Acknowledgments The author expresses special gratitude to Dr. Charles Masinga, District Health Officer in Namutumba, and Ms. Shanifa, Ivukula Quality Improvement Team Leader, for their hard work, professionalism, and commitment to the improvement of healthcare in Uganda and to Ms. Tamara Nsubuga-Nyombi, USAID ASSIST Senior Quality Improvement Advisor in Uganda, and Ms. Joyce Draru, USAID ASSIST Quality Improvement Officer in Uganda, for their leadership in designing and scaling up this improvement effort.

The PHFS initiative described in this case was supported by the USAID Office of HIV/AIDS and the Office of Health Systems through the USAID ASSIST Project, implemented by University Research Co., LLC under Cooperative Agreement Number AID-OAA-A-12-00101.

Chapter 13
Improving HIV Counseling and Testing in Tuberculosis Service Delivery in Ukraine: Profile of a Pilot Quality Improvement Team and Its Scale-Up Journey

Nilufar Rakhmanova Pollard, Igor Semenenko, Uliana Snidevych, Emily Keyes, Roman Yorick, Alyona Gerasimova, and Bruno Bouchet

Abstract This case study describes the experience of a successful pilot team in Chervonograd, a mining city in Lviv Province of Western Ukraine, that participated in an effort beginning in March 2013 to use quality improvement (QI) methods to raise the rates of HIV counseling and testing (HCT) offered to all clients tested for tuberculosis (TB). With a population of close to 67,500, Chervonograd has a higher number of drug users than the rest of the country. State statistics revealed that 75% of AIDS patients diagnosed in the city in 2013 were coinfected with TB, but only 4% of suspected TB cases citywide were offered HIV counseling by TB doctors and only 0.04% were actually tested for HIV. The efforts of Chervonograd's pilot QI team proved critical to both improving the rates of HCT for TB clients in the pilot sites and the overall success of the scale-up of this work throughout Lviv Province.

Keywords Collaborative improvement · Flowchart · HIV counseling and testing · Scale-up · TB/HIV coinfection · Time series charts · Tuberculosis · Ukraine

N. Rakhmanova Pollard (✉)
FHI 360, Phnom Penh, Cambodia
e-mail: nrakhmanova@fhi360.org

I. Semenenko · U. Snidevych
FHI 360, Kyiv, Ukraine

E. Keyes
FHI 360, Durham, NC, USA

R. Yorick
Pact Inc., Dushanbe, Tajikistan

A. Gerasimova
Pact Inc., Kyiv, Ukraine

B. Bouchet
FHI 360, Washington, DC, USA

© University Research Co., LLC 2020   209
L. R. Marquez (ed.), *Improving Health Care in Low- and Middle-Income Countries*, https://doi.org/10.1007/978-3-030-43112-9_13

Background

The health system in Ukraine is especially impacted by one of the highest tuberculosis (TB) disease burdens in Eurasia and by one of the fastest-growing HIV epidemics in the world (UNAIDS 2013). Only half of HIV-positive individuals in Ukraine are aware of their HIV status. Those who test positive for HIV are often diagnosed at a late stage of infection, leading to higher mortality rates. Fifty-three percent of people diagnosed with HIV and enrolled in care were at clinical stages 3 and 4, as defined by the World Health Organization (Ukrainian Center for Disease Control 2015).

The main coinfection and cause of death in AIDS patients in Ukraine is TB, which accounts for 53.5% of all AIDS deaths (Ukrainian Center for Disease Control 2015). In Ukraine, TB and HIV programs, which function separately as vertical programs (i.e., those that focus on specific health conditions), lack true collaboration and integration of services. This often leads to a loss of patients and poor quality of services. Because TB also occurs earlier in the course of HIV infection than many other opportunistic infections, its existence presents a window of opportunity for diagnosing HIV at an earlier phase of infection.

The work described in this case was spearheaded by a United States Agency for International Development (USAID)-funded project, which used QI methodology to improve HIV services for key populations and to strengthen the capacity of government and civil society organizations to reduce levels of HIV transmission among these populations. The study's authors participated on the QI team and documented its progress through observation, coaching reports, and qualitative interviews conducted 18 months after the initiation of the QI work.

Organizing the Improvement Effort

Choosing Improvement Priorities

With technical assistance from a USAID-funded project, Ukraine's Ministry of Health (MOH) in March 2013 launched a collaborative improvement effort to increase HIV counseling and testing (HCT) service coverage and ensure the continuity of HIV care for those who are diagnosed with HIV (Institute for Healthcare Improvement 2003). It was agreed with the MOH from the beginning that the collaborative would start with fewer sites and over time would be extended to more sites with the accumulation of learning, will, and successes of the pilot sites. Three civil society organizations—organizations that advocate for and monitor the implementation of democratic practices and good governance reforms—also partnered with the QI initiative. Participating organizations provided data suggesting that TB providers were missing opportunities to identify the coinfection of HIV among patients with TB, despite the existence of a new regional policy mandating that all TB patients should be offered voluntary HIV testing after counseling.

During a two-day collaborative launch meeting held in Kyiv, participants drafted an improvement charter with the goal of improving HCT and enrollment in care. Since this was the first time that modern QI methods were to be applied to a public health issue in Ukraine, the pilot initiative was limited to Lviv, a province with one of the most severe TB and HIV situations of the 27 provinces in the country. The meeting participants selected two TB clinics in the districts of Chervonograd and Zhovkva to serve as pilot sites, with the expectation of later expanding to more sites.

Health System Culture in Ukraine

In 1991, when the country gained independence, Ukraine inherited an extensive and highly centralized health system (Lekhan et al. 2015). Although considerable decentralization has taken place since independence, the system continues to initiate changes and improvements through issuance of regional orders. Wide gaps exist between hierarchical levels; the system's culture presents challenges to implementing changes at the facility level. Health workers were not used to communicating with higher-level authorities and often expressed to project leaders that their workloads were already too heavy to take on duties for which they had not been trained. Thus, the culture of the system presented inherent barriers to QI projects, which relied on teams of frontline health workers who interacted directly with patients to take actions to improve care quality.

QI Team Formation

During the collaborative launch meeting held in Kyiv, an experienced TB doctor, who served at the province level, emerged as a champion for the project. In the initial months of the launch, she acted as QI mentor and coach for the two pilot sites and guided the selection of the Chervonograd TB dispensary as a pilot site based in part on the doctor's knowledge of the clinic staff.

Chervonograd TB dispensary, a typical TB facility, was staffed by four doctors and four nurses. Before visiting the pilot site, the doctor and two QI experts from the USAID-funded project planned a QI team recruitment strategy that would address the obstacles they faced. The three experts were aware that they would be attempting to recruit staff who were likely to have reservations about taking on additional responsibilities. The team's strategy was to visit the clinic, listen to and address the staff's concerns, and help them envision the potential results of putting QI interventions into place.

Organogram of an Improvement Effort in Chervonograd

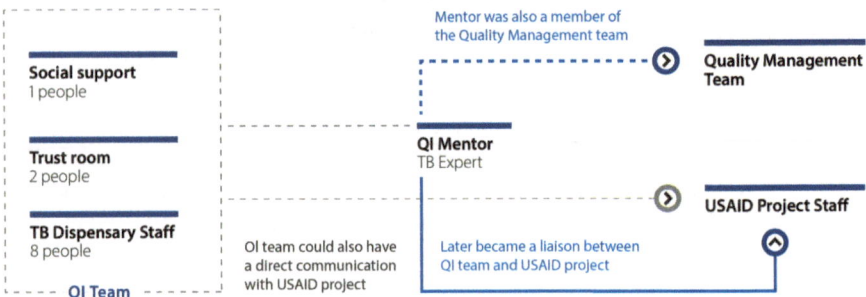

Fig. 13.1 Chervonograd quality improvement team organizational structure

The three visited the Chervonograd dispensary in March 2013 and listened to staff as they presented their concerns and reservations about initiating a project with unfamiliar techniques. Staff members cited an already heavy workload, a lack of resources, the need for rapid diagnostic tests (RDTs), a lack of privacy and confidentiality to conduct tests and counseling, and what they felt was their own lack of competency and knowledge about the HCT procedures. The TB doctor and project representatives generated enthusiasm by describing how QI procedures offer a way in which much-needed HCT procedures could be implemented by the TB dispensary staff. They spoke to what they knew to be the staff's deep commitment to clients' health. The visitors knew that frontline health workers, faced with high rates of TB and HIV coinfection, were acutely aware of the need for HCT. After 2 hours of discussion, a doctor and nurse agreed to serve as initial members of the QI team.

As the project progressed during the first weeks, the initial enthusiasm of the team and support from the USAID-funded project team encouraged others from the TB dispensary to join in the QI effort. Members of other vertical programs, including an infectious disease doctor and nurse from the trust room[1] of Chervonograd's primary health center and a social worker from the province's department of social services, also joined the team.

The TB staff met weekly in the TB dispensary and monthly as an expanded team that included the members from the Chervonograd primary health center and the social services department. They were sometimes joined by the QI mentor/coach and USAID-funded project QI advisors. The organizational structure of the QI effort is shown in Fig. 13.1.

---

[1] Trust rooms, often part of primary care centers, are set up for confidentiality purposes and attended by an infectious diseases doctor and nurse to offer HCT to vulnerable, high-risk patients.

In addition to the other elements of the collaborative, the charter called for a patient's inclusion on the QI team. Project leaders and team members reported that the inclusion of patients proved valuable over time because they brought information about the stigma they experienced and other challenges of navigating the health system to the attention of the medical professionals. The medical staff, in turn, more acutely realized the need to prioritize treating clients with respect and according them dignity. However, QI team members found this requirement challenging to implement in practice and struggled to determine the patient's role. They invited patients to learning sessions but grappled with which sessions were appropriate and how to make the participating patient comfortable in the role.

Quality Management Team

The overall team structure consisted of a facility-based QI team, which interacted with a quality management team, comprised of province-level decision makers as well as with project QI experts (Fig. 13.1). The quality management team's role included establishing collaboration with outside facilities and departments key to the improvement effort. The TB doctor, who acted as the QI team coach and mentor, served on the quality management team and played a major role in developing a local HCT protocol for TB providers and in providing continuous follow-up and advocacy for the scale-up of the improvement effort. In addition, a retired head of the TB facility also served on the quality management team; this team member's extensive network of contacts with health and government officials helped the team navigate government channels and interact with the region's other medical facilities. Quality management team members helped the facility tackle challenges that arose between sites that provided antiretroviral therapy (ART), the AIDS center, and other sites in the province.

Analyzing the Problem

The Chervonograd TB dispensary QI team developed a flowchart to identify problem areas within the delivery of HCT services to patients diagnosed with or suspected of having TB (Fig. 13.2).

The team was able to identify issues leading to patient loss in this fragmented process:

- When suspected or confirmed TB patients reach a TB doctor, the doctor prescribes tests to confirm TB and does not routinely offer HIV counseling. TB doctors are hesitant to counsel because they have not gone through certified HCT training and lack job aids, and TB facilities do not have resources for rapid testing on their own premises.

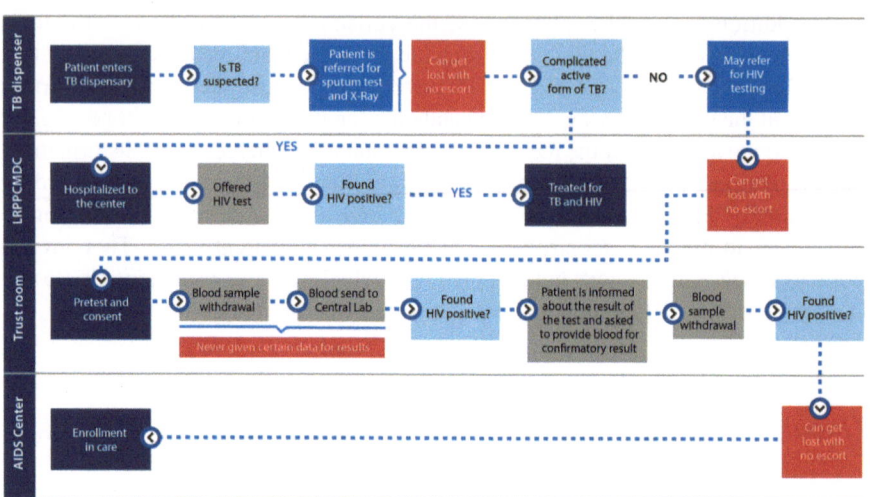

Fig. 13.2 Patient flow for HIV counseling and testing for TB patients in Chervonograd

- If a patient has confirmed TB and has the complicated active form of TB, she/he is referred to Lviv Regional Phthisiatric-Pulmonary Clinical Medical Diagnostic Center for TB treatment. Only at that secondary-level center is the patient offered HIV testing.
- TB doctors potentially recommend that patients go to a separate primary health facility for HCT, which has a trust room and a lab that conducts testing on-site. Often patients did not reach this facility.
- Even if a patient makes it to the trust room, it typically takes approximately 2 weeks to get HIV test results based on the ELISA diagnostic technique, and often the laboratory cannot give an exact date for the patients to return for the results. Some patients who return their results find that they are not yet ready.
- If a patient tests positive for HIV, she/he is referred to the trust room again for posttest counseling and asked to provide blood for the confirmatory test and return for the results. If confirmed HIV positive, patients are asked to go to the regional AIDS center for enrollment in care.

Challenges to the Provision of Quality HCT Services

Under the existing system, the TB clinic was unable to test clients for HIV on-site. As a result, clinic providers referred patients to the primary health-care center, a separate facility. Unlike the TB clinic, the primary health-care center had a laboratory for processing blood samples and a separate area for HCT, referred to as a "trust room," intended to ensure privacy and instill in patients a sense of confidentiality.

The TB clinic's QI team had long felt that an inability to perform HIV testing on-site was the main obstacle to ensuring that TB patients were tested for HIV. Being able to test clients on the clinic's premises, they asserted, would simplify the patient flow and make the process feel more secure. Administering the test to patients as part of TB services would present a more streamlined and efficient process, ensuring that a much greater number of clients would be tested. Without on-site testing, the TB clinic had to ask patients to travel to a different location for the HIV test, the results of which they were likely to be uneasy and fearful about. Asking patients to go to a separate location made it less convenient and more complicated for those who already had reasons to avoid taking the test.

Although no policy barrier existed to TB clinics offering rapid diagnostic testing, clinic staff had not, prior to the QI work, had the time or opportunity to meet as a group to consider how they might obtain a stock of RDTs to use on-site. After the team realized how many clients were being lost as a result of clients having to report to another location for testing, they began to seek ways to obtain a stock of RDTs. Eventually, they applied for and received a grant to receive RDTs from a charitable foundation.

The TB clinic also did not follow up with either patients or the primary healthcare center to confirm that referrals were completed, further contributing to the gap in services. The result was that a majority of TB clients identified for HIV testing never actually received testing. With the guidance of the coach and USAID-funded project team, the facility QI team shifted their focus from budgetary and resource obstacles to putting in place simpler and less costly interventions that were within their budget and ability to implement.

Carrying Out the Improvement Effort

The Chervonograd team adapted the collaborative's original charter to define the aim of its QI intervention as well as to propose improvement objectives, change interventions, and indicators to assess the effectiveness of changes.

Problem Statement

TB dispensary clients are not offered HCT, leading to missed diagnoses and inadequate management of TB and HIV coinfection.

Aim

Integrate HCT into the process of care at TB clinics to address missed diagnosis of TB/HIV coinfection and ensure enrollment in care for HIV-positive patients.

Improvement Objectives

The Chervonograd QI team defined its improvement objectives as follows:

1. Increase the identification of HIV infection in key populations at the early stages of HIV infection.
2. Increase the percentage of clients screened for TB who receive HIV pretest counseling
3. Increase the percentage of TB facility clients (both suspected and confirmed TB cases) who get tested for HIV following HIV pretest counseling.
4. Increase the number of confirmed HIV-positive clients who are enrolled in care at a specialized clinic.

Development, Implementation, and Testing of Change Ideas

Team members used flowcharts to analyze where current gaps in service delivery existed and where changes could be made and used time series charts to track the effects of the changes made.

The team hypothesized that offering HCT to all TB clients—suspected, new, and chronic—at TB facilities would increase timely HIV detection and address TB/HIV coinfection. QI team members decided to address patient loss through offering HCT to TB clients at TB facilities and tracking client flow in the Chervonograd TB dispensary. The team was able to come up with change ideas based on their analysis of the problem and tested these ideas over time.

Proposed Changes

To reach their improvement objectives, the team proposed change ideas that were then validated through testing, regular measurement, and documentation of results.

- Develop a local HCT protocol with counseling messages and a streamlined patient flow.
- Develop checklists from the protocol for providers to use as reminders.
- Conduct on-the-job HCT training for TB doctors and nurses.
- Define inclusion and exclusion criteria for counseling specific groups of patients.
- Offer escorts from the TB dispensary to the trust room of the primary health center for HIV testing.
- Establish a collaboration between TB facilities and the local police to make sure that prisoners are referred for X-ray and HCT when they are released.
- Establish a collaboration with the rehabilitation center for people who inject drugs to offer them counseling and develop escorting and communication mechanisms.

Measuring Improvement

Indicators

To evaluate the effect of the proposed changes, the team tracked the following indicators:

- Percentage of TB patients receiving pretest HIV counseling
- Percentage of TB patients referred for HIV testing
- Proportion of TB patients provided with posttest HIV counseling
- The number of people living with HIV enrolled in care at the regional AIDS center

Moving Toward a Culture of Data Analysis

The TB dispensary head designated a TB nurse to serve as data collector. Project staff developed a data collection form to ensure that data collection of the new improvement indicators was consistent, and the QI team started an HCT logbook to register progress on these indicators. During the initial coaching visits, the USAID project team pretested the data collection form to make sure that indicators were relevant. The data was transferred to an Excel spreadsheet that automatically generated time series charts. Since at least two indicators required comparison of data across vertical programs, the team developed a QI data measurement algorithm that became part of the local HCT protocol. These developments became invaluable in the scale-up process, since they made the start-up for new teams much easier.

During the initial coaching visits, project representatives and the QI mentor conducted sample-based quality assurance of the data and analysis. Initially, the team reacted to this practice with resistance, but very rapidly data became an engaging tool for generating ideas for improvement (see Box 13.1). According to one QI team member, there was not really a culture of data analysis and reflection before the improvement effort: *"Before, we collected some data, but didn't analyze it. We knew nothing about...how to interpret time series charts."*

Box 13.1 A Snapshot: Changing to a Data Analysis Culture
The act of data collection empowered a nurse from the TB facility to link and integrate care across vertical health-care programs. To ensure that all TB clients referred for HIV testing actually reached the trust room laboratory, she spoke with the trust room nurse on a weekly basis. After the first HIV-positive clients were identified, the nurse established check-in calls with the AIDS center to ensure that HIV-positive clients were enrolled in care. The nurse said, *"Measuring motivates people to work better. It makes them more organized and gives them the opportunity to be proud of results."*

Use of Time Series Charts

Initially, project QI experts worked closely with the Chervonograd QI team to help them analyze the data by looking at trends before and after the introduction of changes, brainstorm ideas, and present results and lessons at the learning sessions.

Through the use of time series charts, the QI team was able to identify effective and ineffective changes, honing the program's focus. They used the charts to analyze why the original change package was not yielding the intended results; specifically, they were not identifying many HIV-positive clients. As a result, they decided to target high-risk key populations, such as released prisoners and people who inject drugs, to reach more potentially HIV-positive clients and link them to care.

Once the team narrowed the focus of the interventions, they began to develop criteria to take steps to reach the target populations and measure results. The head of the Chervonograd TB dispensary established referral systems with the local police and with a Chervonograd drug rehabilitation center to refer released prisoners and people who inject drugs for TB and HIV screening. The QI team developed a referral form to simplify and standardize the process.

The QI team also used the charts to identify which changes they had to abandon or change. For example, after finding that patients were unwilling to wait the length of time it took for escorts to arrive from the social services department, the proposed idea of providing escorts was abandoned. Instead, when HIV rapid testing became available in the dispensary, the medical staff provided counseling for HIV-positive patients and then called the trust room to let them know that a new patient should be coming there. If, after a week, the patient did not come to the trust room, TB dispensary staff would follow up by calling the patient.

Analysis of time series charts also helped reveal a problem that if gone unrecognized could have led to an abject failure in the system. At one point, almost no testing was taking place. In analyzing the time series graphs, the QI team quickly noticed this negative trend and began exploring the underlying reasons why it was occurring. They discovered that the cause appeared to be rooted in provider concerns about whether sharing client information between clinics maintained patient confidentiality. The team was able to conduct a conflict resolution process to address staff concerns and define the process for sharing of client information between the clinics.

Table 13.1 presents the issues that were discerned from analyzing the time series charts and the change ideas on which the team reached a consensus after analyzing the results. It shows the interventions tested and introduced over the course of the project.

Support for Improvement

The TB doctor who was key to launching the effort in Chervonograd initially served voluntarily as mentor and coach for the two pilot sites. After 9 months, the project made the QI mentor job a paid position and defined the role more specifically to

Table 13.1 Change ideas introduced over time

Underlying issue or hypothesis	Change ideas tested
Pretest counseling for HIV	
Because TB doctors were not trained in HCT, they were not comfortable with administering tests or providing counseling	On-the-job HCT training for TB doctors and nurses was conducted by the AIDS center, resulting in a larger number of HIV-trained TB medical staff
Some TB providers were still reluctant to offer counseling since they felt that messages were not customized for TB clients	A local HCT protocol with counseling messages and a patient flow diagram were developed
Initially, despite a lot of tests that were performed, very few positive cases were identified. The team then developed more specific criteria for identification and counseling of high-risk groups	1. The inclusion and exclusion criteria for counseling specific groups of patients were defined 2. Established links with the local police to screen released prisoners for TB and HIV 3. Established links with the local drug rehabilitation center to screen people who inject drugs for TB and HIV
Demand for HIV counseling grew, and it was hard for doctors to cope with increasing demand	To cope with a large number of new TB patients that were supposed to be counseled on HIV, doctors started shifting HIV counseling to nurses
Testing for HIV	
After referring to HIV testing, TB facility would not know if all referred patients were actually tested for HIV	1. Regular communication and data exchange were established between TB doctors and the infectious disease specialist from the trust room on the number of patients tested and results received 2. The social workers from the rehabilitation center offered to escort clients from the TB dispensary to the trust room or the AIDS center 3. With support from the USAID project team, the TB dispensary applied for a grant to receive RDTs through a charitable organization and started using them to provide, for the first time, on-site HIV testing
Posttest counseling	
Patients forget when to come for posttest counseling because of the 2–3-week time to get the confirmatory result	1. TB nurse called patients to remind them to come for posttest counseling 2. The TB nurse followed up by phone with the trust room nurse to track whether patients reached the trust room on the same day referred 3. If the patient has not reached the site within 3 days, the patients' contact information was shared with the social service to enable them to find the lost patients
Patients were concerned about confidentiality since they received pretest counseling in the TB dispensary while posttest counseling was provided in the trust room	A regional order was issued that enabled TB dispensary to do both pretest counseling and posttest counseling to TB patients even though testing was done at primary care center laboratory

(continued)

Table 13.1 (continued)

Underlying issue or hypothesis	Change ideas tested
Enrollment in care for HIV-positive TB clients	
Patients forget or are reluctant to go to the AIDS center for enrollment in care	1. TB nurse calls to remind patients to enroll in care 2. If the patient had not reached the AIDS center within 3 days, the patient's contact information was shared with the social service unit and the AIDS center to enable them to find the lost patient
Loss of an HIV patient would go unnoticed because the TB dispensary, AIDS center, and trust room did not have a system of information exchange	A regional order was issued that enabled the TB dispensary, trust room, and AIDS center to exchange regular information of newly identified HIV patients and ensure their enrollment in care

include both mentoring and coaching duties. During the initial visits, the coach supported the team in identifying and assessing indicators and developing plans to address performance gaps. As the project developed, she supported the staff to test and implement changes using a "plan-do-study-act" cycle. The coach conducted 20 visits to the Chervonograd clinic during the year that it served as a pilot site. Using techniques and methods such as role playing, observation, and immediate feedback, the coach mentored team members on how to implement QI change interventions and improve services. She worked with the team to use time series charts to track changes in the data and analyze QI measures.

Initially there was resistance among the TB doctors to provide HCT, a new practice. However, by the third coaching visit, they recognized the groundwork that was being laid for providing improved health-care services, diagnostics, and testing to clients. As they began to recognize the potential of the interventions and saw that the effort might actually bring needed change, their attitudes changed. In fact, the QI mentor reported that TB providers started working together to address technical issues, such as developing a facility-specific local protocol to conduct HCT as a guide for TB staff. By the fourth coaching visit, the QI mentor reported that the QI team had already established a new practice of counseling, testing, and data collection. And, to ensure testing for patients, the team was actively working to improve collaboration with staff at the trust room and social services. Starting from the fifth coaching visit, the QI mentor reported that the Chervonograd team was communicating about their QI efforts with the district and Provincial AIDS Council. By the seventh coaching visit, the team had expanded its relationship with the drug rehabilitation center and internal affairs department in order to reach more members of key populations.

The team was not provided with monetary support other than a minimal payment paid to the QI mentor. Other organizations did provide training and technical support: the local civil society organization provided HCT training; the AIDS center provided training in the use of RDTs; the Lviv social services department conducted an interpersonal communication training; and a charitable foundation provided HIV rapid test kits to the Chervonograd TB dispensary.

QI Team Dynamics

The evolution of the QI team's dynamics and relationships illustrates how changes that take place on the frontline can resonate throughout the system. Since QI team members were from discrete programs and departments, which operated in a vertical system, members' relationships had to develop and evolve. Over time, mutual respect between members grew, as one participant shared: *"Teamwork is no longer my way or the highway...it is more about we and us."* The group eventually emerged as a committed and cohesive team which persisted in its efforts until goals were reached. As it developed and grew, the team faced various challenges which it met with enhanced communication between members and through the guidance of strong leaders.

In follow-up interviews, team members reported experiencing either no conflict within the team, or, if conflicts were reported (usually around miscommunication), they described confidence that the team could come to resolution due to its "open culture." These experiences likely contributed to the individual members functioning effectively, helping to support rapid formation of supportive team norms.

As the team became more organized and cohesive and more experienced with QI, they took on increasingly complex tasks. For example, if initially the group was thinking only about establishing a monitoring system, in later stages, it was implementing complex changes requiring strong coordination with a number of different institutions and programs. Almost from day one, the team demonstrated a willingness to cooperate between units from three vertical programs—the TB dispensary, the trust room, and the social support unit.

Results

Figures 13.3, 13.4, and 13.5 illustrate the effects of change interventions introduced by the Chervonograd QI team on HIV counseling and testing. After providing HIV counseling training to TB providers, the percentage rate of patients who received pretest counseling grew to 60% (Fig. 13.3). In July, after the TB dispensary team began to use the local facility-based HCT protocol and more health providers started to provide counseling, higher numbers of TB patients received services. To manage the higher demand, the team shifted counseling duties to nurses and narrowed the criteria for client selection. At about the same time, the drug rehabilitation center started to participate in the project and brought additional clients to the TB dispensary. The period between June and November 2014 was characterized by a decrease in performance due to a change in the dispensary's head. In January 2015, the TB staff acclimated to new management, and the performance again started to trend upward.

The process of requesting patients to schedule HIV testing at another facility (and travel to that facility for testing) resulted in many patients not following through. Providing a social worker to escort patients to the other site temporarily boosted testing rates, but the intervention proved unsustainable. Additionally, a staff

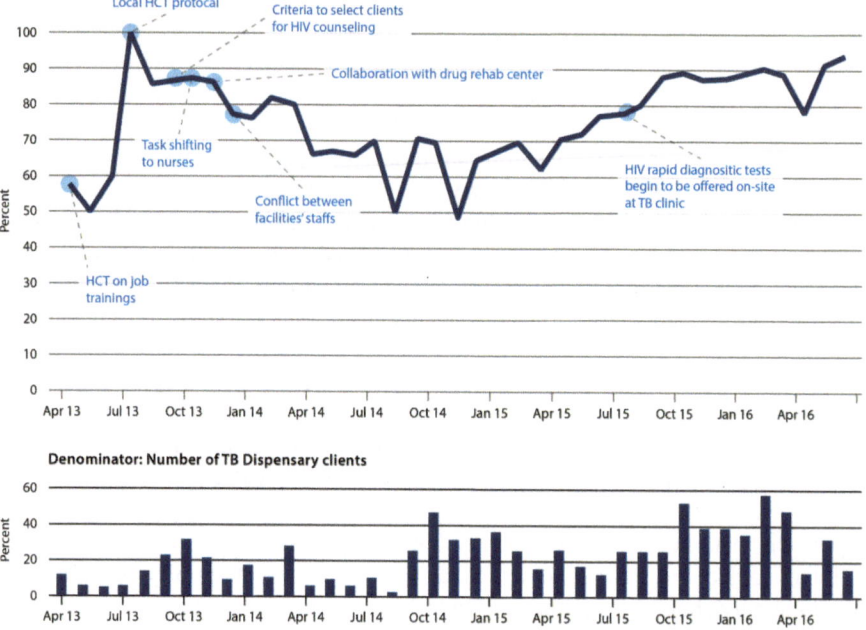

Fig. 13.3 Percentage of Chervonograd TB dispensary clients who received HIV pretest counseling (Apr 2013–Dec 2015)

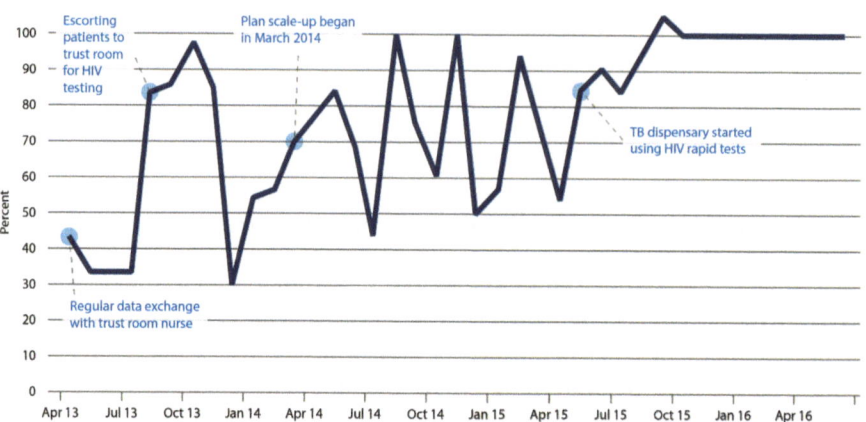

Fig. 13.4 Chervonograd TB dispensary clients who received HIV testing (Apr 2013–Dec 2015)

conflict in fall 2013 between the Chervonograd TB and trust room staff dramatically decreased the number of patients tested.

The number of patients again rose after the conflict was resolved, and the Chervonograd TB and trust room staff were asked to help plan the expansion of pilot work to new districts within Lviv. The request to assume new responsibilities

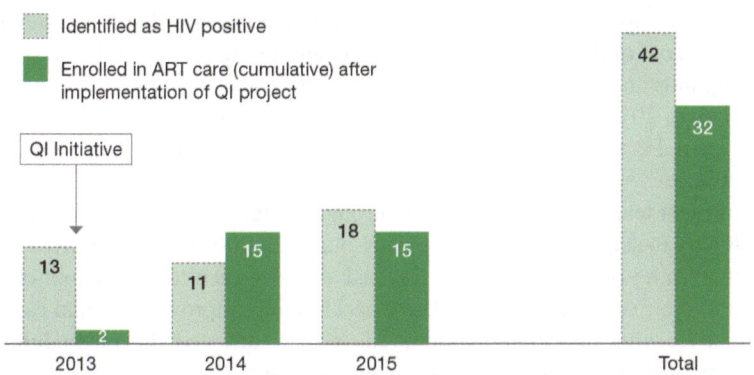

Fig. 13.5 Number of HIV-positive clients enrolled in HIV care by year and cumulative number (2013–2015)

reportedly boosted staff morale and helped to improve performance and ensure that patients were tested.

When the improvement effort started, only civil society organizations applied for funding to purchase and use HIV RDTs in Ukraine. The civil society organizations were Global Fund recipients, which procured rapid tests for them for HIV screening among key populations. Very few government health facilities were recipients of grants from any international organization at that time, and none of the health facilities in Lviv Region were recipients of grants.

To make diagnoses, public health facilities withdrew blood and sent samples to the laboratory for ELISA—a time-consuming diagnostic test process. The Chervonograd TB dispensary recognized that it could provide HCT services on-site to TB clients and, after applying for a grant to fund the initial purchase of rapid test kits, began in July 2015 to provide HCT services to clients on-site and even to offer it to clients of other facilities. Now, TB dispensaries throughout Lviv use on-site rapid testing. The convenience and confidentiality of on-site rapid testing have led to a sustainable and reliable HCT process for all TB clients (see Fig. 13.4) and to an increased number of HIV-positive clients enrolled in care. Initially, out of 24 patients identified as HIV-positive in 2013 and 2014, 17 were successfully enrolled in care. By 2015, this proportion improved to 15 patients enrolled in care out of 18 identified as HIV positive (Fig. 13.5).

Scaling Up the Improvement Effort

In March 2014, 1 year after the QI start-up, four new TB facilities joined the improvement effort; in 2015, an additional six sites came on board. Over the course of the initiative, the project held a QI coach training, five QI learning sessions, and eight trainings on how to administer and practice HCT. Coaches conducted 144 site visits.

The 12 participating sites used rapid tests provided by the charitable foundation or purchased out of their own budget. Chervonograd's successful collaboration with other programs and the province AIDS center led to an issuance of a new province-level policy in 2015 that called for a strong collaboration and exchange of information between TB facilities, the province AIDS center, and trust rooms throughout Lviv Province.

The project team followed the Breakthrough Series Collaborative improvement methodology to scale up the initiative (Massoud et al. 2006). Collaboratives operate on adult learning principles, require focused work by each team to adopt effective changes to their setting, use methods for accelerating improvement, and capitalize on shared learning and collaboration. The project adopted the methodology by intensifying coaching visits between learning sessions.

The scale-up initiative was largely peer-driven with members of the Chervonograd QI team serving as coaches and the QI mentor expanding her role to oversee the entire effort.

An initial training held for the new coaches covered a wide range of duties, such as:

- Working with the QI team to collect accurate data and analyze QI measures using time series charts
- Maintaining regular communication via meetings, email, or phone on QI activities with the quality management team and with the project officer
- Helping prepare teams to present their results (via storyboards or PowerPoint presentations) at learning sessions
- Facilitating discussions during learning sessions
- Reporting to the team, the district, and provincial managers

Under the leadership of the QI mentor, scale-up coaches visited each of the districts to explain the improvement concept and disseminate handouts critical to the process. For example, they provided a blank charter template with their own charter to use as an example and asked staff to develop their own district-specific charter.

Learning sessions presented opportunities to bring together all the teams, novice and experienced, on a quarterly basis to share their experiences with peers, discuss opportunities and challenges, and plan the next steps. Bringing together participants from different districts raised a healthy competition among peers and enabled them to share strategies and common challenges. The initial session focused on sharing learning from application of the QI model, analysis of results, and planning the next steps using plan-do-study-act cycles. An outside QI expert from Russia was invited to share their experience of implementing improvement efforts in HIV services. Subsequent learning sessions focused on the same goals plus sharing best practices and planning scale-up to new sites.

Chervonograd team members were paired with their peers in new districts: the retired TB doctor who was a member of the quality management team shared his experience with other TB doctors; the data collection nurse shared her experience with other potential data collection nurses. Learning sessions played a critical role in strengthening the cohesion of the Chervonograd team. At the sessions, the project team introduced QI concepts and methods as well as ways to plan, implement, monitor, and refine changes in health-care processes. During small-group discussions, the project team supported participants in developing improvement aims, objectives, and changes. Each QI team from the 12 participating sites was oriented on how to use the data collection tools and how to select and analyze indicators that would allow the team to assess the effectiveness of change interventions.

Project staff and the team's QI mentor conducted coaching visits between trainings and learning sessions. The visits served as a mechanism to follow up on how improvement plans were progressing as well as providing an opportunity to discuss and brainstorm creative ideas to improve care processes. Coaches helped new teams to test and implement changes using plan-do-study-act cycles. Coaching visits were made on an almost monthly basis when the QI effort started. Over time, visits gradually became less frequent.

Figure 13.6 presents data showing that the TB facilities which joined the effort during the scale-up period performed better than their predecessors on the first objective (HIV counseling for all TB clients) within 4 months of initiating the work. By December 2014, their performance level for counseling TB patients on HIV reached 90%, whereas the proportion achieved by the pilot sites dropped to 50% during this time. The discrepancies in performance are attributed in part to the Chervonograd site's lack of a separate room for ensuring confidentiality during

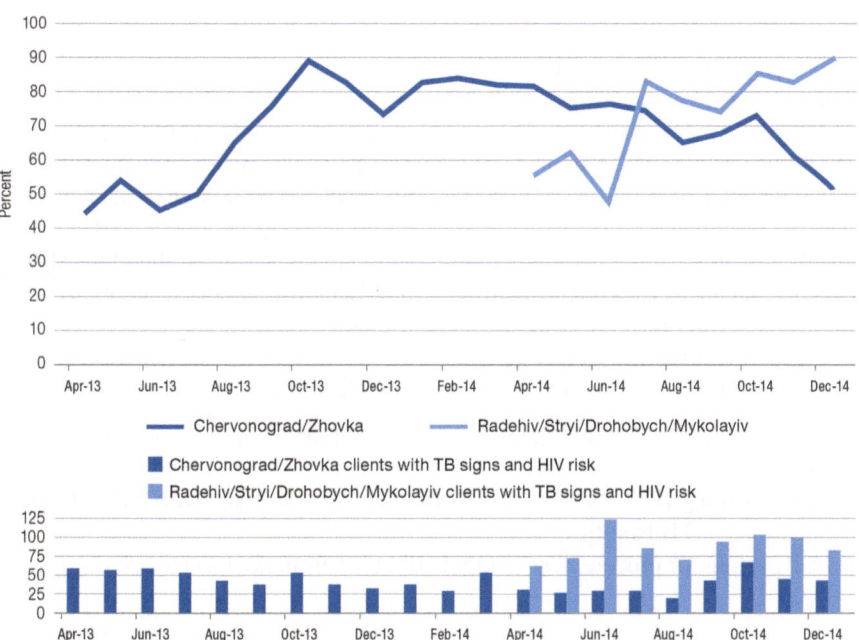

Fig. 13.6 Percentage of TB patients counseled for HIV in pilot and scale-up sites (Apr 2013–Dec 2014)

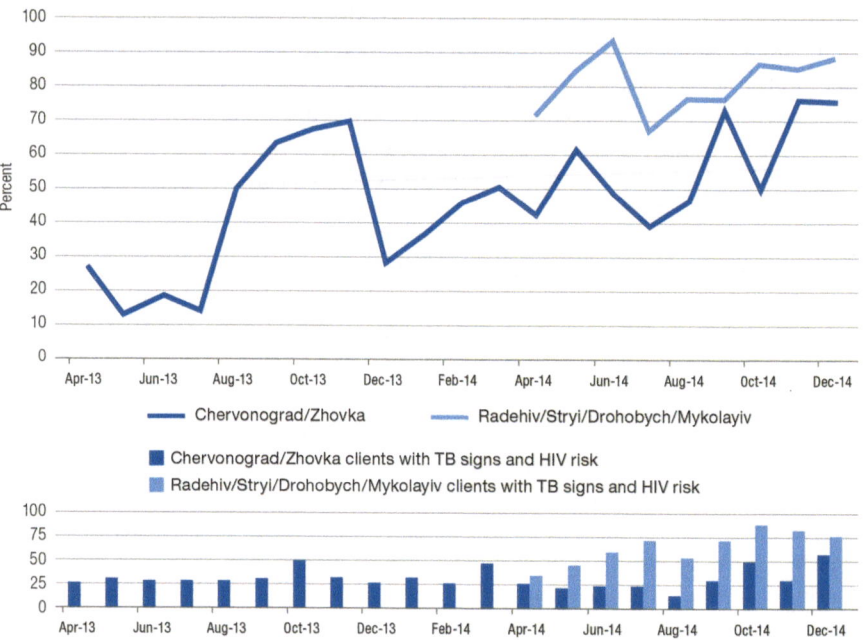

Fig. 13.7 Percentage of TB clients tested for HIV in pilot and scale-up sites (Apr 2013–Dec 2014)

counseling. Most importantly, however, the scale-up sites were more easily able to replicate the effective changes and learning generated by the pilot sites.

Figure 13.7 demonstrates a higher performance level in terms of the percentage of TB clients tested for HIV in the scale-up facilities. The main reason for this result is that the pilot TB facilities, at that time, still needed to refer counseled clients to a separate health facility for testing, while the four scale-up TB clinics started immediately procuring rapid tests using their own budgets and were therefore able to conduct diagnostic tests on the premises, which demonstrates that scale-up facilities went even further than pilot ones in some of their QI efforts.

The USAID-funded project completed its support in the third quarter of fiscal year 2016. The QI mentor continues to oversee the effort through:

- Scaling up of HCT in TB facilities to the rest of the 13 districts of Lviv Province and Lviv City
- Implementing HCT for the sexual partners of people living with HIV who were identified in TB facilities
- Advocating for procurement of rapid HIV tests from the local district budgets

Reflection

Piloting a collaborative improvement effort in a system that is new to QI is a labor- and resource-intensive endeavor. As evidenced by the number of coaching visits and learning sessions conducted and the level and amount of training provided, supplying technical support to pilot teams—especially those new to improvement efforts—requires a rigorous, large-scale effort.

The incremental changes that the Chervonograd team put in place to address the larger and costlier obstacle of being unable to perform testing on-site because they did not have RDTs was critical to the project's success. By demonstrating incremental successes, the clinic was recognized by the charitable organization and the provincial and facility health managers and, as a result, was eventually provided with the RDTs that allowed them to do on-site testing.

The success of the pilot program and the scale-up effort is due in large part to the commitment of the QI team in Chervonograd, a factor that illustrates how critical it is to select, especially for key roles in the scale-up process, a pilot team that has the strongest chance of being successful. It also highlights the very specific role of leadership, especially in the beginning. Without the retired head of the TB facility whose extensive network of contacts with health and government officials helped the team navigate government channels and interact with the region's other medical facilities, the team's effort may have stalled and never moved too far. This leader gave the team confidence to persevere and excel. In addition, it is critical to monitor the success of the team and to empower participants to take on more responsibilities and function more independently. This case shows that empowering high-performing teams to develop leadership potential also enables these same teams to support a spread strategy.

This case also clearly demonstrates that in rigid systems like the health system in Ukraine, it is important to work within the system's constraints to empower the team for changes and spread. Considering the fragmented and vertical nature of the Ukrainian health system, the USAID-funded project team proposed a multidisciplinary team structure with representation from various service delivery organizations. Reaching a balance between organizational structure and procedural flexibility enables teams to more effectively adopt the QI model to hierarchical systems similar to the system in Ukraine.

The Chervonograd team operated in a complex, dynamic environment. Collaboration across multiple vertical programs and among a variety of individuals was required to identify barriers to improvement in the targeted areas and to remove them. The participation of representatives from different public facilities on the Chervonograd QI team increased the effectiveness of the team as each QI team member provided a perspective from a different vantage point. As a QI leader pointed out: *"We worked a little with social services before the QI project started, but during the project we started collaborating with the trust room, the drug reha-bilitation center, and even local police."*

These improvements would not have been possible without day-to-day support from the QI mentor and from the head of the AIDS center, both strong advocates of HCT in TB services. They also played a crucial role in the MOH's issuance of decrees that facilitated the scale-up, and they continue supporting this effort province-wide. The team is certain that this work is sustainable. As one of the inter-viewed team members noted: *"We can't go back to old way of working now. The changes we implemented are already permanent."*

In conclusion, being part of the HCT improvement effort gave the Chervonograd TB team a new vision and, in fact, made them champions among other facilities. We believe that the journey of this team can serve as a role model for an improvement effort that is seeking pioneers that are able to meet the challenges of pioneer QI programs.

Acknowledgments The authors express special gratitude to Natallya Hopyak, Chief of TB Unit, Lviv Regional Pulmonary and TB Diagnostic Center, who served as the QI mentor, and the Chervonograd QI team members—Galina Saharuk, Ulyana Sava, Viktoriya Kozyuk, Irina Zalisna, Maryana Marchuk, Ivan Sinitskiy, Mikola Baklanov, Iryna Zelinkska, Roman Stetsyk, Serhiy Kruhinets, and Iryna Naida—for their hard work, professionalism, and commitment to the improvement of health care in Ukraine.

The authors also express gratitude to

LM Ruck, Head Coordinator of Lviv Province regarding TB and HIV/AIDS;

MB Slouzhinska, Head Doctor at Lviv Province AIDS Center; VV Melnychouk, Phthisiatrician, Lviv Regional Phthisiatric-Pulmonary Clinical Medical Diagnostic Center; AL Sorokoleet, Epidemiologist at Lviv Province AIDS Center; SO Myronyuk, Coordinator of Lviv Oblast AIDS Center; PB Lykhovyd, "Salus" Coordinator; and O Kovalchuk, Social Worker at Salvus (Chervonograd, Zhovkvivskiy rayon).

The AIDS Healthcare Foundation.

Many people contributed to the design and scale-up of this improvement effort: Alyona Gerasimova, Chief of Party of the RESPOND Project, for her vision and support for introducing new QI methods in Ukraine; Roman Yorick, Deputy Chief of Party of the project, for technical support; and Natalya Nizova, Director of the Ukrainian Center for Disease Control, for support at the national level. Three QI experts worked with the teams to grow their capacity in QI: Bruno Bouchet and Nilufar Rakhmanova of FHI 360 and Olga Chernobrovkina (independent QI Consultant). Project QI staff Uliana Snidevich and Igor Semenenko provided continuous support to the team in Chervonograd.

A special thanks to Valentyn Zharkevych, who served as the patient representative on the QI team.

References

Institute for Healthcare Improvement (2003) The breakthrough series: IHI's collaborative model for achieving breakthrough improvement. IHI innovation series. Available at: http://www.ihi.org/resources/Pages/IHIWhitePapers/TheBreakthroughSeriesIHIsCollaborative ModelforAchievingBreakthroughImprovement.aspx

Joint United Nations Programme on HIV/AIDS (UNAIDS) (2013) Global report: UNAIDS report on the global AIDS epidemic

Lekhan V, Rudiy V, Shevchenko M et al (2015) Health Systems in Transition; Ukraine; Health system review. WHO Regional Office for Europe. Available at: https://apps.who.int/iris/handle/10665/176099

Massoud MR, Nielsen GA, Nolan K, Nolan T, Schall MW, Sevin C (2006) A framework for spread: from local improvements to system-wide change. IHI innovation series. Institute for Healthcare Improvement, Cambridge, MA. Available on www.IHI.org

Ukrainian Center for Disease Control (2015) HIV/infection in Ukraine. Newsletter #43, p 34. Available at: https://phc.org.ua/uploads/documents/c21991/2b413308855aa209c676da62a8f562e9.pdf

Chapter 14
Conclusion

Lani Rice Marquez and Alison Lucas

Abstract This concluding chapter summarizes learning from a selection of case studies on improving health care in low- and middle-income countries. This selection of quality improvement (QI) cases exposes students and practitioners to real examples of what health-care improvement efforts can achieve. While not glossing over difficulties, the cases presented seek to show how real teams and organizations dealt with challenges in QI implementation. These 12 cases illustrate the range of settings in which QI methods are effective and focus on different aspects of QI intervention design and implementation. Together, they paint a comprehensive picture of how QI methods have been applied to improve health care in low- and middle-income countries at all levels of the health system and show how different QI methods can be applied by health workers at each level. The cases also offer important insights into factors that facilitate results: a focus on reaching explicit standards, engaging health workers in identifying gaps in meeting standards and taking action to address the gaps, management support for QI and for intervening in the selected care area, tools to support data analysis, and facilitating friendly competition and sharing learning among improvement teams.

Keywords Audit and feedback · Coaching · Guidelines · Low- and middle-income countries · Quality improvement · Shared learning · Standards

This collection of cases from low- and middle-income countries seeks to show what quality improvement (QI) methods can achieve in practice. The structure of the QI initiatives described in the 12 cases ranges from individual facilities testing changes to resolve unique problems to improvement collaboratives with dozens of sites testing changes in the same care area and to coordinated national programs with

L. R. Marquez (✉)
University Research Co., LLC (URC), Bethesda, MD, USA
e-mail: lmarquez@urc-chs.com

A. Lucas
Formerly with University Research Co., LLC, Palo Alto, CA, USA

hundreds of sites measuring quality with the same indicators. Collectively, the cases illustrate the QI process at all levels of the health system—community, health post, health center, district hospital, and referral hospital. The cases included in this book also deal with a wide variety of health-care issues, including HIV treatment, prevention of mother-to-child transmission of HIV, voluntary medical male circumcision, acute respiratory infections, tuberculosis-HIV co-infection, education and social protection of young children, nutrition and health promotion for pregnant women and children under two, antimicrobial resistance due to overuse of antibiotics, Zika prevention, and prevention of maternal deaths.

While all 12 cases took a quality improvement approach to making health care better, the cases applied different QI methods. Several cases relied on audit and feedback systems, assessing medical records for performance to specified care standards (Georgia, Ukraine, the Kyrgyz Republic, Honduras, Uganda). Another used an accreditation system to stimulate improvements in care processes (Kenya). Several cases used a collaborative approach to organize improvement in the same care area across multiple sites (Georgia, Uganda, India, Honduras). Another case emphasized the use of electronic medical records to facilitate real-time audit of HIV care to identify poor health outcomes at the national level and address gaps in care processes at the local level to reach national targets (Haiti). One team created flow charts to analyze where current gaps in service delivery existed and where changes could be made and used time series charts to track the effects of the changes made (Ukraine). Regardless of specific QI method, in general the efforts of health workers described in this book focused on assessing actual care and comparing it to expected standards of care, to understand the gap between the two in order to strategize about what could be done to close the gap.

To illustrate the many different approaches that have been applied to improve quality of care, Table 14.1 summarizes the care focus area and the QI methods applied in each case.

The cases also focus on different aspects of the QI process. Some cases describe in depth the process of forming QI teams and guiding them to conduct comprehensive baseline assessments, often based on detailed standards of care defined at the national level (Georgia, Tanzania, the Kyrgyz Republic, Honduras, Haiti, Mozambique, Uganda). One case from India profiles in depth the roles that different health authorities played in starting up and supporting QI activities, including the documents they developed to guide QI teams as well as the managerial and leadership structures needed to support QI work. Several cases detail the approach individual teams used to develop and test changes to improve care in a particular setting (Georgia, Guatemala, Tanzania, the Kyrgyz Republic, Honduras). One case focused on the use of QI methods to integrate gender considerations in the improvement of services to prevent mother-to-child transmission of HIV (Uganda).

The cases describe a wide range of approaches to training health workers in QI methods, from on-the-job training, as teams audited records to quantify gaps in care, to more formal QI courses lasting 1 or 2 weeks. Some cases emphasized the

Table 14.1 Care focus areas and QI methods applied in each case

Case country (lead author)	Focus areas	QI methods
Georgia (Chitashvili)	Treating respiratory tract infections in children	Audit of medical records in nine facilities and feedback to teams on baseline results showed the scope of overprescribing of non-evidence-based medications. The intervention included biweekly peer review of medical records and discussion of gaps in care and changes needed to improve care
Guatemala (Hurtado)	Improving health and nutrition counseling for mothers of young children	As part of a large-scale national improvement collaborative involving 166 health posts and 429 community centers, provided coaching support to community teams to improve mothers' knowledge of danger signs and appropriate feeding practices and increase the development of emergency birth plans, using lot quality assurance sampling to measure changes in maternal knowledge
Haiti (Bardfield)	Improving HIV patient care and outcomes with real-time access to patient data to guide clinical decision-making	National implementation of an electronic medical record system with a monthly review of reports on performance measures for core areas of care and generation of lists of active patients for care reminders, tracking of retention in care, identification of inactive patients and patients at risk of medication discontinuation, and identification of patients eligible for enrollment on antiretroviral therapy
Honduras (Banegas)	Integrating Zika counseling and screening in services for women of reproductive age	Preparation of national guidelines and implementation of an improvement collaborative involving 42 health facilities to improve Zika counseling in family planning services and prenatal care
India (Livesley)	Improving antenatal care, delivery, postnatal care, and essential newborn care services	Clinical trainings and coaching support to facility teams to identify root causes of poor quality in 4 hospitals, 8 community health centers, and 42 primary health centers in 1 district. Supported teams to test ideas to address these causes on a small scale and apply successful ideas to the entire facility
Kenya (Spieker)	Primary health care (outpatient services), inpatient care, surgical services, laboratory, and medical imaging	Embedding clinical and business quality standards and quality improvement methodology into the process of contracting health-care providers by the National Health Insurance Fund to guide improvement within a facility, incorporating pay for performance and reimbursement based on quality of care
Kyrgyz Republic (Smith)	Promoting the rational use of antibiotics for the treatment of common infections	Nine index conditions where antibiotics were often used inappropriately at primary and secondary care levels were identified, and clinical protocols developed for correct management of the conditions. Three districts were selected to pilot the protocols. Health workers were asked to audit their own medical records against standards of care to self-evaluate their performance and given specific feedback and job aids to promote adherence to standards

(continued)

Table 14.1 (continued)

Case country (lead author)	Focus areas	QI methods
Mozambique (Necochea)	Improving the quality of antenatal, labor and delivery, and postnatal care at health facilities	Application of standards-based management and recognition in 120 maternities: development of performance standards, implementation of the standards through facility assessments and improvement actions (using a tool developed to measure verification criteria for 81 performance standards), measurement of progress through review of the repeated assessments and tracking of selected indicators, and recognition of achievements
Tanzania (Nyagawa)	Improving quality of services for orphans and vulnerable children, including food and nutrition, shelter, family-based care and support, social protection and security, primary health care, psychosocial care and support, education and vocational training, and household economic strengthening	Collaborative approach to pilot national guidelines and QI activities in 31 small communities of 3 wards of one of 169 districts in the country through the efforts of the Most Vulnerable Children Committees and community-based organizations
Uganda (Byabagambi)	Addressing gaps in voluntary medical male circumcision service delivery to prevent HIV infection, using a collaborative improvement approach	In 30 sites, an external assessment team assessed male circumcision performance using a comprehensive quality assessment tool. At the end of each site assessment, the assessment team worked with site staff to develop an action plan that detailed the gaps identified, the interventions selected to fill the gap, the person responsible, and the timeline for implementing the interventions. After the baseline assessments, teams were trained and coached in how to test process changes and monitor the effects on indicators captured in the quality assessment tool
Uganda (Faramand)	Engaging men in prevention of mother-to-child transmission of HIV services	Testing gender-related changes in one rural health center to try to increase retention in care. The health center was one of 22 facilities in 6 districts that participated in the Partnership for HIV-Free Survival initiative to integrate nutrition support and counseling in HIV services
Ukraine (Rakhmanova)	Integrating HIV testing in tuberculosis services	Use of flow charts to map existing processes in order to quantify lost opportunities to test tuberculosis patients for HIV and identify process changes to increase uptake of HIV testing and counseling

collateral skills that health workers developed through the QI work, such as an ability to evaluate clinical evidence to judge whether care was in line with clinical best practices (Georgia, the Kyrgyz Republic).

What Do These Cases Tell Us About QI in Low- and Middle-Income Countries?

This case book shows that a quality improvement approach is effective in many diverse settings. It can work in both complex care settings and community settings. These cases do not point to a single preferred way of implementing QI. They show that many QI methods can yield results—that there is no "best way" to improve care. Many common methods proved effective and were feasible for health workers to implement: process mapping, audit and feedback, electronic medical records, and comparison to national guidelines. Regardless of the method, engagement of health workers in improving care was key.

The cases offer insights into factors that facilitate results, which can be emphasized in future QI initiatives. The most important key to success was a focus on reaching explicit standards and engaging health workers in identifying gaps in meeting standards and taking action to address the gaps. Teams were able to brainstorm and think through ways of improving adherence to standards. Some approaches (like standards-based management and recognition in Mozambique and accreditation in Kenya) introduced rewards for meeting standards, but from the information presented in the cases, it is not clear that such rewards produce better results than simply informing health workers of gaps in care. Similar improvements in care were achieved without explicit rewards for quality.

Data collection was something health workers were used to doing, but data *analysis* was a new skill for many. Tools that helped teams see changes in data in a simple or intuitive way allowed teams to easily understand what worked—and what did not. Electronic databases to automate the calculation of indicators and comparison across points in time facilitated interventions that involved the audit of many indicators or records. For smaller QI projects, use of spreadsheets and electronic databases automated the calculation and display of improvement data.

Building in mechanisms to share learning across QI teams as they tested different approaches improved the impact of QI efforts in many cases, as effective ways for improving care were shared among teams and scaled up to more sites.

QI teams achieved better results with strong support structures around them. We observed in many of these cases that QI initiatives work better with management support, mainly to help teams address system-level problems that are beyond the reach of individual QI teams. Many of the cases also emphasize the value of coaching support to help teams translate standards into practice. A key takeaway lesson for future QI initiatives is to build in adequate support for health workers as they begin to apply QI methods—support in the application of QI methods and support for intervening in the particular care area.

A pilot approach can be useful to demonstrate results on a small scale before scaling up to multiple sites. Results at pilot sites helped create buy-in and political support for the QI approach at the administrative level of the health system, which in turn strengthened the efforts at the ground level.

We do not have data to compare the overall time and costs involved in spreading change ideas to many sites, so we cannot conclude which approaches were more cost-effective in reaching the most sites. We can, however, see that those QI initiatives with an explicit strategy for scaling up results or for achieving national scale with the intervention (India, Uganda, Haiti, Mozambique) were able to achieve results at a larger scale.

For many teams, a little friendly competition was a powerful motivator of change. Comparing performance between facilities and districts, while providing facility-specific feedback, stimulated the efforts of QI teams to modify practices. Health workers were motivated by evidence of how their practices deviated from the established practices or from the mean performance of other facilities in the same region.

These cases do not, however, tell us much about the sustainability of QI initiatives since all were short-term initiatives without long-term follow-up. The cases also involved differing levels of external technical assistance and did not attempt to measure the costs of the interventions, making it impossible to correlate results with the resources invested to achieve or sustain them. Future QI interventions will always be well served by building in measurement of costs to achieve results. In fact, automating and standardizing the documentation of costs of interventions are likely the only way to get at the question of cost-effectiveness of specific QI interventions since implementers' ad hoc cost analyses are likely to be biased in favor of their interventions.

As a collection, we hope these cases provide realistic descriptions of what QI looks like in practice—how actual health workers approached their improvement efforts—and illustrate the many ways that QI methods have contributed to improving health care in these countries. The authors' reflections at the end of each case provide further insights into what factors contributed to results in the specific case and draw on their wisdom to inform future QI efforts. The rich detail provided in these cases can also guide health workers in applying QI methods to specific care areas such as male circumcision, prevention of mother-to-child transmission of HIV, tuberculosis and HIV, and Zika prevention.

Above all, we hope these cases clearly demonstrate that QI methods can be productively applied to many care areas in low- and middle-income countries and that there is a rich body of expertise in QI in these countries that can and should be tapped as part of national efforts to improve care efficiency and effectiveness and produce better health outcomes.

Acknowledgments The development of this case book was made possible by the generous support of the American people through USAID. This chapter was developed with the support of USAID and its Bureau for Global Health, Office of Health Systems, through the USAID Applying

Science to Strengthen and Improve Systems (ASSIST) Project, managed by University Research Co., LLC under Cooperative Agreement Number AID-OAA-A-12-00101.

We are indebted to Dr. James R. Heiby for initiating this case book and to all the authors of the 12 cases presented in this book, particularly the lead authors: Maria Elena Banegas Arnold, Joshua Bardfield, John Byabagambi, Tamar Chitashvili, Taroub Harb Faramand, Elena Hurtado, Nigel Livesley, Edgar Necochea, Flora Nyagawa, Nilufar Rakhmanova Pollard, Barton Smith, and Nicole Spieker.

Index